Telecommunications in Transition

Telecommunications in Transition

Policies, Services and Technologies in the European Community

Edited by
**Charles Steinfield,
Johannes M. Bauer and Laurence Caby**

SAGE Publications
International Educational and Professional Publisher
Thousand Oaks   London   New Delhi

For information address:

SAGE Publications, Inc.
2455 Teller Road
Thousand Oaks, California 91320

SAGE Publications Ltd.
6 Bonhill Street
London EC2A 4PU
United Kingdom

SAGE Publications India Pvt. Ltd.
M-32 Market
Greater Kailash I
New Delhi 110 048 India

Printed in the United States of America

Library of Congress Cataloging-in-Publication Data

Main entry under title:

Telecommunications in transition: Policies, services and
  technologies in the European Community / edited by Charles
  Steinfield, Johannes M. Bauer, Laurence Caby.
    p.   cm.
  Includes bibliographical references and idexes.
  ISBN 0-8039-4606-6 (cloth).—ISBN 0-8039-4607-4 (pbk.)
  1. Telecommunication—European Community countries.
  2. Telecommunication policy—European Community countries.
  3. Telecommunication—International cooperation.
  4. Telecommunication systems—European Community countries.
  I. Steinfield, Charles William. II. Bauer, Johannes M. III. Caby,
Laurence.
HE7700.T46 1994
384'.068—dc20   94-24427

94 95 96 97 98 10 9 8 7 6 5 4 3 2 1

Sage Production Editor: Astrid Virding

Contents

Preface

Throughout this century, telecommunications services in European countries have been provided predominantly by large, government-owned monopolies known as Post, Telegraph, and Telephone Administrations (PTTs). Although great differences in their performance are visible, these organizations are frequently regarded by corporate and residential customers as restrictive and unresponsive. Until recently, the PTTs were embedded in domestically oriented industrial policies of the many sovereign nations in Europe. This has resulted in a fragmented telecommunications market and a multitude of standards, especially in the types and forms of equipment that could be attached to telecommunications networks, the types of transmission permitted on networks, and the applied tariff principles.

Presently, however, the PTTs of Europe are experiencing unprecedented change. National governments are placing more weight on the strategic importance of a dynamic telecommunications sector for economic prosperity and growth. Such national strategies as the liberalization of the regulatory environment or the privatization of government-owned and -operated telecommunications authorities have created pressures that are making it difficult for the traditional PTT structure to survive. These national approaches to telecommunications reform are boosted by the European integration process, aiming at a single common market where goods, services, capital, and people can move freely across national borders. Fully aware of the enormous strategic importance of telecommunications in a global economy, the Commission of the European Communities has undertaken concentrated efforts to foster a more competitive course for European telecommunications policy.

The stakes in the reform process are significant. As the chapters in *Telecommunications in Transition* illustrate, not only will telecommunications network and service providers spend billions of dollars in the coming years to upgrade their infrastructures, but users—companies, public institutions, and private consumers—also will depend heavily on telecommunications services. Many key issues remain unresolved, however, and some constraints indeed remain on those who wish to provide or use telecommunications networks and services.

Understanding the nature and relationships among the many issues surrounding European telecommunications requires a good deal of background information. For this reason, this book examines the players, issues, new developments with regard to emerging services, and policy trends for telecommunications in Europe. The text is divided into four major sections. Part I provides a general introduction, develops a conceptual framework to analyze the shaping of European telecommunications policies, and overviews various approaches to liberalization. Part II introduces the many different institutions that play a role in international telecommunications coordination and discusses key issues in telecommunications policy. Part III explores new technology and service initiatives currently being undertaken in Europe. Finally, Part IV examines the emerging trends and global strategies resulting from the reshaping of European telecommunications.

The topics covered within this book are interdisciplinary and relevant to many fields and areas of study. *Telecommunications in Transition* has been developed to be of use to scholars, students, and practitioners. Scholars and students from such fields as telecommunications, communications, information systems, management, public policy, political science, economics, international relations, and engineering will find that all of these disciplines can inform and be informed by the events shaping European telecommunications. The increasing attention to international topics within nearly all universities suggests the need for a book that can serve as both a textbook and research aid. Although primarily targeted at the graduate level, it also can be effectively used for advanced undergraduate courses on international aspects of telecommunications.

We have also tried to ensure that the chapters would prove interesting and relevant to managers, whether they represent telecommunications users or providers. User firms from a wide array of industries that operate on an international level need advanced information and telecommunications capabilities and thus should have an interest in the factors that influence their organizations' abilities to develop and effectively use international networks.

Representatives from telecommunications service and network providers will also need to be informed about European telecommunications developments, because of the increasingly global nature of their businesses. Liberalization will provide important market opportunities, and those who will be involved in analyzing, planning for, and implementing international telecommunications activities can benefit from the insights and background information in this text. Of course, those involved in the policy process itself can also benefit from exposure to issues and strategies, as many policy initiatives transcend national boundaries.

There are many people and institutions who have played an important and supportive role in helping us edit this book. First and foremost, we thank all of our authors, who prepared original and insightful contributions. Many people also provided helpful advice and guidance; we thank Alain Vallée, Bruno Lanvin, and Herbert Dordick. We are also grateful to Michigan State University and the Institut National des Télécommunications for their financial and administrative support of all the editors. Charles Steinfield acknowledges the additional financial support of a Fulbright Research Award through the Council for the Exchange of International Scholars and the Commission Franco-Américaine D'Échanges Universitaires et Culturels that helped make his contributions possible. Phil Fare and Kathryn Busse are thanked for their diligent and competent help with the preparation of the indexes and other copy. And perhaps most important, we owe thanks to our spouses—Susan Russick, Susan Woods, and Luc Guillet—and our children, who endured the inevitable long hours that producing such a book requires.

Charles Steinfield
Johannes M. Bauer
Laurence Caby

PART I

Introduction and Conceptual Foundations

ONE

An Introduction to European Telecommunications

CHARLES STEINFIELD

American impressions of the telecommunications situation in Europe vary greatly depending on the observer's context. Travelers accustomed to the homogeneity resulting from the common Bell System heritage throughout the United States and Canada find the diversity in calling procedures confusing and are astonished at the costs of international calls from certain countries. For American telecommunications managers who must work with locations throughout Europe, impressions often focus on the difficulties they face in obtaining the same kinds of equipment, services, and prices that they have in their U.S. private networks as well as on the complexities involved in coordinating across different countries. They also frequently express frustration at restrictions that are placed on the use of telecommunications resources (especially leased lines) by a few European public telecommunications operators. Yet another view can be heard from representatives of American telecommunications companies, especially the Regional Bell Operating Companies (or RBOCs), who are often envious of the ability of many of their European counterparts to enter into lines of business from which RBOCs in the past were prohibited, often on a scale that the privately held U.S. companies could never hope to achieve (e.g., French videotex: see Bouwman & Latzer, Chapter 9 in this book). A common perception, however, across most of these diverse groups is the view that telecommunications in most European countries has long been dominated by

AUTHOR'S NOTE: I am grateful to my coeditors, Johannes Bauer and Laurence Caby, as well as Alain Vallée for their comments on this chapter. Any errors or omissions, however, remain my own.

large, monolithic organizations who enjoy a government-sanctioned monopoly over the provision of most, if not all, telecommunications networks and services.

To a certain extent, the kinds of impressions noted above are reflective of old perceptions that now require reexamination. The past half decade has been one of tumultuous change, change due not only to rapid technological development but also arising from significant shifts in the policies of many European countries. Many reforms have been implemented in the hopes of stimulating innovation and efficiency in this sector, although some have questioned whether or not the reforms will significantly alter how the most important services (e.g., voice telephony) will be provided (see Noam & Kramer, Chapter 15 in this book).

In this chapter, I provide a broad introduction to telecommunications in Europe in order to give newcomers to this topic the background necessary for reading the remainder of the book. Those with more exposure to the study of telecommunications in Europe of course may wish to move immediately on to the later chapters. I begin by examining the historical approach to providing telecommunications services in Europe and proceed to an overview of pressures for change, including those arising from technological as well as social and economic sources. Several recent initiatives are briefly highlighted, including political and regulatory efforts arising from international institutions such as those of the European Community. Then I close with a brief look at how individual nations have responded and suggest several emerging issues that may portend even greater changes in the future. The chapter thus serves as a blueprint to the structure of the rest of this book.

The PTT Tradition

In the latter part of the 19th century, as first the telegraph and then the telephone were introduced throughout Europe, a common pattern was followed in many countries. That is, after a brief period in which private companies were allowed to operate very restricted electric networks on a concessionary basis, most governments nationalized telegraph and telephone systems and placed responsibility for provision of these services under some form of administration overseen by a minister of communication (excellent historical analyses can be found in Brock, 1981, and Noam, 1992). Administration of telegraph and telephone networks was often merged with the existing postal authority—hence, the PTT or Post, Telegraph, and Telephone Administration, which was granted a complete monopoly on the provision of telecommunications infrastructure and services.

Several European governments acted to restrict new electric technologies in order to avoid harming existing investments in older technologies (Brock, 1981). For example, Brock notes that a common approach was to permit local telephone exchanges on a concessionary basis but prohibit any interconnection between exchanges, forcing interurban traffic to be converted into telegraphs and carried by the postal authority's telegraph lines.

The nationalization of telecommunications was often justified on the basis of a disappointing experience with private providers, many of whom charged exorbitant prices and provided poor service. The option of government regulation of the industry, which eventually became the model adopted in the United States, did not really exist in most European states because of their specific legal and constitutional structures and traditions. In addition, the view that a telecommunications monopoly could be a secure form of taxlike revenues, as well as concerns from the military that a private telecommunications system could pose threats to national security, also favored nationalization (it is useful to place the introduction of the telephone in its historical context of the pre-World War I military tension throughout Europe).

Nationalization can therefore be seen as a particular European response to an imperfectly competitive young industry around the turn of the century. Similarly, the U.S. approach that emerged gradually at the same time, with federal regulatory jurisdiction first extending to telecommunications in the latter two decades of the 19th century and gaining momentum with the creation of state regulatory commissions in the early 20th century, was a product of the unique conditions there. Without a tradition of public (i.e., government-owned) enterprise in the United States, movements to nationalize telecommunications and other public utilities were not politically successful.

The gradual reintroduction of competition in basic telecommunications services in the United States over the past 30 years or so was perhaps more feasible given the existing ownership structures than it would have been under a national PTT structure. The two distinct models thus lead to questions of the comparative efficiency of the approaches, with some observers questioning how well the bureaucratized PTTs, in the absence of competitive pressures, fully diffused telephone services in the early years (Brock, 1981) and more recently responded to challenges of technological change and to the now much more diversified spectrum of user needs (see Mansell, Chapter 11 in this book).

Some have argued, for example, that the effect of eliminating competition at such an early stage and following a conservative strategy to protect existing investment (e.g., the French held back the electronic telegraph because of their well-developed optical—i.e., semaphore— telegraph network) was that in most European countries telephone penetration grew quite slowly and was mostly confined to urban areas (Brock, 1981). Brock notes that the United States experienced similar slow growth in telephone service during Bell's monopoly period but greatly outstripped most European countries after the expiration of the Bell patents in 1876 opened the field to competitive entry. The only exception was in Sweden, which did permit private companies to compete with a government provider for telephone exchange service (although the long-distance network was nationalized in 1889; Aurelle, 1986) and which still has a higher per capita penetration rate for telephones than any country in the world (see Table 7.1).

Thus, the basic model of public monopoly provision of telecommunications became entrenched throughout Europe and, indeed, throughout much of the world. Just as AT&T and Western Electric enjoyed a monopoly on equipment in the United States, PTT monopoly control over the basic telephone and telegraph networks was further extended in most countries to include the supply of telephone sets and other terminal equipment to subscribers, although generally these were not manufactured by the PTT. The same held true for switching and other network equipment. Often, the manufacturing of such equipment became a tool of industrial policy and was typically provided by one or a very few domestic suppliers to the PTT, as in the case of Siemens and the Deutsche Bundespost, and Alcatel and the former Direction Général des Télécommunications in France.

European PTTs became large and powerful organizations and often were among the largest employers in their respective countries. Moreover, they generated significant income due to their captive markets, which not only paid for their own operating expenses but often subsidized other social programs as well. Although at times this served to limit investment in infrastructure, as in the case of Belgium (Logica, 1989), a strong government role could also permit rapid infrastructure upgrades and/or the offering of new services not likely to provide a return in the short term, if deemed a national priority. France, for example, following the recommendations of the now famous Nora and Minc report (1980), throughout the 1970s and early 1980s substantially digitized their network, dramatically increased telephone penetration, created the world's busiest packet switched network, and implemented what many regard as the world's most successful videotex system (Dupagne, 1990).

Without the deep pockets of the national government, such a coordinated effort would not be possible in such a short period of time. Any threats to their monopoly position were thus vigorously fought—a goal that was easily reached on the domestic front since PTTs generally occupied the triple roles of policymaker, regulator, and operator (Melody, 1991). Potential competition that might arise through the international flow of telecommunications traffic—e.g., countries competing to carry "transit" traffic (i.e., traffic carried across country C in order to get from country A to B)—was constrained by international agreements. In fact, some have argued that the oldest surviving international organization, the International Telecommunication Union (ITU), enabled the established telecommunications administrations to erect a stable regime that effectively preserved their privileged positions (Drake, Chapter 5 in this book). Within Europe itself, an association of PTTs—the Conférence Européenne des Administrations des Postes et Télécommunications (CEPT)—served as a forum for cooperation and, although not an explicit goal, had the effect of minimizing any chance of competitive entry by outsiders or private entities (Besen, 1990).

One potential threat to the revenues of PTTs was the emergence of large-scale private user networks that would carry company traffic over leased facilities. Although not expressly forbidden in most countries, PTTs could and largely did curtail private user networks by prohibiting connection with the public network, sometimes restricting them to data traffic rather than voice, applying a volume charging mechanism rather than a flat rate tariff on leased lines, and prohibiting any form of sharing or resale of excess capacity. In this way, PTTs could easily engage in various forms of cross subsidization to support social objectives without fear of encouraging private users to "leave the public network" or attracting any form of specialized common carrier entry as occurred in the United States when rules regarding use of leased lines were liberalized (see Brock, 1981; Faulhaber, 1987; Shooshan, 1987; and Wiley, 1987, for complete reviews of the U.S. situation).

Beginnings of Reform

Such a system remained stable as long as all members of the "club" (including private monopoly operators such as AT&T as well as the PTTs) adhered to its recommendations (Drake, Chapter 5 in this book). Such was not to be the case, however, as liberalization began to take hold in the United States and, even within Europe, the United Kingdom began to engage in a sort of competition with other countries. Early competition for international traffic occurred when the United Kingdom permitted telex refiling—that is, in order to take advantage of cheaper rates when originating telex traffic from the United Kingdom, a few enterprising companies began collecting telex traffic from the United States and other countries, sending it to London, and "refiling" it to send it on to the intended destination countries. Attempts by the British Post Office to stop the practice, which was vehemently opposed by other club members (most notably Italy), were rebuffed by the European Court of Justice (Vallée, 1992). This practice was an early precursor to more recent competition among major European carriers to have their key cities serve as the telecommunications "hubs" for large multinational private networks. In addition, the attractiveness of London as the major gateway to Europe for multinationals' networks, especially since the privatization of British Telecom and the introduction of competition in the United Kingdom in 1984, had not gone unnoticed among the PTTs on the continent. Finally, and perhaps most importantly, this case established the precedent that public telecommunications operators, even if they were state monopolies, were not exempt from the competition rules contained in the Treaty of Rome and thus could not engage in behavior that in any way served to restrain trade within the European Community (Vallée, 1992).

Other potent forces for change can be noted, including technological developments in both the computer and telecommunications industry. Rapid technological changes altered the traditional barriers to entry by (1) creating new classes of value-added services that can be efficiently offered by other providers as long as nondiscriminatory network access is available (see Bouwman & Latzer, Chapter 9 in this book) and (2) lowering the costs for certain kinds of infrastructure (e.g., satellite networks) and thus creating new incentives for entry by others. Moreover, the highly innovative and unregulated computer industry exposed the inefficiencies of PTT monopolies in the equipment sector and created additional pressures to ease entry restrictions for devices that could connect to the public networks (e.g., data communications equipment).

Economic factors, especially related to the globalization of trade, have also frequently been mentioned as a force for reform of the PTT system (Lanvin, 1989). Increasing attention to trade issues, especially in the area of trade in services, directly exposed the protectionism that historically characterized this sector (see Woodrow & Sauvé, Chapter 6 in this book). Additionally, Europeans began to focus heavily on the "costs of non-Europe," especially in the equipment sector (Müller, 1988; Ungerer & Costello, 1988). The logic here was that the varying standards and protected suppliers in Europe limited the size of the market and hence the economies of scale for European equipment providers, who then could not compete with North American and Japanese rivals supplying much larger markets. Ungerer and Costello (1988) and many others (see Bauer, Chapter 2, and Ypsilanti & Kelly, Chapter 7, in this book) further stress the crucial role that telecommunications is expected to play in the future well-being of each nation's economy, not only because of the direct contribution of the sector to the gross national product (GNP) but also because of its fundamental role in supporting all types of economic activity. In particular, this has led to a new emphasis on ways of stimulating the growth of the value-added services marketplace in Europe, and particularly for pan-European services.

Pressure, too, came from European business itself, which was clearly envious of the relative flexibility and lower costs its U.S. competitors enjoyed in implementing telecommunications networks and incorporating them into overall business strategies (see Keen, 1988; Mansell, Chapter 11 in this book; Rockart & Short, 1991).

Reform of telecommunications in Europe thus became one important element in the efforts to implement the Single European Act, adopted by all European Community member states' parliaments in 1986. The next section introduces the European Community activity in this regard, with more detail provided in Bauer and Steinfield (Chapter 4 in this book) and Ungerer and Costello (1988).

The European Community and Telecommunications

The various institutions of the European Community have collectively embraced the concept of reform in telecommunications as an important goal. Perhaps most important in this area has been the work of the Commission, through its Directorate General for Telecommunications, Information Industries, and Innovation (DG XIII), which drafts much of the legislation for later approval by the Council of Ministers (see Bauer & Steinfield, Chapter 4 in this book). Also important, however, is the Directorate General for Competition (DG IV), which applies the principles embedded in the Treaty of Rome to promote competition within the common market and which has recently targeted monopoly abuses within the telecommunications sector (Amory, 1991).

Even before the passage of the Single European Act, which called for a single European market by 1992, efforts were underway within the community to improve Europe's position in the world market for telecommunications. Strategic research programs engaging in pre-competitive cooperative research were promoted at the Community level, including the European Strategic Program for Research and Development in Information Technologies (ESPRIT) in 1984 and Research and Development in Advanced Communication Technologies for Europe (RACE) begun in 1985 (see Schnöring, Chapter 8 in this book).

In June 1987, however, the most important European Community policy document in the area of telecommunications, the Green Paper on Telecommunications, was published by the Commission (Commission, 1987). This document set forth the blueprint for the kinds of regulatory adjustments member states would have to undertake to achieve the goals of the common market for telecommunications. Using the complex political system of the European Community (see Bauer & Steinfield, Chapter 4 in this book, for an overview of the organizational structure), based on legal principles contained in the 1959 Treaty of Rome, a gradual process of reform has been initiated.

The Green Paper proposed opening the market for terminal equipment as well as the competitive provision of all services that were not reserved for the exclusive provision by telecommunications administrations. The notion of *reserved* and *nonreserved* services was used rather than attempting, as had the FCC in the United States, to find a stable definition of basic and enhanced services. A major concession to telecommunications administrations was the provision that all network infrastructure, and key basic services such as voice telephony, were permitted to remain under monopoly control. In order to liberalize and create a pan-European terminal market, the dual principles of harmonization—i.e., attempting to make rules and standards more similar across member states—and mutual recognition—ensuring that equipment approved for use in one country would automatically be approved for use throughout the EC—were espoused. For services, the Open Network Provision (ONP) doctrine was created (see Bauer & Steinfield, Chapter

4, and Caby & Steinfield, Chapter 3, in this book). Essentially, ONP recognized that if infrastructure remained in the hands of the monopoly providers, then fair and nondiscriminatory access to this infrastructure would have to be ensured for other companies attempting to offer some form of nonreserved service, especially when they would directly compete with the PTT.

To facilitate the creation of pan-European standards, the Commission proposed the establishment of the European Telecommunications Standards Institute (ETSI) (see Besen, 1991; Drake, Chapter 5 in this book). Another goal of this new standards body is to further open the field to more players, by inviting manufacturers and users to participate in addition to the traditional Public Telecommunications Operators (PTOs) (Besen, 1991; Drake, Chapter 5 in this book).

In addition, the Green Paper recognized the inherent contradictions that would arise in the provision of competitive services when regulatory and operational functions were combined into one entity. It called for a clear separation of these functions, although it did not specify any sort of preferred regulatory agency structure (see Caby & Steinfield, Chapter 3 in this book). Since the publishing of the Green Paper, and its formal adoption by the Council of Ministers in 1988, key directives have been issued regarding the opening of the terminal equipment market by 1990, competition in telecommunications services, and the basic framework of Open Network Provision (ONP; see Bauer & Steinfield, Chapter 4 in this book). Other earlier EC decisions further targeted mobile services (see Müller & Toker, Chapter 10 in this book), Integrated Services Digital Networks (ISDNs; see Arlandis, Chapter 12 in this book), and broadband services (see Connell, Chapter 13 in this book). More recent efforts have focused on opening up the market for satellite communications, and now even basic telephone service (Bauer & Steinfield, Chapter 4 in this book).

Although there have been challenges to certain directives from the Commission (Amory, 1991; Bernard, 1990; Falvey, 1989), these have been mostly on procedural rather than substantive grounds, and the telecommunications administrations appear fairly supportive of the overall policy. Initially, important concessions to the administrations (i.e., the preservation of a monopoly on voice telephony and on infrastructure) and the ability to impose "essential requirements" on competitive service providers (e.g., basic data transmission service providers in France must make their service available to all regions of the country and not just in the key markets) served to minimize any threats to their dominant positions. Nevertheless, a process of reform has begun.

Other International Institutions Pursuing Reform

Alongside the European Community, other international fora have pressed for liberalization in telecommunications market. Beginning in the Uruguay Round in 1985, the General Agreement on Tariffs and Trade (GATT) negotiations have included a special round of talks focused on trade in services (the Group of Negotiations on Services or GNS; see Woodrow & Sauvé, Chapter 6 in this book). Telecommunications services have been specifically singled out as a fundamental target for incorporation within the overall GATT framework, which attempts to progressively reduce barriers to free trade.

Although the prospects for an agreement have waxed and waned over the years mostly because of difficulties in other sectors (specifically agriculture, which was also newly introduced into GATT negotiations in the Uruguay Round), the likelihood of some form of eventual compromise suggests that even without the EC there would have to be some reform on the part of the PTTs.

Also pressing for liberalization is the Organization for Economic Cooperation and Development (OECD), to which belong the 24 most industrialized nations of the world. Through its Information, Computer, and Communications Policy (ICCP) division, the OECD has conducted research that highlights the benefits of having more responsive and better performing telecommunications sectors (see Ypsilanti & Kelly, Chapter 7 in this book). Although their recommendations are nonbinding on member countries, they are still influential in exposing inefficient practices among telecommunications operators.

Country Responses

An often overlooked fact by overly enthusiastic supporters of EC initiatives is that Community directives have no real impact until translated into national laws. Thus, a directive stipulating a separation of regulatory and operational functions merely sets forth a basic guideline—the exact implementation will differ according to the individual approaches taken in each country. Throughout the EC, telecommunications legislation has been passed in most countries, although the specific approaches to liberalization vary (see Caby & Steinfield, Chapter 3 in this book; Noam, 1992). Most have acted to separate regulatory and operational functions, although even here important differences remain. The United Kingdom created OFTEL

(Office of Telecommunications), which is independent both from the operators and the government ministry responsible for communications. However, in other countries such as France, the newly created regulatory agencies are directly responsible to the Minister for Communication. In creating an independent operational entity, only the United Kingdom has chosen to have privately financed and managed companies providing telecommunications on a competitive basis across all aspects of the business. Other countries already had some degree of private participation, but only in selected segments of the business (e.g., the private local companies in Finland and formerly in Denmark; minority private participation in concessionary companies in Italy and in Telefónica in Spain). Other countries changed the status of their telecommunications administrations into state-owned companies that would now operate under private law (e.g., France and The Netherlands). Important benefits following from a transition from administration to state-owned company are more flexibility in dealing with employees (as opposed to civil servants) and more flexibility in managing costs and determining investment priorities. Finally, others, because of constitutional restrictions, could not effectively change the status of their administrations but nevertheless attempted to define new operating procedures (e.g., Germany).

Liberalization in services has also proceeded in different ways, with approaches ranging from fairly open competition, as in the United Kingdom, to more restricted views of what the "essential requirements" are that service providers must follow, such as in France. In general, however, EC members have attempted to allow value-added services to be provided on a competitive basis in their new legislation. So far, only the United Kingdom has opted for competition in the basic telephony market, authorizing and helping to establish Mercury as a competitor to British Telecom in 1983. This duopoly structure remained until the end of 1991, after a review recommended allowing in new entrants (DTI, 1990). Many countries have followed a similar duopoly pattern in the provision of cellular telephone services, however. More important, the monopoly provision of reserved services has been reexamined in 1993, and even basic voice telephony will be opened to competitive provision in the not-too-distant future (see Bauer & Steinfield, Chapter 4 in this book).

New Issues

On the horizon are new challenges to the existing structure of European telecommunications. Several authors in recent years have suggested a new type of convergence—that between the electronic media industries (broadcasting and cable television) and telecommunications/computing. If the former convergence posed the problem of conflicts between regulated and unregulated industries, this new convergence suggests conflicts between two very different regulatory regimes (see Burgelman & Pauweis, 1991). Throughout the EC, approaches to the provision of cable television vary immensely, with some operators allowed to install and manage their own infrastructure (as in the United Kingdom) but others forced to lease infrastructure from the telecommunications administration (as in Germany) (see Dutton & Vedel, 1992, for a comparative analysis of cable television policies in the United Kingdom, France, and the United States). The desires of the EC to foster the development of pan-European Integrated Broadband Communications (IBC) services will no doubt pose important new political challenges.

It is also important to avoid the temptation to view the European Community as the only voice for European matters. The EC has 12 members: Belgium, Denmark, France, Germany, Greece, Ireland, Italy, Luxembourg, Netherlands, Portugal, Spain, and United Kingdom. Yet the CEPT membership is now composed of 31 European telecommunications administrations, including new members from Eastern Europe. Policy coordination with the European Free Trade Association (EFTA includes Austria, Liechtenstein, Switzerland, and the Scandinavian countries Finland, Iceland, Norway, and Sweden) is becoming a more visible issue (Bauer, 1990). Moreover, many of the former Eastern bloc countries, all with terribly underdeveloped telecommunications infrastructures, now are petitioning for some form of meaningful association with the EC (see Bauer & Straubhaar, Chapter 14 in this book). Although the potential market size of over 500 million people entices policymakers and service and equipment suppliers, harmonization of policies to make this market a reality represents an even more difficult challenge than before. Moreover, given the EC's attempts to channel resources into less favored regions to help improve telecommunications infrastructures through such programs as STAR (Special Telecommunications Action for Regional Development; see Ungerer & Costello, 1988), associations with the Eastern countries could strain EC funds. The situation is even more desperate in the newly independent republics arising from the former Soviet Union, where underinvestment in telecommunications infrastructure served political goals of the former regime (Bauer & Straubhaar, Chapter 14 in this book).

Conclusions: Europe Between a Patchwork and a Common Market

Future developments in the European telecommunications sector will reflect both the harmonizing influences originating from external forces and more fragmented approaches favored by internal forces. Much of the preceding discussion focused on the former, identifying such external influences on reform as common technological advances, increased emphasis on global trade and the concurrent focus on elimination of barriers to trade in telecommunications services, European Community efforts to create a single market, and efforts by multinational companies to rationalize their global networks. Working against the harmonizing effects associated with these influences, however, are the very different national contexts that collectively comprise Europe.

We must be careful not to make light of the fact that even within the European Community, the 12 countries have very different cultures, economic conditions, and geography, and this serves as an opposing force to the centrifugal tendencies originating in the EC (Vallée, 1990). Thus, there is little justification for assuming that telecommunications could and should be offered in a homogeneous fashion across such diverse contexts. Cultural traditions suggest that people will use telecommunications services in different ways and will have different legal and administrative traditions for managing the sector. Economic conditions will also affect the ways telecommunications will be used as well as the availability of capital to invest in new infrastructure and services. The less favored and more rural economies of Ireland, Portugal, and Greece, for example, may not generate the same requirements for integrated broadband communications as in the United Kingdom, France, or Germany. Geographic conditions such as the type of terrain and population density will influence costs of providing infrastructure and the viability of different services. Such factors, for example, can partly explain the somewhat higher penetration rates for mobile services in the Nordic countries as opposed to elsewhere in Europe. Table 7.1 illustrates, for example, the variability that exists across OECD countries along such factors as population and telephone penetration, and elsewhere in this book we can see important differences in other areas such as ISDN strategy (Arlandis, Chapter 12) and videotex development (Bouwman & Latzer, Chapter 9).

Finally, despite the general trend toward competitive provision of services in Europe, the approaches are neither identical to the U.S.

model nor by definition less optimal. Rather, the question of what the optimal approach to telecommunications should be is an open research question (see Bauer, Chapter 2 in this book). Bauer notes, for example, that although easing restrictions on market entry can have dynamizing effects on the industry, it may also be destabilizing from the perspective of interoperability and network coherence. Moreover, the interaction of forces briefly outlined in this chapter suggests that it would be a mistake to assume that European telecommunications will closely resemble the United States situation in the near future. Different beginning points and present circumstances, even with common external influences, imply a different trajectory for telecommunications development.

References

Amory, B. (1991). *Telecommunications in the European communities: The new regulatory framework*. Paper presented to the Telecommunications in Europe Program, Brussels, July.

Aurelle, B. (1986). *Les télécommunications*. Paris: Editions La Decouverte.

Bauer, J. M. (1990). *Telecommunications policies in the small European countries*. Paper presented to the Telecommunications in Europe Program of Michigan State University, Paris, July.

Bernard, K. (1990). Doing business in Europe. *Telecommunications Policy, 14*(4), 279-282.

Besen, S. (1991). The European Telecommunications Standards Institute: A preliminary analysis. *Telecommunications Policy, 14*, 521-530.

Brock, G. (1981). *The telecommunications industry: The dynamics of market structure*. Cambridge, MA: Harvard University Press.

Burgelman, J., & Pauweis, C. (1991). Growing convergence between broadcasting and telecommunication: Policy problems at the level of the Commission of the European Economic Communities. *Telematics and Informatics, 8*, 135-142.

Commission of the European Communities (1987). *Towards a dynamic European economy. Green Paper on the development of the Common Market for telecommunications services and equipment*. Communication from the Commission of 30 June 1987. COM (87) 290.

DTI (1991). *Competition and choice: Telecommunications policy in the United Kingdom*. London: Department of Trade and Industry.

Dupagne, M. (1990). Electronic directory services: Will the French model work in the U.S.? *Telecommunications Policy, 14*(6), 489-504.

Dutton, W., & Vedel, T. (1992). The dynamics of cable television in the United States, Britain, and France. In J. Blumler, J. McLeod, & K. E. Rosengren (Eds.), *Comparatively speaking: Communication and culture across space and time* (pp. 70-93). Newbury Park: Sage.

Falvey, J. C. (1989). France v. The Commission of the European Economic Community: The power of the Commission to issue a Directive under Article 90. *Virginia Law Review, 29*, 937-967.

Faulhaber, G. R. (1987). *Telecommunications in turmoil: Technology and public policy.* Cambridge, MA: Ballinger.

Keen, P. (1988). *Competing in time: Using telecommunications for competitive advantage* (2nd ed.). Cambridge, MA: Ballinger.

Lanvin, B. (1989). Achieving sustainable growth in an information-based world economy: Trade, information, and development. In B. Lanvin (Ed.), *Global trade: The revolution beyond the communications revolution* (pp. 169-191). Montpellier, France: IDATE.

Logica. (1989). *Telecommunications in Europe.* London: Logica.

Melody, W. (1991). *Telecommunications: Which sectors do we privatize?* Paper presented to the ITU Telecom 91 Economic Forum, Geneva, October.

Müller, J. (1988). *The benefits of completing the internal market for telecommunications services/equipment in the Community.* (Research on the "Cost of Non-Europe." Basic findings, vol. 10.) Luxembourg: Office for Official Publications of the European Communities.

Noam, E. M. (1992). *Telecommunications in Europe.* New York: Oxford University Press.

Nora, S., & Minc, A. (1980). *The computerization of society.* Cambridge, MA: MIT Press.

Rockart, J., & Short, J. (1991). The networked organization and the management of interdependence. In M. Scott-Morton (Ed.), *The corporation of the 90s* (pp. 189-219). New York: Oxford University Press.

Shooshan, H. (1987). The Bell breakup: Putting it in perspective. In H. Shooshan (Ed.), *Disconnecting Bell: The impact of the AT&T divestiture* (pp. 8-22). New York: Pergamon.

Ungerer, H., & Costello, N. (1988). *Telecommunications in Europe.* Brussels: Office for Official Publications of the European Communities.

Vallée, A. (1990, March-April). Les états pourront-il faire l'Europe des télécommunications? *Revue Reseau (CNET), 40,* 93-104.

Vallée, A. (1992). *La loi nouvelle des télécommunications en France.* Montpellier, France: IDATE.

Wiley, R. (1987). The end of monopoly: Regulatory change and the promotion of competition. In H. Shooshan (Ed.), *Disconnecting Bell: The impact of the AT&T divestiture* (pp. 23-46). New York: Pergamon.

TWO

Conceptual Frameworks for the Design of Telecommunications Policy

JOHANNES M. BAUER

The coincidence of technological, economic, political, and social change has created a tremendous challenge for contemporary telecommunications policy. The established policies of the past are crumbling worldwide and give way to new approaches and policy experiments. Recent theoretical and empirical research in such disciplines as economics, political science, sociology, communications, law, computer science, engineering, and management science has notably improved our understanding of the telecommunications industry and contributed to the overhaul of established policies. Telecommunications research has become a rather complex, truly multi-paradigmatic undertaking. Not only do different disciplines address telecommunications policy issues, but different traditions of thought within disciplines contribute to the body of research. Although there seems to be consensus about the weaknesses of the traditional (PTT) approach to telecommunications, significant areas of dispute and controversy exist as to the best course of future action and the specific policy instruments to be employed.

The European telecommunications policy debate shows several unique features. Historically, and enforced by the reforms of the early 1980s, the institutional setting of telecommunications varies greatly between single European nations. For instance, the United Kingdom has established a very liberal telecommunications regime, whereas other countries

AUTHOR'S NOTE: The author wishes to thank Tom Baldwin, Bob LaRose, and Tom Muth for comments on an earlier draft.

still maintain far-reaching special and exclusive rights for the incumbent telecommunication service providers. In addition, the state of telecommunications development varies significantly between European countries (see Ypsilanti & Kelly, Chapter 7 in this book) and therefore the weights attached to different policy goals—such as the development of a basic telecommunications infrastructure versus the deployment of specialized services—also differ. In drafting blueprints for a comprehensive overhaul of European telecommunications, the European Community is somewhat constrained by those diverging national approaches. As a result of these specific conditions, Europe has embarked on a telecommunications policy course that differs in many aspects significantly from U.S. policy. In this chapter, I attempt to review some of the major conceptual frameworks that are underlying the specific design of public telecommunications policy and ongoing telecommunications policy "experiments." My goal is a discussion of core concepts and proposed solutions rather than a comprehensive survey of the existing telecommunications policy literature.[1]

The Telecommunications Policy Problem

Like any other sector of the economy, telecommunications needs a legal and institutional framework for its operations. This framework is defined by *rules* at different levels of societal organization. Some of these rules are defined at a very general societal level, such as in the constitution of a country that provides rules across all sectors of an economy, perhaps guaranteeing the freedom of entrepreneurship and establishment or delineating the jurisdiction of regulatory authorities. Other rules apply more narrowly to the telecommunications industry and are set by statutory law or administrative or court decisions. In addition to rules, telecommunications policy comprises a complex set of *discretionary public policy actions* to influence the course and operation of the telecommunications industries.

The telecommunications policy problem consists of the design of an overall set of rules as well as a set of discretionary actions for the industry (the establishment of a *policy regime* or *governance structure*). Such a policy regime usually defines an institutional framework for the sector (which institutions, at the national and European level, are responsible for telecommunications, their jurisdiction, as well as conditions for interest groups to become party in policy decisions); specifies conditions for market access and the regulation of conduct; and contains rules for the pursuit of social goals in the sector.

For most of the policy choices, a spectrum of alternative arrangements exist: market access can be free or regulated; ownership of service providers can be public, mixed, or private; price control can be accomplished through antitrust oversight (*ex post*) or different forms of regulation (*ex ante*); access to the policy making process can be granted to all interested parties or restricted to an elite; social policy goals can be implemented in the price structure of a service provider or realized through general instruments of tax policy, and so on.

A conceptual framework for the design of telecommunications policy should identify conditions that call for policy action and provide guidelines as to the choice of a specific policy. Such a *normative* approach is necessarily based on reference concepts and policy objectives that, in turn, inevitably incorporate some value elements. These values can be based on general, presumably widely agreed concepts—such as the economic notion of efficiency or concepts of justice (Rawls, 1971) or fairness (Zajac, 1978)—but also on more specific a priori value systems, such as the concept of (distributional) equity.

Among the goals advocated for telecommunications policy, *efficiency* enjoys salient priority and is seen by many as generic to the pursuit of other objectives such as distributional and fairness goals. However, in many cases trade-offs between these goals exist and the different goals need to be balanced against each other. During the years of relative technological stability in telecommunications (from the introduction of the telephone until about 1960), such a "social contract" (Trebing, 1992) was established in most countries and manifested itself, for instance, in the idea of "universal service."[2] The challenge to contemporary telecommunications policy is to establish a new social contract in an environment of rapid technological change and widely differentiated needs of different groups of users.

Approaches to Telecommunications Policy Analysis

After World War II, most social sciences developed a multi-paradigmatic structure. Within each discipline, several approaches employing different methodologies and core research agendas exist in parallel, leading to diverging analyses and blueprints for the design of telecommunications policy.

In terms of its influence on current telecommunications policy making, *economics* (and within the economic discipline the neoclassical school) has to be considered a core paradigm.[3] A central concern of economics is the efficiency of resource allocation and the institutional setting to achieve efficiency.[4] Economists have argued in support of a competitive market organization on several grounds. At a rather formal level it is demonstrated that under ideal conditions (e.g., large number of suppliers, negligible barriers to entry and exit, perfect information) and given technology a resource allocation via markets leads to a maximization of welfare (see Johansson, 1991, for a survey of the literature). It is argued that competition between firms already in a market or between incumbent firms and potential new market entrants forces incumbents to produce at minimum cost, charge prices according to marginal costs, engage in process and product innovations and, in doing so, meet the need of consumers in an optimal way.[5]

Unfortunately, industries frequently do not possess these ideal conditions that maximize individual and social benefits at the same time. The most important cases are the existence of *imperfectly competitive market structures* such as "natural" monopoly[6] or oligopoly situations,[7] or the existence of market failure such as the prevalence of *externalities*,[8] and *public good* characteristics[9] of the products and services produced. In addition, the working of markets is dependent on a complex web of institutions that might not be well specified (e.g., property rights in the electromagnetic frequency spectrum). However, economic analysis has shown that (ideal) public policy can restore the marginal conditions of a welfare optimum or at least accomplish *second best* solutions that minimize welfare losses as compared to the ideal solution.

It has been argued that this theoretical framework of orthodox economics is of limited value in a technologically dynamic industry such as modern telecommunications. Challenges emanate from two sides. A first line of criticism originates from the study of innovation processes in the spirit of Schumpeter (1942), who argued that innovation is best facilitated under conditions of imperfect competition that enable innovating firms to earn temporary innovation premiums through their market power. Therefore, regulatory policy aiming at an imitation of the marginal conditions of perfect competition is necessarily misled and will not optimize innovation in an industry (Schumpeter, 1942). A second, a priori argument in favor of competition is contributed by the Austrian School of economics and its followers. Competition is envisioned as a *discovery process* that facilitates societal learning processes to unravel new technologies, applications, and better ways to serve customer needs (Hayek, 1968; Weizsäcker, 1984, for an application to telecommunications). As a consequence of these different approaches, competing proposals as to the best organization of telecommunications are advocated—but on different and not fully comparable analytical arguments.

The relatively young discipline of *communication* studies human (and machine) interaction through messages. Of particular relevance for telecommunications policy seems the field of *organizational communications*, which studies the relations between organizations and information technologies (Fulk & Steinfield, 1990; Kreps, 1990), and studies of the social impacts of information technologies (Rogers, 1986, p. 150, for a brief survey). Communications research has gained influence in the formation of mass media policy but has not yet developed an endemic normative tradition to guide the telecommunications policy discussion. Indeed, many of the contributions by communication scholars to public *telecommunications* policy issues follow an interdisciplinary approach drawing on concepts of economic, political, or institutional theory.[10] A large number of communication scholars seem to embrace the goal of equal and open access to communications technologies and services to guide policy decisions.

Political science models the institutional structure of policy making more explicitly than orthodox economics. The legal structure of a country, the actors in the policy process and their specific interests, as well as the underlying power structure of a society are studied in their impact on the process of policy formation and its outcomes. Modern political science tends to follow a positive rather than a normative tradition. From a normative perspective, political scientists have stressed the problem of accountability of policy making institutions (Hills, 1991).

Various theoretical traditions in the social sciences have tried to integrate several disciplines to produce more general models of social processes and might be fruitful for a more comprehensive understanding of telecommunications. Among these approaches that try to overcome the limits of partial, disciplinary analyses are *institutional* theories. Like the other theoretical frameworks, contemporary institutional theory is a diverse endeavor employing a range of methodologies such as neoclassical economics (Nelson & Winter, 1982; North, 1990; Williamson, 1985) and systems theory (Hodgson, 1988). The particular promise of institutional approaches lies in its potential to model the process of institutional change and choice and its linkages to the political and cultural framework of a society.

The common denominator of the diverse set of *critical* approaches is their general skepticism as to the heuristic and explanatory power of the "orthodox" approaches across all disciplines of telecommunications policy research. These critical studies are rooted in various approaches, such as Marxist concepts or the Frankfurt school. Orthodox approaches, it is criticized, largely ignore societal power structures and conflicts of interests and, hence, tend to misperceive the ideological role of telecommunications in these social processes (Schiller, 1981; Slack & Fejes, 1987).

The next section reviews some of the normative conclusions for the design of telecommunications policy that emerge from these approaches.

Normative Foundations of Telecommunications Policy

Market Entry and Exit Regulation

Justifications for the regulation of market entry and exit in telecommunications are based on various efficiency- and equity-related grounds, such as the existence of imperfect market structures or the need for infrastructure development. More recent theoretical research has narrowed the conditions under which an imperfect market may justify the regulation of market access to "unsustainable" market structures (Baumol, Panzar, & Willig, 1982). Although the demand and supply conditions leading to such cases seem relatively rare, unsustainable structures in general result if the prices of a supplier contain elements of cross-subsidies, for example, by averaging prices across low and high cost areas. Market access regulation might, therefore, become a necessary companion of infrastructure policies based in cross-subsidization.

In the infrastructure context, some countries such as the United Kingdom have introduced certain service obligations (which amount to barriers to market exit) on the telecommunications providers to accomplish infrastructure development goals. A restriction of market access may also be an instrument to internalize positive network and regional externalities. Some authors have suggested restricting the diversification of dominant carriers into value-added and information services as a safeguard against unfair competition (Garnham, 1990).

The issue of market entry and exit regulation has received renewed attention in the mobile communications area (Müller & Toker, Chapter 10 in this book). Because of the early stage of market development paired with the scarcity of electromagnetic spectrum space, only a limited number of mobile telecommunications systems may be viable at the local, regional, or even national level.

The regulation of market access need not necessarily take the form of exclusive monopoly rights. Various other forms that utilize processes of competition *for* a market, such as auctions, are available and might be superior to other forms of administrative market access regulation.

Price and Conduct Regulation

Price and conduct regulation influences such parameters as the prices and quality of services, the allocation of investment budgets, or the supplier-customer relations. From an efficiency point of view, a regulation of these variables might be justified to avoid the inefficiencies resulting from market power (such as excessive prices or suboptimal service quality) or forms of market failure. Conduct regulation has also been advocated as a vehicle to implement infrastructure or distributional goals.

The "classic" and most studied situation calling for conduct regulation is the market structure of a natural monopoly (Berg & Tschirhart, 1988; Train, 1991). More recent theoretical developments have sharpened our understanding that even a natural monopoly is forced to behave efficiently if its market is "contestable," that is, if it is subject to effective potential competition (Baumol, Panzar, & Willig, 1982). However, the degree of contestability (and, hence, the need for conduct regulation) of submarkets of the sector is widely disputed. Several authors argue that the effects of potential competition take substantial time to become effective, giving the incumbent firm an opportunity to react strategically to potential market entrants and rendering the disciplining force of potential competition less effective (Schwartz, 1986).

Another controversial question is whether technological change in telecommunications and the resulting weakening of natural monopoly characteristics have rendered price and conduct regulation obsolete. Shepherd (1984) has argued that under conditions of imperfect contestability a considerable "transition" zone between a natural monopoly and a workably competitive market exists. During this transitory phase, the market structure will frequently be characterized by natural duopoly and natural oligopoly market structures. Even if technological and economic change would theoretically allow for a competitive market, such a market structure might emerge only slowly because of the advantages of the incumbent firm, for example, because of an installed equipment or customer base. In all these cases, continued price and conduct regulation might be justified.

A liberalization of market entry under these conditions might result in a market environment with one dominant multiproduct firm and a fringe of smaller competitors. In this case, regulation becomes more complicated than in a "natural" monopoly setting since measures will be necessary to prevent the dominant firm from using unfair competitive strategies. Indeed, the design of regulatory approaches to detect cross-subsidies from protected into competitive markets is a major challenge in a more diversified telecommunications industry (Trebing, 1992).

Public Versus Private Production

Given the dominance of publicly owned telecommunications service providers in most European countries, the question of ownership has received considerable attention in the telecommunications policy debate. Recent research (Vickers & Yarrow, 1988, provide a comprehensive treatise) has shown that under competitive conditions public enterprise faces similar efficiency incentives as private enterprise, whereas, in contrast, private enterprise faces strong incentives to inefficient behavior under imperfectly competitive market conditions. Private ownership commonly provides stronger incentives than public ownership for efficient production at the enterprise level ("X-efficiency"). However, in monopolistic market situations, private ownership generates weaker incentives for an allocatively efficient pricing policy.

Although these theoretical results show no clear-cut advantage for any particular form of ownership, a policy choice between public or private production has to consider a number of additional factors that might argue in favor of private ownership. First, because of the characteristics of the political process, the management of public enterprise frequently does not face clear performance objectives (Aharoni, 1986). This can be due to ad hoc political demands (e.g., to support the domestic supplier industry even if imported technology would be cheaper) (Duch, 1991) or to the weak performance incentives of administrative law. Second, if public enterprises are organized as *administrations* they are usually severely restricted in their managerial and financial flexibility. This includes the impossibility of raising equity capital, possibly limited access to credit markets due to public sector borrowing limits, and rigidities in personnel policies. However, most of these constraints are not related to ownership per se and might be overcome, for instance, through the corporatization of the operators.

Industrial Policy

Beginning in the 1970s, against the background of stagnant economic development, the electronics industry and the telecommunications industry received increased attention as possible levers to overcome economic slack and improve the international competitiveness of industries. Many European countries and the European Community institutions have developed industrial policies intended to increase the societal benefits derived from telecommunications. From a normative point of view, such policies can be justified if they serve to improve social welfare. Three important examples are the prevalence of *externalities* in telecommunications, *public good* characteristics of basic research and development, and the existence of *imperfect international trade* conditions.

Several authors have argued that core parts of the telecommunications industry are afflicted with externalities. These can be embedded in the network character of telecommunications services (Allen, 1988; Markus, 1990) or be caused by the wide geographical or intertemporal distribution of benefits from telecommunications investments (Antonelli, 1991; Diewert, 1986). The prevalence of these types of externalities may call for explicit measures to influence the pricing and investment policies of the telecommunications service providers. Katz and Shapiro (1992) have shown that a suboptimally high diversity of products and services might result in markets with externalities, perhaps calling for public policies to reduce the complexity of those markets. However, the underlying issues are not yet fully understood and need further research.

If the results of basic research and development show certain public good characteristics, its organization in private competing entities may lead to suboptimal investment in research activities. In addition, oligopoly industry structures, as they are characteristic for many parts of telecommunications, may lead to a suboptimally low degree of diversity into different research projects. This is largely due to the strategic interdependence of the companies, which induces them to follow similar research strategies (Nelson, 1981, p. 106). In both cases, public policies might be able to improve welfare.

Modern trade theory has provided yet another argument in support of industrial policy measures. It has been demonstrated that under conditions of imperfectly competitive international markets (e.g., due to oligopolistic market structures that are typical for large parts of telecommunications) individual countries or regions may be able to improve their welfare by measures of industrial policy in support of their national industries (Krugman, 1990). In particular, these policies may include initiatives to support R&D in telecommunications, special programs to develop a modern telecommunications infrastructure, or activities to support the diffusion of telecommunications services.

Social Policy

The notion of telecommunications as a vital infrastructure for society has led many countries to adopt policies to foster the availability and affordability of telecommunications services (OECD, 1991) but also to impose measures to control for unwanted effects of telecommunications such as possible impacts on privacy. Examples of such policies include the policies to assist equal access to communications networks, the design of telecommunications services for the hearing or speaking impaired, the support for applications of telecommunications technology to provide decentralized health services, and measures to protect privacy.

Although the prevalence of some form of market failure can create the need for such policies, measures in this area frequently draw on normative concepts that are based on notions of distributional equity, fairness, or individual rights rather than efficiency. Frequently, trade-offs prevail between the goal of efficiency defined in the neoclassical way and social policy measures.

The Choice of Telecommunications Policy Instruments and Institutions

Numerous regulatory mechanisms to cope with the discussed cases of market failure and to accomplish distributional goals in telecommunications have been used in regulatory policy and proposed in the academic literature. In an "ideal" world of perfect information and free of transaction costs, different policy approaches (public regulation, public production, or the use of tax-subsidy mechanisms) all could be designed to implement welfare-maximizing outcomes and would indeed be equivalent in their comparative efficiency properties (Sappington &

Stiglitz, 1987). However, in a world of incomplete information this conclusion does not hold true. Under such real world conditions a key problem of the design of a policy framework is to overcome the prevalence of *asymmetric information* between the regulatory institution(s) and the regulated industry as well as the problem of *uncertainty* as to future developments. Usually, the regulated industry has more and better information on its cost and market conditions than the regulators. The regulated industry can withhold vital information or misinform the regulatory authorities strategically (Owen & Braeutigam, 1978).

Regulatory instruments have different information requirements allowing the regulated industry different leeway to inform the regulators in a strategic way. For instance, rate-of-return regulation requires detailed cost information from the regulated industry that is not easily observable from outside the company. In contrast, price-cap regulation—one major alternative to rate-of-return regulation tried out in several countries—is based on easy-to-observe price data of a company (Einhorn, 1991). One major challenge to telecommunications policy is, hence, the implementation of *incentive compatible* (Dasgupta, Hammond, & Maskin, 1979) regulatory instruments that minimize the potential distortions created by asymmetric information.

Although the goal of efficiency has become a social imperative (Noll, 1986), a number of other criteria to judge regulatory mechanisms have been discussed. Associated administrative costs are an important aspect of regulatory mechanisms. Other things equal, the instrument causing the lowest amount of these transaction costs could be considered optimal. From a legal point of view, the compatibility of a regulatory instrument with the existing legal environment and the established record of court decisions is important. Finally, regulatory instruments and institutions might be evaluated according to criteria of fairness, equity, or their specific accountability structure (Hills, 1991; Isaac, Mathieu, & Zajac, 1991).

Whereas the efficiency properties of regulatory instruments have been studied in some detail (Spulber, 1989, for an overview), their comparative performance with regard to the transaction costs involved or their fairness and equity characteristics are not as well understood yet. In such a view, *trade-offs* between different instruments become visible (Crew & Kleindorfer, 1986).[11] Because of these trade-offs, the choice of an optimal regulatory instrument becomes dependent on explicit (or implicit) weights assigned to different objectives. The efficiency-equity trade-off might be overcome by separating these two goals and pursuing them with different instruments. It has also been discussed to introduce distributional or fairness constraints into the pricing of telecommunications services (Bailey & Willig, 1981; Mitchell & Vogelsang, 1991) and to maximize efficiency subject to these constraints. More research is needed to examine the possible trade-offs between such goals as (procedural) fairness, efficiency, accountability, and associated transaction costs.

An important issue is, therefore, whether regulatory instruments should be designed to optimize one goal (such as efficiency) or multiple goals (such as efficiency and social policy goals). A classic example for the latter case was (and still is) the public enterprise system in Europe. In its ideal version, the management of the PTTs was expected to accomplish a complex bundle of efficiency, industrial policy, and social policy goals. An example of the former case would be a pure market organization of telecommunications as this has been promoted by liberal scholars with corrective policy measures through the general tax system to secure distributional goals. Because of the complexity of factors involved, no clear-cut answer seems to exist to those questions and to the relative performance of the different policy instruments.

Both at the national and the Community level, the institutional framework of telecommunications is being overhauled. One of the major issues in federal or confederal political structures is the assignment of jurisdiction to the different political bodies, for instance, the jurisdiction of the Community versus national institutions. In principle, the same efficiency and equity criteria used to design more specific regulatory instruments can be applied to the design of the overall institutional framework (see Bauer, 1992b, for a more detailed discussion).

Positive Approaches to Telecommunications Policy

Normative approaches have had a considerable influence on the process of policy formation. However, most normative theories do not model the institutional framework of policy making explicitly and frequently assume perfectly functioning markets or perfect regulation. However, the formation of policies and their implementation does not take place in such a vacuum but is shaped by the institutional framework of policy making as well as the specific actors participating in this process and their interests. Moreover, government agencies may rather act in their own self-interest than in the public interest. As a result, public policies may fail to accomplish the stated goals and, instead, be prone to *government failure*. Once established, policies, by favoring particular groups, may generate vested interests in the status quo that have to be overcome in attempts to reform existing policies. Policy reforms, therefore, are always constrained by the status quo ante and, hence, by policies of the past. Not only do they have to meet normative criteria but they also have to be *feasible* under these complex conditions.

Positive studies of regulation and telecommunications policy have employed various methodological approaches, including rational actor models (Peltzman, 1976), public choice models (Buchanan & Tullock, 1962), or game-theoretic approaches (Sharkey, 1983). In spite of the diversity of approaches, these models have produced some common results. Among other things, it has been shown that (a) policies usually do not favor only one group (as has been asserted by the simple "capture" theory of regulation) but rather favor a coalition of several groups, perhaps even including the entire public; (b) policies are promoted by "political entrepreneurs" and may be subject to "political business cycles" in the form of favors to strong interest groups in pre-election periods; (c) policies have a higher chance of success if potential "losers" can be compensated by potential "winners" (Blankart, 1990); and (d) successful coalitions that can dominate policy may change subject to technological, economic, and political change (see Romer & Rosenthal, 1987, for a more comprehensive overview).

One peculiar aspect of European telecommunications policy is the shaping of policy by national and supranational authorities. This specific institutional framework and its influence on the policy outcomes has received some attention at the general level of European policy formation (Keohane & Hoffmann, 1991). Bauer (in press) analyzes this interaction of national and European telecommunication policies showing that the particular feasibility conditions in the European institutional framework (e.g., the particular voting procedures in the European Council, or the practice of the Commission to solicit input from national authorities and interested parties; see Bauer & Steinfield, Chapter 4 in this book) grant national policies considerable influence on European policies.

The formation of European telecommunications policy has also been analyzed from a more global perspective. Changes related to the globalization of trade, the loss of the American hegemonic power, the restructuring of the global centers of power (Cowhey, 1990), as well as the emergence of new global networks of firms (Bressand & Nikolaïdis, 1990) have been utilized as a background for the study of European policies.

Conclusion

The normative theories of telecommunications policy do not fully predetermine an overall "optimal" policy regime. This indeterminacy goes beyond the trade-offs between efficiency, distributional, and equity goals and is not least rooted in the multi-paradigmatic status of the major disciplines that inform telecommunications policy making. The emerging policies are as much shaped by the historical, political, and cultural environment of a society as by scholarly analysis.[12]

Although the benefits of a more competitive market organization are obvious in the areas of terminal equipment and specialized services, the advantages of a competitive market framework are less well understood in the areas of infrastructure development, its impact on the long-run innovation trajectories of the sector, or the overall performance of the telecommunications industry. In these areas, short-run efficiency gains of an opening of market access might be counteracted in the medium and long run by coordination and transaction costs between more fragmented network and service providers.

The governance structures of telecommunications worldwide are being reorganized in a more competitive way, but significant differences remain (Caby & Steinfield, Chapter 3, and Noam & Kramer, Chapter 15, in this book). The European Economic Community and its member states have chosen a particular strategy of telecommunications policy. Their experience should be an important input into future investigations of the comparative dynamics of differing telecommunications policy regimes.

Notes

1. Because of the limitations of space, the following discussion focuses mainly on the debate of telecommunications policy in the social sciences, leaving the contributions by legal or engineering scholars largely beyond its scope. For a more detailed discussion see Bauer (1992a).

2. This does not necessarily imply that the instruments chosen to achieve universal service, such as public regulation in the United States or public enterprise in Europe as well as strategies to average prices, were the most efficient ones. What I want to underline is the social consensus established with regard to these issues.

3. In the United States, *institutional economics* has had considerable influence in the development of the principles of regulation (see, for instance, Bonbright, 1988). In the European context, the related *Gemeinwirtschaftslehre* was influential in developing

principles of the public enterprise system (Snow, 1988; Thiemeyer, 1983). The French *école de la régulation* provides an interesting encompassing approach to regulation but is, so far, of limited influence on practical policy making (see Brenner & Glick, 1991, for a survey).

4. An economic outcome is called *efficient* (Pareto-optimal) if no individual can be made better off through a reallocation of resources without reducing the utility of another individual.

5. Economics defines *competition* as a market situation in which no individual firm has the power to consistently charge prices above (marginal) cost. This use of the term deviates from its everyday use, which interprets *competition* rather as "rivalry" between different suppliers.

6. An industry is said to be a *natural monopoly* if because of economies of scale and/or advantages of joint production it is cheaper to produce the entire industry demand in one firm instead of two or more firms (see Sharkey, 1982, for a rigorous treatment).

7. *Oligopolies* are situations with only a few incumbent suppliers in a market, in which they may enjoy considerable market power.

8. An activity is afflicted with *externalities* if the private gains or costs to individuals or organizations deviate from the social benefits or costs of these activities (see Musgrave, 1973, for an introduction).

9. Important characteristics of *public goods* are zero (or very low) incremental cost to serve additional consumers and nonrivalry between the consumption of different consumers. Although telecommunications does not show those characteristics in a pure form, it still shares some of them—rendering it an imperfect public good (Egan, 1991; Owen & Wildman, 1992).

10. Communications has been influential in shaping the private telecommunications strategies of users and suppliers.

11. For instance, Ramsey-Boiteux prices, which are known to be efficient prices, call for price variation for different customer groups according to the inverse price elasticity of their demand. This implies higher prices for customers with a low price elasticity of demand, which are frequently lower income, captive customers that cannot choose between different suppliers. Such a price policy might, therefore, conflict with a policy of universal service at affordable rates to all groups of the population.

12. In his poignant statement of the relationship between theory and policy, Keynes (1936, p. 383) argued that

> the ideas of economists and political philosophers, *both when they are right and when they are wrong* [emphasis added, J.M.B.], are more powerful than is commonly understood. Indeed the world is ruled by little else. Practical men, who believe themselves to be quite exempt from any intellectual influences, are usually the slaves of some defunct economist. Madmen in authority, who hear voices in the air, are distilling their frenzy from some academic scribbler of a few years back. I am sure that the power of vested interests is vastly exaggerated compared with the gradual encroachment of ideas.

References

Aharoni, Y. (1986). *The evolution and management of state-owned enterprise.* Cambridge, MA: Ballinger.

Allen, D. (1988). New telecommunication services: Network externalities and critical mass. *Telecommunications Policy, 12*, 257-271.

Antonelli, C. (Ed.). (1991). *The economics of information networks.* New York: Elsevier Science.

Bailey, E. E., & Willig, R. D. (1981) Income-distribution concerns in regulatory policy-making. In G. Fromm (Ed.), *Studies in public regulation* (pp. 79-107). Cambridge: MIT Press.

Bauer, J. M. (1992a). *Conceptual foundations of telecommunications policy.* Unpublished manuscript. East Lansing: Michigan State University, Department of Telecommunication.

Bauer, J. M. (1992b). *The regulatory framework for European telecommunications: A critical examination.* Unpublished manuscript. East Lansing: Michigan State University, Department of Telecommunication.

Bauer, J. M. (in press). Telecommunication in post-1992 Europe. In H. Oniki, T. H. Oum, & R. Stevenson (Eds.), *International perspectives in telecommunications policy.* Vol. 5 of *International Journal of Comparative Public Policy.*

Baumol, W. J., Panzar, J., & Willig, R. D. (1982). *Contestable markets and the theory of industry structure.* San Diego: Harcourt Brace Jovanovich.

Berg, S. V., & Tschirhart, J. (1988). *Natural monopoly regulation. Principles and practice.* New York: Cambridge University Press.

Blankart, C. B. (1990). Strategies of regulatory reform. An economic analysis with some remarks on Germany. In G. Majone (Ed.), *Deregulation or re-regulation. Regulatory reform in Europe and the United States* (pp. 211-222). London: Pinter.

Bonbright, J. C. (1988). *Principles of public utility rates* (2nd ed.). Arlington, VA: Public Utility Reports.

Brenner, R., & Glick, M. (1991). The Regulation Approach: Theory and history. *New Left Review, 18*, 45-119.

Bressand, A., & Nikolaïdis, K. (1990). Regional integration in a networked world economy. In W. Wallace (Ed.), *The dynamics of European integration* (pp. 27-49). London: Pinter Publishers for the Royal Institute of International Affairs.

Buchanan, J. M., & Tullock, G. (1962). *The calculus of consent.* Ann Arbor: University of Michigan Press.

Cowhey, P. F. (1990). Telecommunications. In G. C. Hufbauer, (Ed.), *Europe 1992: An American perspective* (pp. 159-224). Washington, DC: The Brookings Institution.

Crew, M. A., & Kleindorfer, P. R. (1986). *The economics of public utility regulation.* Houndmills, UK: Macmillan.

Dasgupta, P. S., Hammond, P. J., & Maskin, E. S. (1979). The implementation of social choice rules: Some general results on incentive compatibility. *Review of Economic Studies, 46*, 185-216.

Diewert, W. E. (1986). *Measurement of the economic benefits of infrastructure services.* Berlin, Germany: Springer-Verlag.

Duch, R. M. (1991). *Privatizing the economy: Telecommunications policy in comparative perspective.* Ann Arbor: University of Michigan Press.

Egan, B. L. (1991). *Information superhighways: The economics of advanced public communication networks.* Norwood, MA: Artech House.

Einhorn, M. A. (Ed.). (1991). *Price caps and incentive regulation in telecommunications.* Boston: Kluwer Academic Publishers.

Fulk, J., & Steinfield, C. (Eds.). (1990). *Organizations and communication technology.* Newbury Park: Sage.

Garnham, N. (1990). *Capitalism and communication. Global culture and the economics of information* (Ed. by F. Inglis). London: Sage.

Hayek, F. A. von (1968). *Wettbewerb als Entdeckungsverfahren.* Kieler Vorträge N.F. 56. Kiel, Germany: Institut für Weltwirtschaft an der Universität Kiel.

Hills, J. (1991). Regulation, politics and telecommunications. In J.-P. Chamoux (Ed.), *Deregulating regulators? Communication policies for the 90's* (pp. 99-115). Amsterdam: IOS Press.

Hodgson, G. M. (1988). *Economics and institutions. A manifesto for a modern institutional economics.* Philadelphia, PA: University of Pennsylvania Press.

Isaac, R. M., Mathieu, D., & Zajac, E. E. (1991). Institutional framing and perceptions of fairness. *Constitutional Political Economy, 2,* 329-370.

Johansson, P.-O. (1991). *An introduction to modern welfare economics.* New York: Cambridge University Press.

Katz, M. L., & Shapiro, C. (1992). Product introduction with network externalities. *Journal of Industrial Economics, 40,* 55-83.

Keohane, R. O., & Hoffmann, S. (Eds.). (1991). *The new European community: Decision-making and institutional change.* Boulder, CO: Westview Press.

Keynes, J. M. (1936). *The general theory of interest, employment, and money.* New York: Harcourt Brace.

Kreps, G. (1990). *Organizational communications: Theory and practice* (2nd ed.). New York: Longman.

Krugman, P. R. (1990). *Rethinking international trade.* Cambridge: MIT Press.

Markus, M. L. (1990). Toward a "critical mass" theory of interactive media. In J. Fulk & C. Steinfield (Eds.), *Organizations and communication technology* (pp. 194-218). Newbury Park: Sage.

Mitchell, B. M., & Vogelsang, I. (1991). *Telecommunications pricing: Theory and practice.* New York: Cambridge University Press.

Musgrave, R. A. (1973). *Public finance in theory and practice.* New York: McGraw-Hill.

Nelson, R. R. (1981). Assessing private enterprise: An exegesis of tangled doctrine. *Bell Journal of Economics, 12,* 93-111.

Nelson, R. R., & Winter, S. G. (1982). *An evolutionary theory of economic change.* Cambridge, MA: Belknap Press.

Noll, R. G. (1986). The political and institutional context of communications policy. In M. S. Snow (Ed.), *Marketplace for telecommunications: Regulation and deregulation in industrialized democracies* (pp. 42-65). New York: Longman.

North, D. C. (1990). *Institutions, institutional change, and economic performance.* New York: Cambridge University Press.

OECD (1991). *Universal service and rate restructuring in telecommunications.* ICCP No. 23. Paris: OECD.

Owen, B. M., & Braeutigam, R. R. (1978). *The regulation game: Strategic use of the administrative process.* Cambridge, MA: Ballinger.

Owen, B. M., & Wildman, S. S. (1992). *Video economics.* Cambridge, MA: Harvard University Press.

Peltzman, S. (1976). Toward a more general theory of regulation. *Journal of Law and Economics, 19,* 211-240.

Rawls, J. (1971). *A theory of justice.* Cambridge, MA: Harvard University Press.

Rogers, E. M. (1986). *Communication technology: The new media in society.* New York: The Free Press.

Romer, T., & Rosenthal, H. (1987). Modern political economy and the study of regulation. In E. E. Bailey (Ed.), *Public regulation: New perspectives on institutions and policies* (pp. 73-116). Cambridge: MIT Press.

Sappington, D. E. M., & Stiglitz, J. E. (1987). Information and regulation. In E. E. Bailey (Ed.), *Public regulation: New perspectives on institutions and policies* (pp. 3-43). Cambridge: MIT Press.

Schiller, H. I. (1981). *Who knows: Information in the age of the Fortune 500.* Norwood, NJ: Ablex.

Schumpeter, J. A. (1942). *Capitalism, socialism, and democracy.* New York, NY: Harper & Brothers.

Schwartz, M. (1986). The nature and scope of contestability theory. *Oxford Economic Papers, 38*(Supplement), 37-57.

Sharkey, W. W. (1982). *The theory of natural monopoly.* New York: Cambridge University Press.

Sharkey, W. W. (1983). Outline of a positive theory of regulation. In J. Ordover & O. Grandy (Eds.), *Proceedings from the Tenth Annual Telecommunications Policy Research Conference* (pp. 235-250). Lexington, MA: Lexington Books.

Shepherd, W. G. (1984). "Contestability" vs. competition. *American Economic Review, 74*, 572-587.

Slack, J. D., & Fejes, F. (Eds.). (1987). *The ideology of the information age.* Norwood, NJ: Ablex.

Snow, M. S. (1988). The state as stopgap: Social economy and sustainability of natural monopoly in the telecommunications sector. *Review of Social Economy, 46*, 1-23.

Spulber, D. F. (1989). *Regulation and markets.* Cambridge: MIT Press.

Thiemeyer, T. (1983). Deregulation in the perspective of the German Gemeinwirtschafts-lehre. *Zeitschrift für die gesamte Staatswissenschaft, 139*, 405-418.

Train, K. E. (1991). *Optimal regulation: The economic theory of natural monopoly.* Cambridge: MIT Press.

Trebing, H. M. (1992). *Regulatory reform in telecommunications: Beyond price-caps and ideology.* Paper presented at the Telecommunications Faculty Seminar, Michigan State University, East Lansing, MI, January 30.

Vickers, J., & Yarrow, G. (1988). *Privatization: An economic analysis.* Cambridge: MIT Press.

Weizsäcker, C. C. von (1984). Free entry into telecommunications. *Information Economics and Policy, 1*, 197-216.

Williamson, O. E. (1985). *The economic institutions of capitalism.* New York: Free Press.

Zajac, E. (1978). *Fairness or efficiency.* Cambridge, MA: Ballinger.

THREE

Trends in the Liberalization of European Telecommunications

Community Harmonization and National Divergence

LAURENCE CABY
CHARLES STEINFIELD

Despite the common characteristic throughout Europe of a strong government role in the provision of telecommunications infrastructure and services, the specific structure of the sector has traditionally varied from country to country. The past was characterized by national standards (e.g., technical interfaces for connecting to the network were so variable that telephones manufactured for one country would not function in another; Ungerer & Costello, 1988) and very comprehensive monopolies that often covered all infrastructure, services, and equipment. Nevertheless, the unique cultural, economic, and geographical circumstances in each nation encouraged diversity between countries (Steinfield, Chapter 1 in this book; Vallée, 1990).

Whereas, for instance, some countries had only licensed one major telecommunications provider (e.g., France, Germany, Spain) the Italian telecommunications system is run by five major companies whose responsibility is divided along geographical and functional characteristics. Finland even had established 57 local and 3 interregional service providers. Some countries provided telecommunications services jointly with postal and banking services (e.g., Germany until 1989,

AUTHORS' NOTE: We are grateful to Alain Vallée for his comments on an earlier version of this chapter.

England until 1981, Austria, Switzerland); others, such as Sweden, never integrated those services. Some countries clearly supported their domestic telecommunications manufacturers through procurement and standardization activities (e.g., Spain, Germany); others, such as Denmark (not least because of the lack of a significant national telecommunications manufacturing industry), traditionally followed an internationally open procurement strategy. Finally, to give a last example, some countries organized telecommunications as a public administration, and others, such as Spain and Italy, relied on private or at least mixed public-private corporations (Bauer, in press; Noam, 1992).

Given different preexisting national structures, we should not expect the approaches taken in each country to liberalize the sector to be homogeneous. However, efforts to develop a harmonized approach to the regulation of telecommunications throughout the European Community are directed at counterbalancing this diversity in national structures so that a common market for telecommunications services and equipment can be created.

In this chapter, we identify several basic trends in the liberalization of the telecommunications sector throughout Europe. By *liberalization*, we refer to efforts to introduce competition into the telecommunications sector (see Noam & Kramer, Chapter 15 in this book, for a definition of liberalization as well as a discussion of the differences between liberalization and deregulation). We begin by first recognizing the common regulatory approach emanating from the European Community, primarily through the legislative activity of the Commission of the European Communities (CEC; see Bauer & Steinfield, Chapter 4 in this book, and Ungerer & Costello, 1988, for more complete analyses of CEC initiatives in the telecommunications sector). Clearly, the harmonizing effect of the European Community on national approaches to telecommunications has and will continue to be significant. However, the flexibility for individual nations to define their own unique telecommunications approach still exists. We therefore devote the remainder of the chapter to an analysis of the basis of this flexibility, using several country illustrations.

From the Treaty of Rome to the Green Paper: The Emergence of a Communitywide Regulatory Framework

For the past four decades, the member states of the European Community have worked at the construction of a new economic area that would eliminate all barriers to the free flow of goods, services, people, and capital across borders. The principles and procedures set forth in the 1957 Treaty of Rome provided a broad set of guidelines for the creation of a common market, the implementation of which was accelerated in the Single European Act of 1987. Five key articles within the Treaty of Rome provide the basis for the European Commission's specific application to the field of telecommunications in the 1987 Green Paper:

- Article 30 prohibits any measures that would have the effect of restricting imports.
- Article 59 calls for a progressive abolishing of restrictions on the provision of services across borders.
- Articles 85 and 86 focus on competition policy, with the former establishing a prohibition on anticompetitive behavior that could serve to restrain trade and the latter prohibiting the abuse of a dominant position.
- Article 90 specifically indicates that even public undertakings or companies with exclusive rights granted by the state must comply with the Treaty's provisions (importantly, only insofar as it does not obstruct the performance of the particular tasks assigned to them). It further gives the Commission the authority to address specific directives and decisions to member states in order to ensure the application of this provision.

Because the telecommunications sector has traditionally been considered on a national level to be of strategic importance, until the mid 1980s in Europe it had been excluded from market liberalization efforts and remained a protected area dominated by monopoly operators and "national champions" in the industrial equipment field.

There has, however, been a gradual change of attitude based on two main observations (Ungerer & Costello, 1988): First, European telecommunications services are going to play a vital role in improving European economic competitiveness and in creating the internal market as defined in the Single European Act. Second, telecommunications is attributed a substantial influence not only on services in general—such as financial, transport, and tourist services—but also on commodity exchanges and industrial cooperation in Europe.

As described elsewhere in this volume (Bauer & Steinfield, Chapter 4), a comprehensive framework for applying Treaty of Rome principles to telecommunications appeared with the publication in June 1987 of the Green Paper on telecommunications (Commission, 1987). Based on the Green Paper (and the related decisions, directives, and recommendations that have been issued), it is possible to outline three broad targets of EC liberalization and harmonization efforts in telecommunications: terminal equipment, services, and the structural reform of telecommunications administrations.

Terminal Equipment

Even before the publication of the Green Paper, the Commission had begun efforts to open up the market for terminal equipment, which included such devices as telephone handsets, modems, and all other attachments to the network (Commission, 1988). In many European countries (as in the United States until the 1975 FCC Terminal Equipment Decision), telephones and other terminal equipment could only be obtained from the PTT and often could only be rented and not purchased. PTTs obtained their equipment only from preferred national suppliers and used national standards and type approval processes to keep foreign equipment providers from entering the market. But such a market structure foreclosed national equipment providers from capitalizing on economies of scale, discouraged the equipment industry from engaging in the kinds of rapid innovation such as was occurring in the computer industry, and resulted in higher costs and lower benefits to end users.

The Terminal Equipment Directive initiated the market opening process by abolishing all special or exclusive rights to selling terminals. Moreover, it required all member states to publish their specifications and approval rules for terminals to facilitate foreign supplier entry into the market. Simply ending exclusive rights on the selling of equipment is only a first step to creating a pan-European market. If member states persist in employing national standards, then the positions of domestic suppliers can be bolstered, but all suffer from the lack of sufficient economies of scale. Thus, the Commission has pushed for a policy of European standardization, with ETSI (see Drake, Chapter 5 in this book) created to help implement this policy. Member states are obliged to inform the European Commission about their planned projects for technical regulation and standards, and the Commission is able to intervene if it considers that such projects could constitute barriers to intercommunity exchanges. Finally, to add teeth to the policies above, the EC has directed that the principle of mutual recognition be applied to approval requirements and terminals. This means that once a terminal has obtained approval in one of the member states, it can be freely marketed and connected to public networks in any of the others without being subjected to other procedures. To enjoy this freedom, terminals must meet certain "essential requirements"—safety for the user and for the network operator's personnel, protection of the network, and inter-functioning with the network and possibly with other terminals.

At this point, the terminal equipment market has been opened to competition nearly everywhere in Europe. In a related sector—network equipment—an attempt was made to force PTTs to sever relations with national champions by opening up public procurement to foreign bidders (Council, 1990b). Although the language in this bill to a certain degree favors EC companies by allowing PTTs to choose an EC bid over a non-EC bid if within 3% in price, the overall effect is to further liberalize the equipment sector.

The equipment sector was perhaps the easiest in which to begin liberalization efforts, primarily for the reason that the directives from the EC were in fact recognizing what had already been occurring in the marketplace (see Noam & Kramer, Chapter 15 in this book). Nevertheless, the complex of initiatives by the EC has formalized the opening of this market and over time will result in a more harmonized equipment market throughout Europe.

Services

As noted above, Articles 59 and 90 of the Treaty of Rome call for the progressive abolition of restrictions on the provision of services within the EC, even when provided by state-sanctioned monopolies. To open the domestic markets in this part of the telecommunications sector, the EC has adopted a "progressive liberalization" posture—one that explicitly recognizes a need to guarantee the financial viability of existing telecommunications administrations in order for them to fulfill their public service obligations. Thus, the Commission first established the distinction between "reserved" and "non-reserved" services in the Green Paper, with the former allowed to remain under monopoly control of the telecommunications administrations if a country so desires and the latter to be open to competitive supply. Reserved services originally referred only to basic telephone and telex service—with data transmission moving from reserved to non-reserved in 1993 (although member states with poorly developed national data networks can petition to extend their monopolies in data transmission for several more years). New decisions call for the opening of even basic telephone service, beginning as early as 1996 in some countries (see Bauer & Steinfield, Chapter 4 in this book). In addition, member states can also maintain the exclusive provision of all infrastructure by telecommunications administrations, thereby separating the concept of services provision from network provision and operation. These important concessions guaranteed that the lion's share of the market could remain under control of the telecommunications administrations, given that the switched voice market represents more than 90% of all revenues (Noam & Kramer, Chapter 15 in this book).

The commission was clearly interested in stimulating the growth of value-added services, which have come to refer to nearly all services beyond basic switched telephony (see Bouwman & Latzer, Chapter 9 in this book, for a definition and categorization of value-added services). To allow for a competitive market in this area, while at the same time permitting exclusive control of infrastructure by telecommunications administrations, requires that service providers must have fair access to networks. Their customers must be able to access the service, either by dedicated lines or via the public switched network. Moreover, a policy of restricting the entry of existing telecommunications administrations into the value-added services market was not envisioned. Thus, some means was needed of ensuring that administrations would not use their control over the network to gain an unfair advantage over external service providers (e.g., by charging higher prices than they incur themselves for the provision of the same service, or by placing restrictions on access or use that compromise the ability of a service provider to compete).

The two directives issued by the European Commission and Council to accomplish the opening of the services market were the Services Directive (Commission, 1990) and the Open Network Provision (ONP) Framework Directive (Council, 1990a) (see Bauer & Steinfield, Chapter 4 in this book). The former effectively called for the application of the Treaty of Rome to services, granted exemptions for reserved services (at least temporarily), and, after a compromise, allowed member states to employ some form of licensing regime to manage the conditions by which service providers entered the market. The directive required, however, that licensing procedures be designed in accordance with clear, objective, and nondiscriminatory criteria.

The ONP directive dealt with the means of ensuring open access to network infrastructures, for all who desire to provide nonreserved services. Issues discussed in the document include the need for standardized technical interfaces to networks, fair conditions of supply and usage of network resources, and cost-based tariff principles for access and interconnection (Council, 1990a; see Bauer & Steinfield, Chapter 4 in this book, for more details on ONP).

Specific ONP directives will follow, applying the principles in the framework to specific types of network infrastructures. Initial efforts are directed at liberalizing leased line provision, which would permit service providers to offer information and other types of value-added services without facing crippling usage sensitive charges from network operators (which would, in effect, make it impossible to compete with a telecom administration offering the same service, because their costs would not go up with higher traffic on a circuit). Later directives will extend the principles to public-switched telephone networks, public-switched packet data networks, mobile services, intelligent networks, ISDN, and eventually to future broadband communications networks.

Most countries in Europe, following Green Paper recommendations in advance of the ONP directives, have authorized the competitive provision of value-added services. In addition, in most countries, mobile services are provided by at least two competing operators. However, leased line provision remains highly variable, and a full opening of the services market in some countries will take time (OECD, 1990).

Structural Reform of Telecommunications Administrations

The Green Paper did not attempt to dictate in any specific way how the telecommunications administrations should be structured. It did, however, suggest that a clear separation of regulatory and operational functions was necessary. The Commission felt that allowing a network operator to have the authority to set standards, approve equipment, act as the licensing authority for service providers, and so forth, could result in discriminatory practices that disadvantaged the new competitors. Nearly every country has now created some form of regulatory authority, although the degree of separation from the operating side of the administration varies.

Summary

The liberalization trends initiated at the European Community level have thus focused on (a) creating an open and competitive market for telecommunications equipment, (b) progressively opening national markets to competitive supply of value-added services, and (c) curtailing the power of existing telecommunications administrations to use their regulatory authority to constrain competition in services or equipment. Despite these harmonizing efforts, each country continues to maintain its own unique approach to the provision of telecommunications. In the next section, we consider the various means by which country approaches can differ in significant ways.

The Bases for Different Country Liberalization Approaches

National flexibility to organize the telecommunications sector can include (but is not limited to) variations in (a) the specific structure and function of the regulatory authority, (b) the status/ownership of the public telecommunications operator, (c) the degree to which services competition is extended into formerly reserved services, and (d) the authorization of competitive infrastructures. Each is discussed briefly below.

Structure and Function of the Regulatory Authority

The Green Paper on telecommunications called only for a separation between the regulatory and operational functions of telecommunications administrations—it did not contain any specific guidelines as to how this separation should be achieved. Regulatory functions may remain within the government ministry in charge of telecommunications, or they may be given over to a new, independent agency with no explicit link to the ministry. With the exception of the United Kingdom, which has created a regulatory agency, OFTEL, that is independent of the Department of Trade and Industry, the remaining EC countries have kept their regulatory function within the relevant ministry.

Several issues can be raised regarding these two approaches. First, some observers question whether a ministry is capable of acting in an unbiased manner when dealing with competitors to an operator dependent on the ministry. They wonder whether ministers themselves (if they are the "chief regulator") would be willing to make unpopular decisions that might have negative consequences in upcoming elections (remembering that in some countries the telecommunications administration is one of the largest employers and has one of the most powerful unions). In contrast, others argue that such functions need to be part of an elected government office rather than part of an agency that is not formally associated with elected officials. They argue that without this link, regulators might have little or no accountability and may be less inclined to place their decisions within a context of existing social and political realities (see both Carsberg, 1991, and Melody, 1991, for discussions of these issues).

The objectives of the regulation can include such goals as ensuring universality of services, availability of services, efficient management of scarce resources (such as radio spectrum), and fair competition in those areas where permitted. The tools for meeting these broad objectives in general include control of licenses, tariffs, and, increasingly, interconnection requirements and usage conditions, but these tools vary as well from country to country. The United Kingdom and France, for example, employ a price-cap scheme, which limits any price increases to the rate of inflation minus some percentage (although France's cap is less severe than the U.K.'s). The U.K. has also experimented with implementing other "incentive regulation" schemes, which call for financial penalties on poor performance quality of the dominant operator, British Telecom. In this way, they hope to counter a price-cap regime's potential incentive to maximize short-term returns by avoiding investment and allowing performance to deteriorate.

The Status/Ownership of
the Public Telecommunications Operator

Other than the separation of regulatory and operation functions, there are no specific EC guidelines regarding the status of public telecommunications operators (PTOs). PTOs can, for example, be administrations that remain a part of a ministry, state-owned companies that may operate under the same legal framework as private firms, or privately owned companies. Each solution implies a very different context for telecommunications liberalization.

In several European countries, the PTO has retained the status of public administration tied to the relevant ministry. This is the case in Germany and Austria, for example, with Germany limited in its structural reform by a constitutional constraint on any change in the Bundespost's status (although the costs of reunification have now led Germany to move toward privatization to raise sorely needed capital). The Belgium telecommunications operator, now known as Belgacom, is in the process of moving from administration to state-owned company status. Maintaining this structure has several implications for the operator. First, it gives the operator less control over investment strategy, because it is dependent on government budgets, whereas operating revenues are in essence state income that may be earmarked for other programs. Employees can have civil servant status, reducing flexibility in dealing with the labor force. For these reasons, it may be difficult to reconcile administration status with competition in the service sector, as new competitors will not have the same constraints.

A much more common approach is to change the PTO's status from administration to state-owned company, often called *corporatization* (see Noam & Kramer, Chapter 15 in this book). These new companies, which are created out of the operating side of the administration, are generally able to finance investment out of their own revenues. They can thus respond more quickly to market opportunities. Some state-owned companies, such as The Netherlands PTT, operate according to private business laws and have stock, even though the government owns 100% of the shares. Others, such as France Telecom, have a more ad hoc and unique status and are not fully subject to private business laws. Some observers view corporatization as a "pre-privatization" step, which can help improve the value of a private share offering by enabling the operator to become more efficient and accustomed to functioning more like a company than a government bureaucracy (O'Neill, 1991).

Privatization, often confused with such terms as *liberalization* and *deregulation*, means that some or all of the operations, management, and/or ownership of the PTO is sold to private investors (see Noam & Kramer, Chapter 15 in this book). The underlying objectives of privatization are to (a) improve management and operational efficiency and thereby reduce costs, (b) increase access to and quality of basic services as well as provide new services, and (c) generate adequate capital for provision of new services and expansion and upgrade of the basic network.

It would be a mistake to view all privately held operators as alike, however (see O'Neill, 1991, for a discussion of the diverse approaches to privatization of operators around the globe). In fact, one crucial question is the degree to which the government maintains some stake in a private telecommunications operator. The British government, for example, held on to 51% of the shares of British Telecom following its widely publicized privatization in 1984, although it will sell off the remainder shortly. Other European governments hold some stake in their supposedly private operators, including the Spanish government with a significant stake in Telefónica and the Italian government through its holding company IRI-STET, with a majority ownership of SIP (the local telephone service provider) and Italcable (the intercontinental service provider).

Nevertheless, privatization of telecommunications operators does relate to processes of liberalization and regulation in key ways. First, all things being equal, it is usually assumed that a private firm will have a greater incentive (that is, profits to shareholders) to be efficient in its use of resources. However, the unconstrained pursuit of profits might conflict with social objectives—so regulation in the form of price controls and universal service obligations often remain (as in the case of the United States, where the privately held AT&T agreed to such regulatory oversight in return for protection from competition throughout much of the 20th century). Thus countries cannot simply privatize their telecommunications administration without the addition of some form of regulatory framework (O'Neill, 1991).

Even in this case, however, there are few incentives in a private monopoly situation to improve quality and innovate with regard to new technologies and services, as demonstrated again by the U.S. situation. To achieve these objectives, some form of competition is generally introduced. In the United Kingdom, a second private operator, Mercury, was introduced to compete with the newly privatized British Telecom, creating an exclusive duopoly that was authorized for 7 years. Mercury was licensed to provide leased line services in 1982 and switched services in 1985. The exclusivity provision is a frequent one when dealing with newly privatized operators and new facilities-based entrants, in order to promote investor confidence (O'Neill, 1991). However, in terms of regulation, the mere presence of a competitor has proven to be inadequate to control the power of the incumbent former monopoly provider (Carsberg, 1991). New regulations become necessary to control attempts at cross-subsidization by the incumbent and to ensure fair interconnection arrangements (in particular between the incumbent's local access network and the competitor's trunk network).

Extension of Competition Into Reserved Services

Although the European Commission's policies allow member states to maintain the exclusive monopoly provision of basic telephony and telex, there is no restriction against authorizing competition in these services if a country so desires. As of this writing, only the United Kingdom has been willing to permit competition in these so called reserved services, beginning first with the creation of a duopoly between Mercury and British Telecom. Following the duopoly review of 1991 (DTI, 1991), other network operators will be authorized to offer voice telephony services, and resale of leased capacity is now allowed. As previously noted, however, new decisions have laid the groundwork for opening voice resale to competition, soon eliminating this area as a basis for country differentiation.

Competitive Provision of Network Infrastructure

As in the above case, a monopoly on network provision is allowed but not mandated, and an individual country may authorize competitive operators. Likewise, as noted above, within Europe only the United Kingdom permits such facilities-based competition (although theoretically Sweden's market is open to facilities-based competition—the possibility of which is now being tested by Cable & Wireless, parent corporation of Mercury) (Solomon, 1991). Again, as noted above, a decision to authorize facilities-based competition introduces the need for new regulatory initiatives aimed at nurturing new entrants and protecting them from the overwhelming market power of established PTOs (Carsberg, 1991).

Interestingly, facilities-based competition is becoming most fashionable in the formerly communist-controlled Eastern European countries and the new republics of the former Soviet Union. These countries have allowed foreign operators to build voice, data, and mobile networks in cooperation with the PTTs in their haste to extend basic service penetration beyond the meager levels achieved under their former regimes (Solomon, 1991).

Conclusion

Two countervailing forces—tendencies towards divergent approaches at the national level vs. forced convergence at the European level—will shape the future of European telecommunications. The establishment of a Europewide regulatory framework is a long and delicate process and must deal with these often contradictory centrifugal and centripetal forces. As the recommendations contained in the Green Paper are implemented, a Europewide framework is coexisting with national liberalization measures that curtail or outright abolish national monopolies. This framework is a minimum framework, which gives countries that wish to go further along the liberalization road the freedom to do so and has thus engendered important divergences in national approaches. A key question is whether these differences in rhythm will gradually converge into a stable Europewide system, or whether they will persist, reflecting political ideologies too far apart to ever become homogeneous.

References

Bauer, J. M. (in press). Telecommunication in post-1992 Europe. In H. Oniki, T. H. Oum, & R. Stevenson (Eds.), *International perspectives in telecommunications policy.* Vol. 5 of *International Journal of Comparative Public Policy.*

Carsberg, B. (1991). *Telecommunications policy in the U.K..* Paper presented to the ITU Telecom 91 Regulatory Symposium, Geneva, October.

Commission of the European Communities. (1987). *Towards a dynamic European economy. Green Paper on the development of the Common Market for telecommunications services and equipment.* Communication from the Commission of 30 June 1987. COM (87) 290.

Commission of the European Communities. (1988). Commission Directive of 16 May 1988 on competition in the markets in telecommunications terminal equipment (88/301/EEC; OJ L 131/73).

Commission of the European Communities. (1990). Commission Directive of 28 June 1990 on competition in the markets for telecommunications services (90/388/EEC; OJ L 192/10).

Council of the European Communities. (1990a). Council Directive of 28 June 1990 on the establishment of the internal market for telecommunications services through the implementation of open network provision (90/387/EEC; OJ L 192/1).

Council of the European Communities. (1990b). Council Directive of 17 September 1990 on the procurement procedures of entities operating in the water, energy, transport and telecommunications sectors (90/531/EEC; OJ L 297/1).

DTI. (1991). *Competition and choice: Telecommunications Policy in the United Kingdom.* London: Department of Trade and Industry.

Melody, W. (1991). *Telecommunications: Which sectors do we privatize?* Paper presented to the ITU Telecom 91 Economic Forum, Geneva, October.

Noam, E. M. (1992). *Telecommunications in Europe.* New York: Oxford University Press.

OECD. (1990). *Telecommunications network-based services.* Paris: OECD-ICCP.

O'Neill, J. (1991). *Privatization of public telecommunications operators.* Paper presented to ITU Telecom 91 Regulatory Forum, Geneva, October.

Solomon, J. (1991). *Competition in telecommunications in the U.K.* Paper presented to the ITU Telecom 91 Regulatory Symposium, Geneva, October.

Ungerer, H., & Costello, N. (1988). *Telecommunications in Europe.* Brussels: Commission of the European Communities.

Vallée, A. (1990, March-April). Les états pourront—il faire l'Europe des télécommunications? *Revue Reseau (CNET), 40,* 93-104.

PART II

European Telecommunications Institutions and Issues

FOUR

Telecommunications Initiatives of the European Communities

JOHANNES M. BAUER
CHARLES STEINFIELD

Unlike other integration issues such as energy or agriculture, telecommunications became an integral part of the European Communities' agenda only in the 1980s. During this past decade, the institutions of the European Communities[1] have developed into a major force in the reform of European telecommunications. In this chapter, we analyze this role and the major initiatives launched by the European Communities.

Policy Formation in the European Communities

The European Communities are a unique political construction, neither federation nor confederation. Although part of the sovereignty of the member states is "pooled" in European institutions, the member states play a decisive role in the process of policy formation and implementation (Keohane & Hoffmann, 1991, p. 10; Schneider & Werle, 1990).

The major formal policy making institutions at the Community level are the Council of Ministers, the Commission, and the European Parliament. The Council is formally composed of one representative of each member state. The composition of the Council varies depending on the specific issue and in 1991 23 such sectoral Councils existed (Wessels, 1991). For instance, the Telecommunications Council is comprised of the 12 respective ministers with jurisdiction over telecommunications. The Commission currently consists of 17 commissioners, appointed "by common accord" of the member states in the European Council.[2] In addition to one seat in the Commission for each member state, the larger countries (France, Germany, Italy, Spain, and the United Kingdom) are allowed a second commissioner (Ludlow, 1991, p. 88). On appointment, commissioners must commit themselves to act independently of their national governments and to be loyal to the Community as a whole. The European Parliament currently has 518 members, designated in Europe-wide elections, who do not act as national delegations but as members of Communitywide political parties. Although not formally part of the policy making process, the decisions of the European Court of Justice have been decisive for the development of European policies because of its power of judicial review.

Legislative, executive, and judicial powers are not as clearly sepa-rated among these institutions as in most Western democracies. Both the Council and the Commission have important legislative powers, whereas the European Parliament is severely limited in its functions as compared to national parliaments. De facto, because of its right to initiate legislation that only can be amended by the Council unani-mously, the Commission plays the major role in the development of European legislation. The Commission is also the major executive power and has some jurisdictional functions.

In relation to the member states, the European institutions can apply several legislative instruments. *Directives* are addressed to all member states and are indirect forms of legislation. Directives lay down policy objectives to be realized by member states through national legislation. If member states fail to enact such legislation within the specified time-frame, each individual can apply to the national courts to demand action in accordance to a directive. *Regulations* are also addressed to all member states but do not require intermediate national legislation and can be applied by the courts directly. *Decisions* are of a more specific character and can be directed at member states, companies, individuals, or groups of individuals. They serve to implement Treaty obligations and are immediately legally binding. Although the general power to issue directives, regulations, or decisions is given to the Council, the Commission also has this power in pre-specified cases, most of all the enactment of the competition rules of the Treaty of Rome. In addition to these legally binding measures, the Council and the Commission may issue legally non-binding *resolutions*, *recommenda-tions*, *opinions*, and *communications*.

Since the Single European Act, most legislation is approved by the Council with "simple majority," which means 54 out of the total 76

votes of the Council.[3] To assure the necessary cooperation, the formation of European policies takes place in a complex network of formal
and informal consultations and contacts between the European institutions and national governments. Policies, therefore, reflect a "compromise" between many different forces and have to prove feasible under
these institutional conditions.

The Evolution of Telecommunications Policy at the Community Level

Telecommunications policy evolved within this general framework.
Throughout the 1970s, the Commission of the European Communities
had attempted to integrate the then exempted procurement of telecommunications equipment into the more liberal, general rules for public
sector procurement but failed to reach the necessary national support.
Loose cooperation between the European PTTs took place in the European Conference of Postal and Telecommunications (CEPT) and also
through the International Telecommunications Union (ITU).

At the end of the 1970s, the conjunction of several factors facilitated
the launching of European telecommunications policy initiatives. The
Nora and Minc (1980) report to the French government had increased
the awareness of policymakers of the economic importance of telecommunications and the unsatisfactory state of the European electronics
industry. For both the telecommunications supplier industry and telecommunications users, the obstacles of a fragmented European market
became visible and weakened the existing national coalitions between
PTTs, domestic suppliers, and users. At a more general level, the 1970s
had led to a breakdown of the "Keynesian consensus" of macroeconomic
demand management by national governments and a disbelief in regulation. Gradually, inspired by U.S. policy, deregulation was embraced
as a panacea to revive economic growth and international competitiveness. Finally, this period saw the emergence of a new world political
economy. Together, these factors led to a convergence of national
preferences and facilitated the pursuit of a European telecommunications policy (see Keohane & Hoffmann, 1991, for a general analysis of
these developments).

In 1983, the Commission created a Task Force on Information Technology and Telecommunications to develop the emerging consensus
into an active policy approach (Ungerer & Costello, 1988, p. 130).

However, for this policy to be feasible, it had to be tied to the existing status quo ante and forms of cooperation in European telecommunications. In 1984, the Senior Officials Group on Telecommunications (SOG-T), attended by representatives of the member states' telecommunications operators, was created to advise the Commission on all aspects of telecommunications policy, thus establishing a major link to the national policy authorities. In addition, the Senior Officials Group on Information Technology Standards (SOGITS), the Senior Officials Advisory Group for the Information Market, special committees within the RACE and ESPRIT programs (see Schnöring, Chapter 8 in this book), and a great number of other groups—such as the ESPRIT Round Table of industrial companies, the Standards Promotion and Application Group (SPAG), and the European Workshop for Open Systems (EWOS)—were established as formal and informal networks for European policy coordination. In cooperation agreements with CEPT and CEN-CENELEC, the Commission linked with the existing bodies of trans-European cooperation in telecommunications in 1984. For purposes of standardization and on EEC proposal, CEPT created a new body, the Technical Recommendations Applications Committee (TRAC), in 1984 and, 4 years later, the European Telecommunications Standards Institute (ETSI).

On the basis of the work of SOG-T, the Commission submitted its proposed lines of action to the Council on Telecommunications (Council, 1984), setting out for the first time a consistent program in telecommunications. Based on the positions of this program and initiated by the Commission, the Council started to adopt a series of directives, decisions, regulations, and recommendations (*Telecommunications for Europe 1992*, 1988). In 1986, the Task Force was integrated with the other organizational units of the Commission with jurisdiction over telecommunications issues and merged into the Directorate General for Telecommunications, Information Industries, and Innovation (DG XIII). At the same time, the Commission's Directorate for Competition (DG IV) assisted by the European Court of Justice, intensified its campaign to open up the telecommunications market for competition. Although with a much lower profile, the Directorates General for Information, Communication, and Culture (DG X), Internal Market and Industrial Affairs (DG III), and External Relations (DG I) have gained some influence on the telecommunications policy of the Community. In all, the process of European telecommunications policy formation evolves in a complex network of formal and informal contacts.

Redefining the Institutional Framework of Telecommunications

Following a proposal by the Commission, the Council of Ministers issued a recommendation concerning the implementation of harmonization in the field of telecommunications in November 1984 (Council, 1984). The positions of this first important policy statement were then absorbed and amended in the major blueprint for the future European telecommunications policy, the Green Paper on the development of telecommunications (Commission, 1987). After another round of intensive public policy debate, the Green Paper was followed by a schedule for its implementation, published by the Commission in February 1988 (Commission, 1988a). These documents, as well as the subsequent legislation, address among other issues the areas of terminal equipment, services, standards, regulatory structures, procurement, and type approval.

The Green Paper on Telecommunications

By delineating the major characteristics of the future European telecommunications environment, the Green Paper identifies the areas in which Community action shall be undertaken. In all other areas, the member states are free to pursue their own policies as long as they are compatible with the Treaty of Rome and the Single European Act, most of all the provisions about fair competition. The Green Paper outlines a future European telecommunications market characterized by an increased reliance on competitive forces but leaves sensitive areas largely untouched. The main positions provide for the following:

- A full liberalization of the supply of terminal equipment is called for (Position F).
- All restrictions of competition in the value-added services area (defined negatively as all "non-reserved" services) are eliminated (Positions B and C).
- The member states may specify exclusive or special rights for the provision of the network infrastructure by the telecommunications administrations (Position A) and for the exclusive provision of a restricted number of basic, or "reserved," services as far as this is considered essential for the safeguarding of public service goals (Position B).
- To guarantee a level playing field in such a mixed monopoly-competitive environment, the Green Paper pleads for communitywide standards and

interoperability conditions (Position D), the development of common principles of Open Network Provision (Position E), the separation of regulatory and operational activities of the Telecommunications Administrations (Position G), and provisions to monitor the competitive behavior of public and private providers of telecommunications services, especially to avoid anticompetitive practices of cross-subsidization (Positions H and I).

- The Green Paper suggests the formulation of consistent Community positions in international negotiations (especially within the ITU and GATT) as well as with Third Countries (Position J).
- The Green Paper recommends the monitoring of the social impact of telecommunications developments.

Within these boundaries, the Green Paper leaves a number of policy issues to the discretion of national governments. These include the introduction of competitive conditions in the areas of network infrastructure and reserved services, the ownership form of the major telecommunications providers, and the specific regulatory arrangements to oversee the industry. Unlike the Modified Final Judgment in the United States, which prohibited the Bell Operating Companies from providing information services until 1991 and still prohibits them from the manufacturing of telecommunications equipment, the Green Paper envisions the incumbent telecommunications authorities as potential competitors in every telecommunications market segment, even if this should create difficult regulatory problems.

Implementation of the Green Paper

The Green Paper has the status of a legally nonbinding communication by the Commission, which requires subsequent legislation to implement its provisions. The public policy debate after its publication largely supported the Green Paper's positions and both the Council and the European Parliament passed backing resolutions (Council, 1988). Nevertheless, during the process of drafting legislation some compromises became unavoidable, weakening somewhat the original positions.

Opening of the Terminal Equipment Market

Terminal equipment policy in the EC is based on the principle of open competitive provision subject to the fulfillment of "essential requirements" and the principle of mutual recognition of certificates stating the conformity of equipment with these essential requirements between member states. Already in 1986, the Council had issued a directive on the initial stage of mutual recognition of type approval for telecommunications terminal equipment (Council, 1986a). This document introduced the idea of "one-stop testing" (Delcourt, 1991, p. 17) of terminal equipment and was repealed effective November 1992 by the Council Directive of 29 April 1991 on the approximation of the laws of the member states concerning telecommunications equipment (Council, 1991a). In 1988, the Commission laid down the framework for the introduction of Europewide competition in the provision of terminal equipment in a directive based on Article 90 of the Treaty (which gives the Commission jurisdiction over competition issues concerning public monopolies) (Commission, 1988b).

"Essential requirements" to be met by terminal equipment shall guarantee user safety as well as the safety of public telecommunications network operators; electromagnetic compatibility requirements; protection of the public network from harm; effective use of the radio frequency spectrum where appropriate; and the interworking of terminal equipment with the public telecommunications network (Council, 1991a, Article 4). The Commission shall identify the type of terminal equipment for which common technical regulations are required. In this task it is assisted by a newly created advisory committee, the Approvals Committee for Terminal Equipment (ACTE), composed of representatives of the member states and chaired by a Commission representative. The respective technical standards are to be developed by the relevant standardization bodies and transferred into common technical regulations, which then become mandatory guidelines for all certification procedures. Manufacturers of equipment can either apply for an EC-type examination at any approved testing facility or, given appropriate in-house testing facilities, provide a production quality assurance of conformity with the technical regulations.

In all, the new terminal equipment regime greatly simplifies the process of type approval. However, whether this policy will effectively open the terminal equipment market or still contain elements of strategic standardization will heavily depend on the specific common technical requirements that will be drafted.

Services Liberalization and Open Network Provision

The policies of telecommunications service liberalization and Open Network Provision (ONP) are closely related. ONP can be seen as a

necessary precondition to effectively liberalize the segment of nonreserved services and to provide a level playing field in an environment
where the suppliers of the network infrastructure and reserved (basic)
services are allowed to fully compete in the nonreserved services
markets. During the deliberations to implement such policies, considerable differences between the member states regarding the delimitation
of reserved versus competitive services, the time schedule for service
liberalization, as well as the legal instrument for their implementation,
surfaced. Whereas the Commission argued in favor of open markets,
influential members of the telecommunications Council of Ministers
placed a higher weight on public service goals.

The ensuing stalemate could be overcome in a compromise reached
in December 1989 between the Commission and the Council that resulted in the adoption of the Services and Open Network Provision
Directives in June 1990 (Commission 1990a; Council, 1990a). This
compromise confirmed the intention to rapidly and fully open the
value-added services markets for competition. A more cautious strategy
was proposed for data communication services. First, member states
with poorly developed data communication networks were granted the
possibility to extend the deadline for the introduction of simple resale,
originally envisioned for the beginning of 1993, until 1996. Second,
yielding to the vigorous demand of France and the poorer European
countries, member states were allowed to impose public service obligations such as quality and coverage requirements on providers of data
communication services if they are in the general economic interest (see
also Woodrow & Sauvé, Chapter 6 in this book). The Commission
scrutinizes such obligations on a case-to-case basis to ensure they are
based on objective criteria, are nondiscriminatory, and are proportion-
ate to the specific stated objectives.

The solution to the services issue also enabled progress in the implementation of provisions for Open Network Provision. The basic principles of ONP are the opening and harmonization of conditions of access
to the public network infrastructure and services for new service providers as well as for users. Harmonization covers the three areas of technical interfaces, usage conditions, and tariff principles. These conditions of ONP must not restrict access to networks and services except
for narrowly defined public interest reasons (these include, for instance,
the security of network operations, network integrity, the interoperability of services, and the protection of data). Conditions for Open Network Provisions must be based on objective criteria, be transparent and

published in an appropriate manner, and guarantee the equality of access and be nondiscriminatory in accordance with Community law.

Based on these general principles, more detailed legislation will be drafted. The Council enacted a directive on the application of Open Network Provision to leased lines in 1992 (Council, 1992). The Commission proposed a Council recommendation for packet-switched data services (Commission, 1991b), and further directives specifying ONP conditions for voice telephony and ISDN will follow. The development of ONP conditions can also be expected for mobile services, intelligent networks, and broadband services.

Tariffs

The goals of building-up an ubiquitous telecommunications infrastructure—distributional goals—and also political demands for the generation of subsidies for loss-making postal services or for general financial contributions to the public budget have led to a substantial divergence of telecommunications tariffs from the cost of their provision throughout Europe. Not only do such rate structures lead to allocative welfare losses, they are also incompatible with the objective of introducing a higher degree of competition into parts of the telecommunications market.

In its Resolution of 30 June 1988 on the development of the common market for telecommunications services and equipment up to 1992 (Council, 1988), the Council made explicit that Telecommunications Administrations will have to move toward a greater cost orientation of tariffs. During the first half of 1992, the Commission conducted a review of the progress achieved on this issue.[4] In addition to considering the national tariffs, the Commission has launched a formal investigation into the practices of international tariff-setting after a preliminary examination has unveiled information pointing to anticompetitive arrangements between telecommunications organizations.

Other Provisions

The position of the Green Paper to separate regulatory and operational activities was included in both the terminal equipment (for type approval) and the services directives (for the authorization of services). However, the specific approaches chosen in the member countries vary, with some such as Germany or The Netherlands relying on ministerial departments and others such as the United Kingdom creating formally independent regulatory bodies (Caby & Steinfield, Chapter 3 in this book).

Another proposal for the creation of a European Telecommunications Standards Institute (ETSI) has resulted in a major reform of the standards-setting process in the sector. ETSI was founded in April 1988 in Sophia-Antipolis near Nice, France, and has evolved to become the main body in the creation of European telecommunications standards (Besen, 1991; Drake, Chapter 5 in this book).

After several failed attempts during the 1980s, the Council succeeded in September 1990 in adopting a directive on the procurement procedures of entities operating in the water, energy, transport, and telecommunications sectors (Council, 1990c). The implementation of this directive is gradually opening the formerly highly protected telecommunications procurement markets to bidders from other member states.[5]

The Emerging European Satellite Policy

With the exception of a provision to liberalize receive-only earth stations, the Green Paper on telecommunications has made the entire satellite issue contingent on further study. The background document, the Green Paper on satellites, was published in 1990 (Commission, 1990d). In accordance with the consensus achieved in the telecommunications council in December 1989 on the proper balance between harmonization and liberalization, the Green Paper on satellites proposed four major changes of the existing regulatory environment in order to exploit fully the potential of satellite communications in Europe (Commission, 1990d, p. 128):

1. Liberalization of the earth segment for both receive-only and two-way terminals. All exclusive or special rights need to be abolished. However, terminals are subject to type approval procedures if they are connected to the public switched network or if this is justified to implement necessary regulatory safeguards.

2. Free (unrestricted) access to space segment capacity, subject to licensing procedures in order to safeguard exclusive or special rights (such as a monopoly on the provision of reserved services or special obligations for providers of data communication services as defined in the services directive; Commission, 1990a), with regulatory provisions set up by member states in accordance with Community law and based on the consensus achieved in Community telecommunications policy.

3. Full commercial freedom for space segment providers, including direct marketing of satellite capacity to service providers and users, subject to compliance with the mentioned licensing procedures and, in particular, the competition rules of Community law.

4. Harmonization measures as far as required to facilitate the provision of Europewide services. These include the mutual recognition of licensing and type approval procedures, frequency coordination, and the coordination of services provided to and from countries outside the Community.

As compared to the status quo, these positions will lead to a significant opening of the satellite-based services market, although the need for compatibility with established exclusive or special rights in individual member states will limit the overall affect. Legislation to implement these basic provisions of the Green Paper on satellites is currently being drafted.

Industrial Policy

An integral part of the European approach to restructure the institutional framework are various supply-and-demand industrial policy measures. These include measures to develop Europewide networks and services and to support innovative applications of telecommunications, research and development programs (see Schnöring, Chapter 8 in this book), as well as policies to support disadvantaged regions.

The Community has embarked on a number of specific programs aimed at the coordinated introduction of Europewide networks and services. Among the further developed projects is the introduction of pan-European digital mobile communications (GSM; Council, 1987a, 1987b); the introduction of a land-based European radio paging system (European Messaging System or ERMES; Council, 1990b, 1990d); and the introduction of a unified Digital European Cordless Telephone (DECT) system (Council, 1991b, 1991c).

In several initiatives to facilitate the construction of "electronic highways" for 1992, recommendations were issued regarding the gradual coordinated introduction of an Integrated Services Digital Network (ISDN) (Arlandis, Chapter 12 in this book; Council, 1986b), although the progress in this area is slower than originally expected. Rather ambitious areas are the initiatives aiming at the development of an integrated broadband communications network in the framework of the

RACE program as well as the (in 1993 suspended) policies in the high-definition television area (Slaa, 1991). Both the Commission and the Council initiated measures to support the development of Trans-European Networks in infrastructure areas, including telecommunications, during 1990 (Commission, 1990e; Council, 1990e).[6]

These measures are accompanied by policies aiming to support advanced applications of telecommunications. As major users of telecommunications and to facilitate their enormous information exchange, the Community institutions launched several programs themselves. The Interinstitutional Integrated Services Information System (INSIS) aims at the development of an interinstitutional electronic mail system, videoconferencing techniques, and the buildup of a specialized information system for members of the European Parliament. The CADDIA (Cooperation in Automation of Data and Documentation for Imports/Exports and Agriculture) program, launched in 1985, aims at replacing paper documentation relating to Community procedures (such as customs matters) by electronic data interchange. In addition to these in-house projects, the Community has adopted measures such as the Trade Electronic Data Interchange Systems (TEDIS) program, which attempts to avoid a proliferation of closed user EDI systems with particular attention to the needs of the small and medium business community (Council, 1987c).

To alleviate concerns that these initiatives would primarily benefit the more developed regions within Europe, the Council issued a recommendation in 1986 (Council, 1986c) establishing STAR (Special Telecommunications Action for Regional Development), a 5-year program to support the deployment and use of advanced telecommunications technologies in less favored regions of the European Community. STAR was financed by the Regional Development Fund of the European Communities with matching funds from the member states, totaling some 1.3 billion ECU (approximately 1.6 billion U.S. dollars). Although STAR was phased out in 1991, telecommunications development projects continue to be financed by the Regional Development Fund and the European Investment Bank.

EC Competition Policy in Telecommunications

The various legislative initiatives by the European Commission with regard to telecommunications are inseparable from Community competition policy. Such directives as those on terminal equipment and services are rooted in Treaty of Rome provisions espousing competition in goods and services (see Caby & Steinfield, Chapter 3 in this book, for a brief summary of relevant Treaty of Rome articles). The directives merely attempt to implement the provisions in a way that is consistent with the goals of the Treaty of Rome and is specifically focused on the equipment and services sectors. However, two additional aspects of the Treaty are important to point out. First, in Article 90, it specifically permits the European Commission to issue directives directly to member states in order to ensure the application of competition policies to public undertakings or situations where member states grant exclusive privileges. Second, Articles 85 and 86 prohibit various forms of anticompetitive behavior within the Community, including agreements that may affect trade (such as price fixing) and any abuses of a dominant position. Both of these points have been instrumental in influencing the shape and pace of telecommunications reform above and beyond the general legislative processes outlined in previous sections.

With regard to the first point, the Commission relied on the provisions in paragraph 3 of Article 90 to directly issue the Terminal Equipment and Services Directives to the member states. Although not disagreeing with the substance of the directive on terminal equipment, France deeply opposed the use of Article 90 to bypass the need for review and approval by the Council of Ministers on such an important topic (Amory, 1991). France appealed, along with Belgium, Italy, Germany, and Greece, to the European Court of Justice to have the directive annulled and to force the Commission to submit future directives to the Council of Ministers. However, in March 1991, the European Court of Justice largely upheld the Commission's right in this particular case to issue the directive in question (Blandin-Obernesser, 1992). Their decision was tied to the specifics of the terminal equipment directive and not meant to serve as a blanket endorsement to the Commission for future directives to member states. However, as a result, a similar case against the Services Directive did not materialize, and the Commission's efforts to speed the reform process were strengthened.

In the area of enforcement of the Treaty's competition rules, the Commission, through the DG IV, has on occasion initiated actions on a case-by-case basis against those entities deemed in violation of specific directives or more general provisions in Articles 85 and 86. In 1991, the Commission published general guidelines to inform the member states about its future interpretation of the competition rules in telecommunications (Commission, 1991a) that generalized and expanded decisions developed in previous cases. One key problem is the delineation of cases that, for their redeeming benefits, justify exceptions from the general competitions rules of the Treaty.

One of those cases, based on Article 86 of the Treaty of Rome, was an action brought against the Belgian Regie des Telegraphes et Télécommunications (RTT, now known as Belgacom) in response to a complaint filed by a private value-added services provider. The RTT had refused to provide international leased lines to this company on the grounds that it was carrying third-party traffic. Under Belgian law at the time, the transport of third-party traffic over leased lines was not allowed without prior authorization by the RTT. Such a restriction was in direct violation of the Services directive, and the Commission informed the RTT that its refusal to grant the lines could amount to an abuse of its dominant position. The RTT subsequently granted the circuits to the company in question and later was forced by the Commission to end their restrictive policies regarding provision of such lines (Amory, 1991).

In another case, the European Conference of Postal and Telecommunications Administrations (CEPT) issued a recommendation in 1989 that PTOs impose a 30% surcharge on all leased circuits that interconnect with the public switched network or that carry third-party traffic. Such a surcharge was not in keeping with the spirit of the services and ONP directives, as it was not cost-based, and would act as a barrier to competitive value-added service providers. The Commission viewed the CEPT recommendation as an agreement of the type prohibited by Article 85 of the Treaty of Rome, in that the PTOs were clearly coordinating their prices, usage conditions, and so forth. Under threat of EC intervention, the CEPT dropped their controversial recommendation in early 1990 (Amory, 1991).

Not all international agreements between PTOs have been rejected by the Commission. Article 85 in the Treaty of Rome states that such agreements can be allowed if deemed to be for the benefit of the consumer or supportive for technological and economic advance. Thus the Commission reacted favorably to agreements that were designed to stimulate pan-European service offerings and facilitate the formation of pan-European networks. One such agreement was on the ill-fated Managed Data Network Services agreement (MDNS) (Scherer, 1991, p. 28). MDNS would have enabled PTOs to cooperate on a pan-European enhanced data network that would have provided users with one-stop shopping (ordering of all circuits from a single PTO, which then coordinates with the others to provision the network) and network management. Although the project failed for other reasons, the case is indicative for future Community policy in the areas of one-stop shopping and network management.

Protection of Personal Data and Privacy

The effective protection of personal data and privacy was repeatedly recognized by the Council and the European Parliament as a necessary precondition for the social acceptance of new telecommunications services. The new digital networks and services in particular allow the processing and linkage of subscriber-related data, only possible with substantial additional technical effort in analogue networks. One of the key problems in developing a common European policy are the widely diverging approaches in the member states of the Community. Germany, for instance, follows a rather restrictive approach based on the principle of *prior consent* of the affected individual to authorize the storage, linkage, and retrieval of personal data. England, in contrast, has established a rather liberal regime of data protection based on the principle that the use of personal data is considered authorized unless it is explicitly *protested*.

Within the framework of its general policy on the protection of personal data, the Commission has issued several proposals to create a European legal framework for privacy protection and information security (Commission, 1990b). It has submitted a proposal for a Council directive concerning the protection of personal data and privacy in the context of public digital telecommunications networks, in particular the Integrated Services Digital Network (ISDN) and public digital mobile networks to the Council (Commission, 1990c). The original draft directive establishes a right to strict confidentiality of personal data processed in connection with telecommunication networks and services and relies on the principle of prior consent for the disclosure of this data to third persons. The draft has caused substantial criticism (most of all from the direct marketing business community). It can be expected to be weakened before a final version will be adopted.

Conclusions

In the past decade, the institutions of the European Communities, most of all the Commission, emerged as one of the major actors in

European telecommunications policy. The addition of this quasi-federal, supranational level of decision making, somewhat removed from the established coalitions of interest at the national level, has added considerable momentum to the ongoing reform debate at the national level. Emerging from an intense formal and informal consultation between policymakers at the European and national levels, these policies are best characterized as feasible compromises between actors arguing for a higher degree of liberalization and actors more rooted in a public-service-oriented tradition. Nevertheless, this process has significantly reduced the fragmentation of European telecommunications through the harmonization of technical and regulatory conditions and through the increasing use of the principle of reciprocity between the member states, and has reshaped telecommunications in a more competitive way.[7]

As Europe evolves beyond 1992, it becomes more transparent that the process of European integration will pose continuing challenges after the completion of the Common Market. In the area of competition policy, reliable indicators to detect, and measures to eradicate, unfair competition in the more complicated telecommunications environment, with some suppliers both in monopoly and competitive markets, will have to be developed. The convergence between telecommunications and broadcasting can be expected to create new regulatory problems. The Commission has announced that it will periodically review established policies such as the delimitation of reserved and competitive services or tariff principles. At the institutional level, a continued discussion of the balance between European versus national jurisdiction and the accountability of European policymakers seems probable and might be complicated by a possible expansion of membership in the Community. In all, it can reasonably be expected that the present telecommunications approach has the character of a temporary equilibrium that will need to be adapted to the future developments of the Community.

Notes

1. The European Communities comprise the European Economic Community (EEC), the European Coal and Steel Community (ECSC), and the European Atomic Energy Community (EURATOM). The Maastricht Treaty, which is currently in the process of ratification, foresees a change from the plural to the singular *European Community*.

2. Although the terminology is misleading, the *European Council* must not be confused with the *Council of Ministers*. It consists of the heads of government of the European Communities and meets twice a year but is no formal part of the European institutional structure as set up by the Treaty of Rome of 1957 and the Single European Act of 1987.

3. The current distribution of votes in the Council is: Germany, France, Italy, United Kingdom each 10 votes; Spain 8 votes; Belgium, Greece, Netherlands, Portugal each 5 votes; Denmark, Ireland each 3 votes; Luxembourg 2 votes.

4. On June 16, 1993, the Telecommunications Council of Ministers endorsed a policy to open voice services for full competition by 1998. The poorer countries of the Community will be granted an extended time period to realize this goal. In addition, the Commission was asked to prepare a Green Paper on network infrastructure and universal service to assess the impacts of a liberalization of the provision of the network infrastructure.

5. Tenders made by parties from outside the EEC may be rejected if the proportion of the product originating in third countries exceeds 50% of the total value of the tender (software used in telecommunications networks is considered a product in this terminology). In cases of otherwise equivalent offers, products from third countries can be rejected if they are less than 3% cheaper than EEC products (Council, 1990b, Article 29).

6. Basic provisions concerning the establishment of Trans-European networks are also included in Articles 129b, 129c, and 129d of the Maastricht Treaty.

7. In May 1992, the European Communities and the seven members of the European Free Trade Association (EFTA)—Austria, Finland, Iceland, Liechtenstein, Norway, Sweden, and Switzerland—signed a treaty to establish a European Economic Area (EEA) which will extend most of EC telecommunications legislation to the EFTA countries (Bauer, 1992). Although the Swiss public opted out of the EEA-Treaty in a referendum in December 1992, it will become effective for the six other EFTA members.

References

Amory, B. (1991). *Telecommunications in the European communities: The new regulatory framework*. Paper presented to the Telecommunications in Europe Program, Brussels, July.

Bauer, Johannes M. (1992). *Implications of the creation of a European Economic Area for telecommunications in EFTA countries*. Unpublished manuscript, Department of Telecommunication, Michigan State University, East Lansing.

Besen, S. M. (1991). The European Telecommunications Standards Institute: A preliminary analysis. *Telecommunications Policy, 14*, 521-530.

Blandin-Obernesser, A. (1992, June). Legal basis of the European telecommunications policy in light of the "terminal" judgement. *Communications & Strategies* (Special Edition), 171-185.

Commission of the European Communities. (1987, 30 June). Towards a dynamic European economy—Green Paper on the development of the Common Market for telecommunications services and equipment.COM(87)290 final, Brussels.

Commission of the European Communities. (1988a, 9 February). Towards a competitive community-wide telecommunications market in 1992—Implementing the Green Paper. COM(88)48 final, Brussels.

Commission of the European Communities. (1988b, 27 May). Commission directive of 16 May 1988 on competition in the markets in telecommunications terminal equipment (88/301/EEC), OJ L 131/73.

Commission of the European Communities. (1990a, 24 July). Commission directive of 28 June 1990 on competition in the markets for telecommunications services (90/388/EEC), OJ L 192/10.

Commission of the European Communities. (1990b, 5 November). Proposal for a Council decision in the field of information security (90/C 277/05), OJ C 277/18.

Commission of the European Communities. (1990c, 5 November). Proposal for a Council directive concerning the protection of personal data and privacy in the context of public digital telecommunications networks, in particular the Integrated Services Digital Networks (ISDN) and public digital mobile networks (90/C 277/04), OJ C 277/12.

Commission of the European Communities. (1990d, 20 November). Towards Europewide systems and services—Green paper on a common approach in the field of satellite communications in the European Community (COM(90)490 final), Brussels.

Commission of the European Communities. (1990e, 10 December). Towards trans-European networks. For a Community action program—Communication from the Commission to the Council and the European Parliament (COM(90)585 final), Brussels.

Commission of the European Communities. (1991a, 6 September). Guidelines on the application of the EEC competition rules in the telecommunications sector (91/C 233/02), OJ C 233/2.

Commission of the European Communities. (1991b, 7 June). Proposal for a Council recommendation on the harmonized provision of a minimum set of Packet-Switched Data Services in accordance with Open Network Provision (ONP) principles (COM(91)208 final), Brussels.

Council of the European Communities. (1984, 16 November). Council recommendation of 12 November 1984 concerning the implementation of harmonization in the field of telecommunications (84/549/EEC), OJ L 298/49.

Council of the European Communities. (1986a, 5 August). Council directive of 24 July 1986 on the initial stage of the mutual recognition of type approval for telecommunication terminal equipment (86/361/EEC), OJ L 217/21.

Council of the European Communities. (1986b, 31 December). Council recommendation of 22 December 1986 on the coordinated introduction of the Integrated Services Digital Network (ISDN) in the European Community (86/659/EEC), OJ L 382/36.

Council of the European Communities. (1986c). Council Regulation of 27 October 1986 instituting a Community program for the development of certain less-favored regions of the Community by improving access to advanced telecommunications services (STAR program) (86/3300/EEC), OJ L 305/1.

Council of the European Communities. (1987a, 17 July). Council recommendation of 25 June 1987 on the coordinated introduction of public pan-European cellular digital land-based mobile communications in the Community (87/371/EEC), OJ L 196/81.

Council of the European Communities. (1987b, 17 July). Council directive of 25 June 1987 on the frequency bands to be reserved for the coordinated introduction of public pan-European cellular digital land-based mobile communications in the European Community (87/372/EEC), OJ L 196/85.

Council of the European Communities. (1987c, 8 October). Council decision of 5 October 1987 introducing a communications network Community program on trade electronic data interchange systems (TEDIS) (87/499/EEC), OJ L 285/35.

Council of the European Communities. (1988, 4 October). Council resolution of 30 June 1988 on the development of the common market for telecommunications services and equipment up to 1992 (88/C 257/01), OJ C 257/1.

Council of the European Communities. (1990a, 24 July). Council directive of 28 June 1990 on the establishment of the internal market for telecommunications services through the implementation of open network provision (90/387/EEC), OJ L 192/1.

Council of the European Communities. (1990b, 9 November). Council directive of 9 October 1990 on the frequency bands designated for the coordinated introduction of pan-European land-based radio paging in the Community (90/544/EEC), OJ L 310/28.

Council of the European Communities. (1990c, 21 October). Council directive of 17 September 1990 on the procurement procedures of entities operating in the water, energy, transport and telecommunications sectors (90/531/EEC), OJ L 297/1.

Council of the European Communities. (1990d, 9 November). Council recommendation on the coordinated introduction of pan-European land-based public radio paging in the Community (90/543/EEC), OJ L 310/23.

Council of the European Communities. (1990e, 6 February). Council resolution of 22 January 1990 concerning trans-European networks (90/C 27/05), OJ C 27/8.

Council of the European Communities. (1991a, 23 May). Council directive of 29 April 1991 on the approximation of the laws of the member states concerning telecommunications terminal equipment, including the mutual recognition of their conformity (91/263/EEC), OJ L 128/1.

Council of the European Communities. (1991b, 8 June). Council directive of 3 June 1991 on the frequency band to be designated for the coordinated introduction of digital European cordless telecommunications (DECT) into the Community (91/287/EEC), OJ 144/45.

Council of the European Communities. (1991c, 8 June). Council recommendation of 3 June 1991 on the coordinated introduction of digital European cordless telecommunications (DECT) into the Community (91/288/EEC), OJ L 144/47.

Council of the European Communities. (1992, 19 June). Council directive of 5 June 1992 on the application of open network provision to leased lines (92/44/EEC), OJ L 165/27.

Crack in services market. EC recommends voice, infrastructure changes. (1992, 9 November). *Communications Week International*, p. 3.

Delcourt, B. (1991). EC decisions and directives on information technology and telecommunications. *Telecommunications Policy, 14*, 15-21.

Keohane, R. O., & Hoffmann, S. (Eds.). (1991). *The new European Community. Decisionmaking and institutional change*. Boulder, CO: Westview Press.

Ludlow, P. (1991). The European Commission. In R. O. Keohane & S. Hoffmann (Eds.), *The new European Community. Decisionmaking and institutional change* (pp. 85-132). Boulder, CO: Westview Press.

Nora, S., & Minc, A. (1980). *The computerization of society: A Report to the President of France*. Cambridge: MIT Press.

Scherer, J. (1991). Telecommunications laws in Europe. In J. Scherer (Ed.), *Telecommunications laws in Europe* (pp. 1-32). Frankfurt, Germany: Baker & McKenzie.

Schneider, V., & Werle, R. (1990). International regime or corporate actor? The European Community in telecommunications policy. In K. Dyson & P. Humphreys (Eds.), *The political economy of communications: International and European dimensions* (pp. 77-106). London: Routledge.

Slaa, P. (1991). HDTV as a spearhead of European industrial policy. *Telematics and Informatics, 8.*

Telecommunications for Europe 1992. The CEC Sources (1988, 1991). 2 vols. Amsterdam: IOS Press.

Ungerer, H., & Costello, N. (1988). *Telecommunications in Europe.* Luxembourg: Office for Official Publications of the European Communities.

Wallace, H. (Ed.). (1991). *The wider Western Europe. Reshaping the EC/EFTA relationship.* London: Pinter (for The Royal Institute of International Affairs).

Wessels, W. (1991). The EC Council: The Community's decisionmaking center. In R. O. Keohane & S. Hoffmann (Eds.), *The new European Community. Decision making and institutional change* (pp. 133-154). Boulder, CO: Westview Press.

FIVE

The Transformation of International Telecommunications Standardization
European and Global Dimensions

WILLIAM J. DRAKE

International technical standards are central to the upheaval in European telecommunications described elsewhere in this book. In engineering terms, standards are design specifications shared by the industry to determine the degree and means of interoperability between both networks and the component on which they are based. In political-economic terms, standards are also a central strategic element in the industry's balance of power. During the monopoly era, international standards were defined by the national administrations and major manufacturers of the industrialized capitalist countries via coordination in the International Telecommunications Union (ITU). Today this arrangement and the power relations underlying it are things of the past. Global liberalization over the past decade has radically increased the number and diversity of stakeholders in the standards game, as new service suppliers, manufacturers, and corporate users vie to interwork a multitude of components and networks into a heterogeneous information fabric that is increasingly geared toward the demands of transnational corporations (TNCs). This process has, inter alia, redefined the procedures and outputs of ITU programs in the regulatory, operational, and standards domains alike. As such, the transformation of international

AUTHOR'S NOTE: For their helpful comments on a previous version of this chapter, the author would like to thank Suzanne Neil, Anthony Rutkowski, James Savage, and Charles Steinfeld.

standardization is best assessed in the context of the wider transformation of the multilateral regime that shaped the old standards order.

It is impossible in this short chapter to examine either particular standards choices or the general causal theories that could be used to explain them. Instead, my purpose is merely to map out the broad contours of the changing global standardization *process* and its European dimension. I argue that corporate pressures and the spread of new ideas about governance of the global information economy have catalyzed a deep power shift from the public to the private sector. This in turn has altered players' incentive structures and unleashed pressures that have revolutionized the standards game. Further, the ITU's purported inadequacies in the new environment has led key players to pursue some types of international standardization in other, more market-oriented fora. Hence, the ITU's once dominant authority has been dispersed to a new global standards architecture in which it remains the favored site for certain large-scale programs such as public switched network development while the more dynamic standardization of advanced business systems often takes place elsewhere.

International Standardization
Under the *Ancien Régime*

Ironically, there is no universally accepted definition of standards. One of the more frequently adopted strategies is to define them in terms of functions, that is, as shared design parameters that ensure the compatibility and quality of systems while reducing their variety and providing industry participants with information (Drake & McKnight, 1988). These functions aside, it is necessary to stress the "sharing" part of the definition. Standards are essentially communicative, injunctive, and procedural in nature; they are both shared cognitive constructs about comparability and behavioral rules. These aspects are important in telecommunications, where standards communicate to diverse players which components and networks can or cannot be interworked with each other. And they are especially critical at the global level because of standards' position in the ITU-based regime.

International regimes "can be defined as sets of implicit or explicit principles, norms, rules, and decision-making procedures around which actors' expectations converge in a given area of international relations. Principles are beliefs of fact, causation and rectitude. Norms are standards of behavior defined in terms of rights and obligations. Rules are specific prescriptions or proscriptions for action. Decision-making procedures are prevailing practices for making and implementing collective choice" (Krasner, 1983, p. 2). This definition underscores that regimes function as intersubjective communication media, coordinating players' expectations about appropriate behavior and what their counterparts are likely to do in a given circumstance; and that regimes comprise a logical hierarchy of interrelated injunctions, in that broad principles and norms about the overarching purposes of cooperation inform and give meaning to more situationally specific rules and decision making procedures.

The *ancien* telecommunications regime that lasted from the 1850s until the late 1980s rested on three overarching principles. First, each independent state had a right to absolute sovereignty over its national system. The vast majority opted for monopoly control via a governmental Ministry of Post, Telegraph, and Telephone (PTT) as the means to exercise that right. A few others—notably the United States, Canada, and parts of Latin America—relied instead on regulated private common carriers or a mix of public and private operators, and for many years both groups used private submarine cable companies for intercontinental telegraphy. Nevertheless, everywhere the state retained the right to regulate and control its market, and the vast majority of ITU members took sovereignty and monopoly to be synonymous. As such, regime policies justified in terms of the former implicitly served to preserve the latter.

However, the universal demand for sovereignty had to be balanced with measures to facilitate cross-border transmissions. Hence, the second principle was the joint provision of services. Revenues from international calls were shared by sending, receiving, and transit carriers in a manner that precluded competition. The third major principle was the need to achieve interconnection and interoperability between national networks via technical standardization. From these overarching objectives flowed a number of lower-order principles, norms, and rules that indicated how they should be operationalized. For example, to maintain their sovereignty and monopolies, governments established regime provisions allowing them to monitor, suspend, and stop transmissions deemed contrary to their national security and public order, to restrict the use of private leased circuits and networks, and other like measures. To maintain joint provisioning, states established an accounting and tariff system that allowed them to set their own access and collection charges, to prevent arbitrage, and so on.

The third principle of interconnection via standardization is of interest here, and it too involved the reconciliation of sovereignty and collective action. Before the rise of standards, cross-border communications involved substantial transaction costs. Consider the situation at the border between France and the Grand Duchy of Baden in 1850: "A common station was established at Strasbourg with two employees, one from the French Telegraph Administration, the other from Baden. The French employee received, for example, a telegram from Paris. . . . This message he wrote out by hand onto a special form and handed it across the table to his German colleague. He translated it into German, and then sent it again on its way" (International Telecommunications Union [ITU], 1965, p. 45).

Two problems were evident: the lack of a common language and of network connectivity. In the former case, ITU members easily settled on the Morse code already in use. The latter case was more difficult, because the Europeans who controlled the ITU saw the promotion of domestic manufacturers as a sovereign right. Full standardization of their networks and services would be divisive if this required choosing one manufacturer's technology over others as the basis for specifications. However, "standardization in those early days was restricted to a few points in the networks. Because of manual operation, only the international operators had access to international circuits, whereas the equipment in the national network was practically not involved in international standardization" (Irmer, 1987, p. 45).

ITU members were generally able to sidestep the development of rigorous and comprehensive standards until quite recently. Standardization concentrated primarily on the gateways, signaling and transmission *between national extensions*. This minimalism left administrations and their manufacturers free to employ internationally incompatible systems within their national networks and to use closed standards as nontariff barriers to equipment trade. Sharply delineating between the national and international realms and applying regime rules only to the latter, states had it both ways: monopoly control *and* lucrative cross-border communication. That standardization stopped at the gateways whenever possible reflected states' collective demand for total control over their national systems. *Hence, ITU standards should be seen as situationally specific regime rules,* just like the detailed accounting and settlement arrangements and restrictions on private networks, by which the higher principles of sovereignty and interconnection were balanced and operationalized. And when the meaning of those principles changed in the 1980s, so did standardization.

Beyond this general logic of political control, the two-level framework of national monopolies and the international regime had more specific effects on standardization. From 1865 until after World War I, ITU members organized a series of conferences at which the regime's governing instruments, the International Telegraph Convention and the accompanying International Service Regulations, were repeatedly amended and adopted. Theses documents and the negotiations behind them were largely devoted to general principles and norms of correspondence and detailed tariff schemes, with the primary standards decision being the adoption of the Morse code and its successors. But as institutionalized research and development began to yield new opportunities, the need for expert standardization became palpable. When France and Hungary first proposed in 1903 that engineers from member administrations should meet regularly to address this need, "the fear that such meetings might sap the authority of the central administrations killed the proposal" (Valensi, 1965, p. 9). Governments relented once the economic incentives and the technical ability to restrict standardization to the international segment became clearer, and so they launched the International Telephone Consultative Committee (CCIF) in 1924, the International Telegraph Consultative Committee (CCIT) in 1926, and the International Radio Consultative Committee (CCIR) in 1927. This chapter focuses on networks and service standardization under the telecommunications regime; readers interested in the CCIR and the radio regime may consult other sources (Savage, 1989).

All ITU members had a right to participate, but the committees were dominated by the European PTTs and, indirectly, their preferred manufacturers. Lacking the Europeans' levels of network development, traffic, revenue, manufacturing capabilities, expertise, and political clout, independent developing countries and colonies alike were excluded de facto from effective participation. Paralleling this horizontal asymmetry among nation-states was a vertical asymmetry with respect to subnational players, in that potential competitive suppliers, users, labor unions, and so on were excluded de jure. Not surprisingly, the standardization of gateways and transmission and the elaboration of tariff rules and operating procedures for intra-European correspondence were the committees' dominant concerns.

This Eurocentrism attenuated somewhat after American Telephone and Telegraph (AT&T) joined the CCIF in 1928 to improve the new intercontinental telephony, even though the United States government did not join the ITU until its reconstitution as a "telecommunication" union in 1934. The United States viewed the ITU as overly statist and European and, after joining, adopted a selective approach to the regime's injunctions. Indeed, it did not sign all the Regulations until 1973. Canada and some of the Latin American countries adopted similar stances. In contrast, the United States devoted greater attention to the radio regime, where military concerns and the treaty allocation of spectrum were considered more compelling. But AT&T and American private record carriers worked closely with the committees to achieve interconnection and service provision, albeit while refusing to implement those ITU Recommendations regarded as insufficiently applicable to America's unique market structure and network requirements.

In 1956, the CCIF and CCIT were consolidated into the International Telegraph and Telephone Consultative Committee (CCITT) to facilitate more coherent planning. The rapid growth of intercontinental telephony, the new non-voice services made possible by the merging of computers and telecommunications, the expansion of electronic components to be integrated into networks, the growing number of administrations with stakes in standardization, and other factors combined to make the CCITT a more active and less Eurocentric body. The CCITT became the locus of an increasingly worldwide standardization effort, albeit one still controlled by the advanced capitalist countries.

The CCITT adapted its structure and procedures to meet the exploding demand for standards. It comprised a series of Study Groups containing specialized Working Parties that met several times a year to draft Recommendations, or voluntary regime rules. The work was divided into 4-year Study Periods that ended with Plenary Assemblies at which the Recommendations were formally adopted. As in the days of the CCIF and CCIT, decisions were normally taken by consensus; votes occurred on only the most divisive issues. Hence, the CCITT process during the *ancien* regime was: slow, since final standards took at least 4 years, and often more; consensual, so as to maximize input from and minimize later noncompliance by leading members; reactive, as it largely involved existing national technologies brought in "bottom up" for international standardization; and power-based, as the only system specifications being considered were those advocated by the dominant carriers and manufacturers of a few industrialized countries.

If success is defined as the ability to formulate agreements that most participants abide by, the CCITT and its predecessors were among the most successful of international bodies. The Recommendations facilitated the coordinated expansion of worldwide networks and services and achieved the regime's purposes. Where possible, they were crafted to provide broad compatibility in international connections while leaving many details unspecified so carriers could choose varying technologies within their national networks. But compromise was not always possible. The most obvious factor separating success from failure was whether major players had made substantial investments in competing systems prior to undertaking coordination. In such cases, the committees might settle for oxymoronic "dual" or "multiple" standards listed together in a Report, rather than achieving a single Recommendation. For example, incompatible designs for international videotex, color television, and high definition television were accepted in the CCIR, while similar problems arose at times on pulse code modulation, signaling, and digital transmission in the CCITT. Alternatively, a majority of members might agree on a single Recommendation, but important players would pursue different implementation "options" that it blessed. And in still other cases, members might agree to a purportedly universal Recommendation but implement it in dissimilar ways, as happened with the X.25 packet switching protocol and many aspects of Integrated Services Digital Networks (ISDNs). When competing preferences could not be reconciled, market players had to undertake complicated and costly interworking via gateway translator technologies or settle for a lack of compatibility. But in the broad sweep of ITU history, such occurrences, although significant, were more the exceptions than the rule.

International Regime Transformation and the New Standards Game

The political-economic analysis here contrasts with most of the traditional standards literature, as exemplified by articles in the ITU's in-house *Telecommunication Journal*. Written predominantly by committee engineers, this literature typically positions technological change and expert rationality as the causal forces explaining cooperation (Wallenstein, 1979). It is true that technological progress imposes functional parameters on standardization, that systems complexity requires expertise, and that engineers have styles of reasoning and criteria for evaluating options that can distinguish their interaction from other types of negotiations. But does it follow, as one CCITT veteran argues, that standards-makers constitute "an independent suprapower," and that "high-level managers, business elite's 'decision-makers,' have little influence on standards and must accept them as decided by people at lower levels of their own organizations" (Wallenstein, 1990, p. 1)? This and similar participant accounts sidestep questions of power and interests, thereby ignoring the fact that standards experts work for organizations with material stakes that impose strong compulsions and constraints on their actions.

Technological change expands the range of options from which actors may choose in pursuing their objectives, but it does not autonomously define those objectives. The telephone was introduced in some countries in the 1870s, but international standardization was not pursued until the 1920s in large part because administrations preferred to protect their prior telegraph investments. Other new services languished for decades without enabling standards; organizational decisions paced the technology's diffusion. More generally, the key innovations of the information control revolution's early years—for example, the digitized merging of computers and telecommunications, and the later spread of microelectronics and software-based functions—did not in themselves alter the carriers' objectives. To the contrary, CCITT members expected until the 1980s to expand their existing monopolies into advanced services. But innovation did alter their incentive structures regarding the precise approach best suited to new opportunities. For example, they had to extend some standardization into their national networks to reap the economic benefits of automatic direct dialing in international telephony. That made coordination and compliance more difficult, especially for unenthusiastic governments such as those in the Soviet bloc. New technology complicated the search for standards, but the decisions about whether to adopt them in the first place were matters of organizational power and interests.

The availability of new technical possibilities also altered the incentives for other players. In the United States, military procurement combined with unregulated and potentially vast commercial markets to spur computer and electronics firms into developing an expanding range of systems that could interwork with telecommunications. New service providers saw the possibility of carving out niches in untapped markets, and large corporate users saw that leased circuits could be upgraded to advanced private networks that enhanced their efficiency and control. But institutional barriers stood in the way of realizing such opportunities, so an assault on the domestic regulatory regime of the Federal Communications Commission (FCC) and the dominance of AT&T was launched. Beginning in 1959, the FCC incrementally responded to the call for deregulation, not only because of pressure from this highly mobilized coalition but also because of its own learning process. Natural monopoly conditions were eroding, and telecommunications was increasingly seen as a strategic business resource for an information-based economy. Preserving the old rules seemed contrary to the national interest, a view being echoed by academic and industry analysts.

The deregulatory coalition began pressing foreign administrations for "flexibility" akin to what was being attained in the United States. By the early 1980s, the United States government had moved firmly behind the global liberalization cause. This alliance also teamed up with an influential expert community in calling for the establishment of a trade in services regime to include telecommunications. The multilateral discussions that would later lead to drafting of a treaty in the Uruguay Round negotiations lent further weight to the worldwide rethinking of telecommunications policy (Drake & Nicolaïdis, 1992). But the most direct force for change became large corporations in Europe and other industrialized countries that, after initially varied and hesitant reactions, made the Americans' agenda their own and pressed their respective home governments for liberalization. For new service suppliers, manufacturers, and users alike, competing globally with American-based counterparts that had benefited from institutional change required comparable freedoms. And over the next 10 years they progressively achieved many of their key objectives, first in the industrialized world, and then in the developing world.

Within the ITU, the CCITT's regulatory Recommendations on private leased circuits and networks, value-added networks and resale, customer premise equipment (CPE), switching, routing, tariffs, and a host of other issues came under attack from the American/corporate alliance. Some PTTs attempted to dig in their heels, especially in the preparatory discussions for the World Administrative Telegraph and Telephone Conference (WATTC) set for 1988. There they attempted to insert into the Regulations, one of the regime's two governing treaty documents, language that could provide a legal rationale not only to preserve their dominance in existing markets but also expand it into new domains of network-based service provisioning (Drake, 1988). But by the time the conference was held, a corporate ground swell against the draft necessitated backpeddling, and negotiators reached an agreement that actually undercut the intellectual and political foundations of continued monopoly control. Two years later, CCITT members took the process further by substantially liberalizing the regulatory Recommendations on both private circuits and networks and on the accounting rates and tariffs associated with joint provisioning (Drake, in press).

The message of this quick overview is that the international regime is undergoing transformation. Although sovereignty as a constitutional concept remains, the assumption that it must be operationalized via monopolies has been jettisoned. There is now a broad consensus that varying mixes of public and private control are viable means to economic and social ends. Joint provisioning by administrations is no longer viewed as the singular solution for service provision, as end-to-end carriers have proliferated in advanced services and are seeking entry into basic telephony. And most important here, the third overarching regime principle of interconnection via standardization has also been reconstituted. Liberalization and private control have altered the substantive nature of the standards in demand and the process by which they are supplied. This is evident if we consider four key dimensions of the transformation: commercialization, globalization, differentiation, and integration.

Commercialization comprises the processes of market entry liberalization for service providers and manufacturers, applications liberalization for users, and the competitive repositioning of administrations. Its impact on international standardization in the 1980s was threefold. First, there was rapid growth in the number and diversity of firms seeking to influence CCITT decisions. Some members of the liberalization coalition, especially users and nondominant manufacturers, had fewer resources than the PTTs and their big suppliers with which to participate effectively in the details of standardization. Nevertheless, they affected the general tenor of the process by constantly invoking the need for standards that were market-oriented, rapidly devised, open, and flexible, and by damning as protectionist nontariff barriers any specifications that did not meet these criteria. Second, commercialization affected the character of technical change by greatly increasing its rate while shortening product life cycles, pushing its substantive direction toward the customized systems and services demanded by TNCs and accelerating its diffusion across national and regulatory boundaries.

Third, commercialization compelled the carriers controlling the CCITT to undertake painful reorientations. Their historical preference was for architecturally closed and administratively centralized networks in which they retained monopolies or at least dominant positions in services, as per the original vision of each constructing "the" national ISDN (the United States being a notable exception). Commercialization made this impossible by forcing open selected market segments to competitive provisioning and enhancing users' ability to attain and manage private leased circuits and networks. And since the mid-1980s, the spread of "open network" concepts and regulatory frameworks across the industrialized world has redefined their identities as "network operators" that provide underlying resources that can be drawn on and customized by competing providers and users. Accordingly, with varying degrees of enthusiasm they are being pushed toward more open multi-vendor standards and hoping that paid access to their networks offsets any revenue losses from service competition. Similarly, large manufacturers that once thrived by offering customers integrated families of products based on closed standards and proprietary technologies are also being pushed toward open systems, in turn creating new market niches for smaller entrants who are no longer relegated to being mere "standards takers."

The *globalization* of strategies, systems, and services is a response to the market incentives of commercialization. Its primary impact on standardization is a growing demand for end-to-end interconnectivity and interoperability that transcends the national gateways and jurisdictional delineations of the past. As noted above, there were instances under the *ancien* regime era when new economic opportunities led administrations to extend ITU standards into their national networks. For decades this pertained primarily to aspects of record transmission, where a low tolerance of errors required performance standards. Beginning in the 1960s, direct dial telephony and subsequent innovations provided further incentives for "a gradual penetration of worldwide compatibility standardization into the sacred territories of national telecommunication operators" (Wallenstein, 1990, p. 72). Engineers may perceive this to have been a direct result of technical change, since "progressive automation coupled with growing volume and diversity of traffic has brought about a need for specified compatibility of the national system and the local systems within it" (Wallenstein, 1990, p. 73). But changes in traffic depended on prior organizational choices about how to expand capacity, service offerings, and revenues in light of new opportunities. And in the 1980s, commercialization led TNC users to demand direct end-to-end connectivity instead of being forced to adopt cumbersome gateway translation functions between national systems. Administrations struggled to accommodate these lucrative customers via more thorough standardization. This was clearly reflected in CCITT programs including, inter alia, universal personal telecommunications and ISDNs. Indeed, in many Recommendations one finds standards for "inter-network" rather than "inter-national" relations.

The radical *differentiation* of systems and services associated with commercialization has also affected standardization. For a century, telegraph, telex, and telephone services were rather homogeneous in substance and mode of provision across countries. The major categories of networks and equipment were also comparable, even if the precise specifications employed within each varied among major producers. But in recent years, suppliers have responded to new incentives by generating increasingly specialized systems and applications. The incorporation of microelectronics and software intelligence into all aspects of telecommunications to satisfy users' demands for customization in a commercialized marketplace resulted in an exponential growth in systems heterogeneity that raised serious problems of interoperability.

Hence, the flip side of the differentiation coin is *integration*. As vendors around the world began to generate more and more varied systems, there was a growing need for "not only the broadening (more elements to be standardized) but at the same time also the deepening (more details to be standardized)" of specifications (Irmer, 1987, p. 46). From a technical standpoint, networks and their components needed either direct compatibility built in or the intelligent capability to overcome the inadequacy or absence of truly harmonizing standards. From a political-economic standpoint, the procedural and substantive issues this raised were who would set which terms for integration. In the pre-competitive era, the problem involved establishing boundaries between the unregulated computer and regulated telecommunications industries, as FCC attempted in its First Computer Inquiry.

At the international level, the CCITT encountered the dilemma in the 1960s that its work was beginning to overlap with that of the International Standardization Organization (ISO) and the International Electrotechnical Commission (IEC). Sharing turf meant sharing power; even the adoption of common terminologies was difficult. Slowly, the organizations evolved a division of labor based more on traditional jurisdictional delineations than inherent technological properties. For example, the 1964 Plenary Assembly adopted a Recommendation for cooperation on data transmission stating: "Clearly, it will be the responsibility of the CCITT to lay down standards for transmission channels. . . . The standardization of signal conversion terminal equipment (MODEMS) is the province of the CCITT; the standardization of the junction (interface) between the MODEM and the data terminal equipment is a matter for agreement between the CCITT and the ISO or the IEC" (International Telegraph and Telephone Consultative Committee [CCITT],

1964, p. 207). But as the technology evolved and commercialization spread, the organizations were drawn into closer working relations. They jointly undertook initiatives such as the X.400 protocols for electronic message handling, and sometimes adopted in parallel identical but renumbered standards for data networks, telematics services, terminals, and the like.

Reconciling differentiation and integration also led to a growing trend toward a priori standardization. Since the 1920s, the usual practice had been for members to bring their preferred national standards to the committees for international adoption. This reactive enterprise often produced broadly framed compromise specifications involving multiple "options," and so on. More recently, the CCITT has responded to the new challenges above by proactively standardizing large-scale systems on which members had a common interest. Technologies that had not yet been tested but could reinforce their dominant positions were drawn up from scratch in committee in order to preclude competing designs. This was attempted for aspects of digital transmission, signaling public data networks and such, but the exemplar was the ISDN, which when first discussed in the CCITT, was "frequently represented . . . with nothing more than a simple cloud-like diagram" (Rutkowski, 1985, p. 41). Engineers also began to emphasize layered reference models and protocol suites, building up from the hardware to users' applications, which could serve as flexible architectural frameworks accommodating multi-vendor systems. Thus they attempted to meet the technical imperatives of integration while sidestepping the divisive problem of picking one player's technology over others as a basis for "the" international standard.

These efforts to cope with complexity took on a different character with the spread of commercialization in the 1980s. Now the problem was not merely to establish flexible architectures but also to make them more open and transparent to all players. The pressure for openness was political and economic; the technology itself could support closed models as well and was hence causally indeterminate. The shift began in the computer industry. In the 1970s, International Business Machines (IBM) established its proprietary Systems Network Architecture and the United States Department of Defense sponsored the development of the Transmission Control Protocol/Internet Protocol (TCP/IP) suite as a vendor-independent framework for computer communications. European governments and manufacturers wanted alternatives to IBM and "DOD/IP" that would allow communication between their own products, and in 1981, launched efforts in the ISO to establish an Open

Systems Interconnection (OSI) reference model. OSI assumptions were subsequently incorporated into CCITT work on ISDNs and related topics. By the mid-1980s, the FCC, the EC Commission, and the Japanese government had expanded open architectural concepts into telecommunications regulations in order to facilitate access to and use of network resources by service suppliers and customers as well.

The shift to open standards is a continuing and conflictual process. Where they can bypass regulatory and antitrust policies, public network operators and major manufacturers still have strong incentives to seek standards favoring their interests over those of competitive suppliers and users. In turn, the latter often contend that OSI and related models are in fact less friendly to competition and customized applications than their names suggest. Even so, the very establishment of openness as a normative and conceptual baseline against which standards are measured facilitates continuing pressure for further gains by advocates of commercialization. The outstanding question is whether the market will wait for the dominant players gathered in the CCITT and ISO to negotiate standards for open global interconnection. Given the exponentially increasing range of differentiated technologies and the sometimes divergent interests of administrations and major manufacturers, the elaboration of layered protocol sets and other standards has become an increasingly complex and time-consuming task. CCITT programs expanded radically in the 1980s and now involve thousands of experts in seemingly endless meetings and over 20,000 pages of Recommendations.

Nevertheless, by the time participants hammer out agreements in the 4-year Study Periods, liberalized technological and market changes frequently render them obsolete. The industry joke that the CCITT specializes in "yesterday's standards with tomorrow's availability" indicates why competitive suppliers and users are increasingly opting to glue together their own "unofficial" interworking solutions through software-based functions or outsourcing this task to systems integration specialists rather than waiting for "official" standards to be issued from on high. Alternatively, they may choose to make do with de facto standards. Nowhere is this more evident than in the booming field of computer internetworking, where an estimated two thirds to three quarters of global implementations are based on TCP/IP, which is readily available, rather than on OSI, for which many of the key standards have yet to be defined. Consequently, the TCP/IP-based Internet has experienced truly spectacular growth worldwide in recent years through market adoption rather than CCITT planning.

In sum, international standardization is undergoing a profound transformation in the context of the new international regime. Commercialization, globalization, differentiation, and integration are proceeding rapidly in a manner that challenges the continuing efficacy of official intergovernmental standardization. Dominant national carriers continue to rely on the CCITT to plan public switched networks and related large-scale projects, such as the plodding development of narrowband ISDN. But unleashed by commercialization, other players are moving to devise the advanced systems and services demanded by TNCs through market coordination and self-defined solutions and by attempting to shift the locus of committee standardization to other, purportedly more efficient fora. It is to the last of these options, in which Europe figures prominently, that we now turn.

Europe and the Decentralization Dynamic

Given its members' historical preference for limiting CCITT rules to the international segment where possible, more detailed standards for national networks were always needed. Responsibility for these standards rested with the carriers rather than the national standards bodies that held jurisdiction over most other industries. One consequence was the adoption of internationally incompatible systems and their use as nontariff trade barriers. In Europe, some half-hearted efforts to lessen these conditions were made in the European Conference of Postal and Telecommunications Administrations (CEPT), a loose organization of 26 PTTs formed in 1959. But CEPT concentrated primarily on achieving a broad measure of regional comparability for tariffs and operating procedures through CCITT-like consensual decisions and voluntary recommendations.

In 1975, the Commission of the European Communities (CEC) called on the CEPT to pursue firmer regional standardization. Its objective was not yet comprehensive liberalization but simply greater harmonization in accordance with its Treaty of Rome. CEPT responded by establishing the Harmonization Coordination Committee for Standardization (CCH). It is difficult to assess the CCH's effectiveness because of the CEPT's infamous secrecy; it is among the least transparent of international organizations. Indeed, even the big manufacturers were locked out of this closed grouping. But if the proof is in the pudding, it is clear that the PTTs had so many incompatible systems and implementations that a true "European market" did not exist.

The turning point was in 1984. The EC issued two key Recommendations aimed at its members in CEPT, one broadly endorsing further standardization, the other requiring the opening to competition of at least 10% of public procurement contracts. The new relationship would become strained, as "throughout the 1980s CEPT struggled to guard its position against encroachment by the Commission" (Temple, 1991, p. 63). But backed by its constitutional authority with respect to key governments, the EC persisted, and the CEPT had to work out a modus vivendi that would reduce the pressure. Accordingly, CEPT ministers endorsed the objectives of greater harmonization among European networks and industrial policies and strengthened the CCH. By this time CEPT was also facing strident demands for competition from the United States government and its corporate allies; the United Kingdom was deviating from the monopoly consensus and pressuring other members by serving as a liberalized hub for transatlantic traffic; and some continental PTTs were beginning incremental reforms tailored to national conditions. The CEPT majority attempted to collectively fend off external pressure and keep errant members in line, but their cartel-like coherence was eroding on many issues and the EC was threatening a jurisdictional coup.

The EC Council of Ministers passed a resolution in 1985 endorsing a "New Approach to Standards," in which "reference to voluntary standards is seen as giving technical expression to . . . Community directives. Under this approach the EC legislation confines itself to laying down the essential requirements with which a product must comply. European standards are then developed under each directive in order to provide manufacturers with a set of technical specifications recognized in the directive as giving a presumption of conformity with the essential requirements" (Temple, 1991, p. 21). The EC was assuming the authority to set binding regional regime principles on overarching objectives while leaving the precise delineation of standards rules operationalizing them to the PTTs and manufacturers. That same year, the European Court of Justice upheld a Commission decision liberalizing telex retransmission, thereby heralding the application of EC antitrust law to telecommunications. The CEPT's authority would be vulnerable to further attack if it did not act to strengthen harmonization. At a 1985 meeting, members signed a Memorandum of Understanding (MOU) that adopted weighted voting to break inertia in the standardization process and created a Technical Recommendations Application Committee with the power to set mandatory "Normes Européennes des Télécommunications" in certain instances.

These steps, although important, did not go far enough for the EC Commission. After a further series of piecemeal initiatives, it launched its comprehensive commercialization program with the Green Paper of 1987. As part of the "1992" agenda of creating a single market for all goods and services among its 12 members, the EC began to put pressure on the PTTs. The Green Paper set the stage for a variety of initiatives that are detailed elsewhere in this book. The key point here is that it contained a broadly worded call for a new regional standards body capable of producing strong, market-oriented standards that administrations would actually implement in a like fashion.

In the United States, the Exchange Carriers Standards Association had launched Standards Committee T1 in 1984 to fill the void left by the divestiture of AT&T. T1 is open to all players in the industry, including carriers, service suppliers, users, research organizations, and even foreign-based firms. Consensual decision making is the normal method, and compliance in the implementation stage is voluntary. But it also has a mechanism for majority voting to break deadlocks, and its activities are relatively transparent, in that draft standards are circulated for comment by interested parties. In pursuit of its own liberalization objectives, officials from Japan's Ministry of Posts and Telecommunications went on a fact-finding mission to the United States. After intensive consultations, they persuaded Japanese companies to launch a Telecommunications Technology Committee (TTC) in 1985 based on comparable principles. Somewhat confusingly, the ministry also established its own similarly acronymed Telecommunications Technology Council. The latter coordinates input fed "upstream" to the CCITT, and the former takes the "downstream" Recommendations and details them for national application. The EC Commission followed with its own fact-finding mission to T1 during 1986, and its assessment fed into the Green Paper's call for a new regional body. The hand was well played: although it had not been formally proposed, the worst possible outcome for the CEPT would have been the creation of a competing, constitutionally stronger organization under the EC. In this implicitly contested market for jurisdiction, the CEPT needed a preemptive strike.

In September 1987, the CEPT decided to create a new European Telecommunications Standards Institute (ETSI). Turf battles made it a difficult birth. Internally, many PTTs wanted the ETSI to serve merely as a research facility providing inputs to the CEPT, which would retain ultimate authority over standards. But that could mean a conflictual division of labor and do little to address the EC's demand that standardization be controlled by a broader cross-section of the industry. Hence the January 1988 MOU formally establishing the ETSI transferred to it all the activities formerly under the CEPT's CCH. Externally, the ETSI endured over the next few years a laborious jurisdictional battle with both the European Committee on Standardization and the European Committee for Electrotechnical Standardization. The former comprises pan-industry standards bodies and the latter specialized electronics standards bodies from member states of the EC and the European Free Trade Association. Both committees were stridently opposed to creating a new organization for telecommunications standardization, which they now argued should be their turf. The EC has mediated efforts to attenuate these strains, and a high-level consultative mechanism has been established comprising the three groups' leaderships. However, the Commission's Green Paper of 1990 on the Development of European Standardization proposes, inter alia, extending the ETSI model by restructuring all standardization along sectoral rather than national lines. Although a logical step in the single-market program, the initiative could engender further turf wars.

Organizationally, the ETSI echoes the T1 principles of pluralistic corporate participation, due process, transparency, and weighted voting where necessary. And although initially there were no provisions for participation by foreign-based TNCs, United States demands that ETSI not become a "standards fortress" have resulted in their admission as nonvoting "associate members." The EC Commission also participates as a "Counsellor" which, under its Directives, may require notification of standards actions, potentially block any deemed to have trade restrictive effects, and make them mandatory for its member states. The ETSI comprises over 200 members drawn from 21 of the countries represented in CEPT, of which roughly 60% are manufacturers, 14% are national administrations, 11% are public network operators, and 10% are users and service providers (Temple, 1991, p. 6). Management issues are addressed in the General Assembly, and the Director and Secretariat handle the day-to-day operations. The highest authority is the Technical Assembly, which sets the budget, allocates resources, and approves final European Telecommunications Standards (ETS). Below the Assembly are the Technical Committees, which coordinate standards initiatives, and below the committees are the Project Teams tasked with drafting the ETS.

This organizational structure reins in somewhat the PTTs' power and sets the stage for pan-European standardization. Voting rights were initially weighted on a national basis according to country size, but this was revised in 1991 to allocate votes among individual members weighted by their sales or, for administrations, their country's gross domestic product. Together with the project team approach, that means "the drafting *and approval* of standards in ETSI is done directly from scratch at the European level. This bypasses the national standards production machinery," and provides TNCs and the EC greater latitude in integrating markets (Temple, 1991, p. 52). This transnational corporate pluralism is not matched by participation from other potential stakeholders, for example, labor unions and public interest groups.

In parallel with this horizontal restructuring of power away from the state is a vertical restructuring of power within the state. At the outset, liberalization partisans complained that despite constituting only 14% of its membership, the PTTs retained disproportionate influence in the ETSI. They noted that the same PTT personnel who had worked in the CCH were simply relocated to ETSI and charged that the PTTs could still parlay their control over switched networks into control over standardization. Moreover, manufacturers were anxious to avoid conflict with their largest purchasers, and users found it difficult to participate effectively in the details of standards design. But here, too, significant changes are now underway. Nationally, European governments are separating their PTTs' regulatory and network operation functions and creating a quasi-adversarial relationship between operators and regulators charged with promoting some competition. Regionally, the carriers correspondingly have been removed from the CEPT and regrouped into a new European Telecommunications Network Operators organization. In the ETSI context, this two-level split may reduce the carriers' power and facilitate standards more attuned to other, corporate interests.

Finally, the use of flexible project teams to draft standards is especially novel. The teams are comprised of experts chosen on the basis of their competence on a given topic. They can be quickly constituted to generate specifications demanded by business and can be disbanded or reallocated when a draft is ready for public comment and subsequent adoption by the Technical Assembly. This task-oriented working method, in which standards may be produced in just a few months, contrasts sharply with the CCITT's 4-year study periods. ETSI has already produced a wide variety of standards recognized by all players on many of the key technologies in the rapidly changing market.

If the boundary lines between national, regional, and international standardization had remained stable, the rise of ETSI, T1, and the TTC might not be a problem for the ITU and its more diverse membership. The CCITT would then continue to set broad parameters for inter-network interfaces, services, and so on while national and regional bodies fleshed out detailed implementations catering to local conditions. Such a division of labor is diplomatically endorsed by the leadership of all three organizations; none wants to be perceived as undermining ITU multilateralism and further concentrating power. But the new transnational systems and corporate practices are blurring the boundary lines. Moreover, some players frustrated in the CCITT are pursuing certain initiatives in the quicker and more market-responsive T1, ETSI, and the TTC, thereby drawing them into international standardization. This is underscored by the fact that all three are now referred to as "regional" standards organizations (RSOs). T1 and TTC are attaining de facto influence across their home countrys' regional spheres of political influence, and the former is now involved in discussions about creating a formal pan-American organization.

Since the late 1980s, the "regionalization" trend has generated substantial debate. On one side are those who argue that a devolution of authority away from the CCITT and toward the RSOs is desirable, as the CCITT is too weighed down by its history, broad membership, public intergovernmental culture, dominant carrier orientation, and comparatively slow procedures to respond effectively to TNC's rapidly changing requirements. Hence, it is better that the RSOs take the initiative and set flexible, market-oriented standards to be fed upstream to the CCITT for renumbering and multilateral adoption. On the other side are those of us who worry that this would undermine multilateralism and reduce the CCITT to rubber-stamping RSO decisions. Even though most CCITT initiatives still originate from the industrialized countries, some (primarily upper income) developing countries have played increasingly active roles during the 1980s. Further, the rest of the ITU's 171 member governments can at least have access to the standardization process and product and exert some diffuse normative influence if the CCITT remains the focal point. Some observers add that despite the demands of large users and competitive suppliers for global interconnectivity, uncoordinated RSO programs and parochialism on the part of large carriers and manufacturers could result in balkanized standards blocs that favor their members' needs over those of outsiders. Suppliers and users would then be faced with the choices of accepting inadequate connectivity or devising resource-consuming translation mechanisms.

The ITU's leadership and countries outside the three blocs have taken the second view. Fearing its bypass, the former launched a two-pronged campaign to reform the CCITT and buttress its authority. Internally, the CCITT Plenary Assembly of 1988 adopted a number of structural and functional changes designed to speed standardization, which have been described elsewhere (Drake, 1989). Most relevant here was the Resolution on "accelerated procedures." The Plenary of 1968 had decided to allow the use of Provisional Recommendations when a simple majority of at least half the carriers in a study group gave their unanimous consent within 3 months. This was revised in 1988 to allow for the final, rather than provisional, adoption of key Recommendations between plenaries if 70% of members agree. The procedure has been used to quickly finalize a number of standards and to liberalize the key regulatory Recommendations.

Further restructuring may occur as a result of the special Plenipotentiary in 1992 prompted by a High-Level Committee Report (ITU, 1991). Under consideration are proposals, inter alia, to regroup all CCITT and CCIR standards activity into a new Standardization Sector; replace the plenaries with a World Telecommunication Standardization Conference to be held at 4- and sometimes 2-year intervals; apply the accelerated procedures more widely; create a corporate Advisory Group on Standardization; encourage the use of electronic networks for rapid document exchange; and allow the rapid deployment of ETSI-like project teams in exceptionally pressing cases. These measures could speed standardization somewhat, although liberalization partisans contend they fail to redress the power and club culture of the dominant carriers. Moreover, opposition in the CCIR to ceding control of radio standards could kill the proposal, as occurred when a similar idea was considered at the Plenipotentiary of 1989.

Externally, the CCITT has tried to define a new working relationship with the RSOs. The Plenary of 1988 adopted a Resolution trumpeting the CCITT's "pre-eminence" in global standardization, a principle ritualistically affirmed by the RSOs. More important, leaders of the CCITT, CCIR, and RSOs established an ongoing consultative process to be guided by an annual Interregional Telecommunications Standards Conference (ITSC). The first ITSC was hosted by T1 at Fredricksburg, Virginia, in 1990 and attempted to establish a division of labor that would not undermine CCITT "pre-eminence." Hence it is interesting and indicative of the CCITT's problems that the most radical proposal was made by its director, Theodore Irmer. Solely national or regional standards would require no coordination. For cases of clear international import, Irmer suggested a three-stage process in which the RSOs would set and compare their programs, prepare draft standards while the CCITT deferred parallel action, and then submit the drafts to the CCITT for global adoption. Irmer acknowledged that "under no circumstances should CCITT members from other regions have the feeling to be merely treated as simple 'observers' in a standardization process already concluded in, or between RSOs," and emphasized that the latter's submissions would only be drafts that the full CCITT membership had the right to modify (Irmer, 1990, p. 7). Nevertheless, he felt it essential to give the power of initiative to the quicker and more market-driven RSOs.

However, the RSOs did not want to take the divisive step of formally assuming this authority. Instead, they successfully argued for a modified version of an ETSI proposal for expanded information exchange in the early stages of development to help the CCITT "strengthen" its market orientation. The Fredricksburg Plan also adopted English as the sole working language, in contrast with the CCITT's slow multiple translations process; the use of electronic networks to circulate drafts, in contrast with the CCITT's slow and expensive printing and distribution practices; and the pursuit of more precisely defined standards within set time frames. The second ITSC, hosted by ETSI at Sophia Antipolis in September 1991, further elaborated this framework, addressed such problems as the tension between transparency and intellectual property rights, and set programmatic priorities, including, inter alia, broadband and intelligent networks, universal personal services, and telecommunications management networks, all of which are notably also under study in the CCITT.

It is too early to determine whether the RSOs will make global interconnectivity more difficult. Mixed motivations abound, as players that might benefit in some respects from semi-exclusionary blocs also have incentives to ensure market access abroad; a "standards war" would not suit their interests. Moreover, other players are demanding open markets and end-to-end connectivity. Given these cross-cutting pressures and the empirical difficulties of assessing how "open" the emerging standards will be in practice, it is no surprise that the debate about "regionalization v. globalization" is marked by abstraction and extrapolation.

What is clear is that some of the CCITT's authority is devolving toward other organizations. RSO members may not want to undermine the CCITT, which had always been "their" club. Indeed, their standards experts often have years of experience building the CCITT and continue to participate in both types of fora. Nevertheless, those experts now work for competitors in commercialized and globalized markets, and there are strong pressures to respond quickly to the pressures thereof. Given the choice, there may be cases when the incentive to shop between standards bodies is overwhelming. "Although the major participants in the RSOs are also important players in the ITU, we suspect that, because of the slowness of the ITU process and the need to coordinate with a larger number of countries, they will often prefer to negotiate within a (perhaps informal) RSO consortium rather than at the ITU" (Besen & Farrell, 1991, p. 316). Much of the long-term planning of large-scale projects such as ISDNs and public networking generally could remain in the CCITT. But at least the initiation of standards geared toward the advanced systems and services demanded by TNCs could become concentrated in the RSOs. Is this bifurcation likely?

On the one hand, the incentive does exist to undertake pressing initiatives first in the RSOs and later bring draft standards to the ITU for multilateral consideration. The ITSCs have not formalized this but did acknowledge that the RSOs can serve as "upstream" sources of draft Recommendations. Irmer admitted at Fredricksburg and the Australian observers complained at both meetings that such a practice could result in countries outside the RSOs being marginalized in the drafting stage and faced with essentially "done deals" thereafter. When and where that will occur is an empirical question that can only be examined once there is more experience to go on. On the other hand, whether the CCITT will be confined to rubber-stamping RSO work depends in part on the fate of current and future reform efforts. Opponents of liberalization may believe that the ITU should go no further in accommodating corporate demands, but the cat is not only out of the bag, it is out of the building. Either the ITU lures it in and finds a way to balance corporate demands with public interest objectives, or it will become a less central forum for standards and related issues. If that happens, it could be even harder to protect social concerns, developing country interests, and so on. The ITU leadership already recognizes the urgency of the task; it is not yet clear when the dominant administrations will.

The future prospects of global standardization are clouded by another factor. Beyond the rise of the RSOs, there are now many other industry bodies from the computer networking side of the market that have moved onto the turf of specialized "telecommunications." In general, they are developing information applications standards layered on top of switched network resources that are geared toward the advanced service requirements of TNCs, research institutions, and so on. They include, among many others, the Corporation for Open Systems (COS), Open Software Foundation (OSF), EDIFACT electronic document interchange group, European Workshop for Open Systems (EWOS), Réseaux Associés pour la Recherche Européene (RARE), Cooperation for Open Systems Interconnection in Europe (COSINE), Standards Promotion and Application Group (SPAG), Promoting Conference for OSI (POSI), the X/OPEN Group, and most notably, the Internet Engineering Task Force (IETF).

Many of these bodies have struggled to push forward OSI-based multiprotocol specifications, although the global Internet explosion has compelled them to accommodate the Internet's TCP/IP in their planning. Leaving aside the OSI versus TCP/IP religious war, it is notable that all are acting outside the "official" CCITT, RSO, and ITSC mechanisms in which they are largely unrepresented and the comparatively "old guard" cultures of which their members often deride. In sum, we are moving toward a decentralized global standards architecture involving many fora with varying degrees of interaction. It is because of this multiplicity of fora around the world involved in various aspects of standardization that this chapter uses the encompassing term "decentralization" rather than "regionalization" to characterize the challenge to CCITT multilateralism.

Two unresolved questions conclude our analysis. First, while dominant national carriers developing public switched networks are committed to some sort of balance between the CCITT and RSOs, advanced networking is being pursued both in those bodies and in other industry fora. How effectively their programs can be coordinated, the impact on global interconnectivity and interoperability, and to what extent all players' competing interests will be accommodated in this policy architecture remain unclear. It might be useful to bring all the organizations into the ITSC process, but the dominant carriers and manufacturers have not been willing to take this step.

Second and related, the time is ripe for a broad and open global discussion about the efficacy of alternative standards models. For example, the IETF and the Internet Society have employed a model in which standards are produced extremely quickly via cooperation within the electronic network environment, rather than through committee meetings stretched over time. How generalizable might this be to areas beyond computer internetworking? What types of systems under what conditions are best addressed through formal committees, market voting, or networked interaction? Can a shared set of criteria and typologies be reached that would facilitate a more efficient and yet representative approach to planning?

As the nominally preeminent body representing all countries, if not all industry players, a reformed ITU could play a leading role in fostering discussion and forging consensus on these and related problems.

Conclusion

This chapter has argued that the transformation of the international telecommunications regime has revolutionized standardization. Under the *ancien régime*, standards were usually limited to the international segment and broadly designed to maintain administrations' autonomy while supporting their favored manufacturers. The consensual coordination process was largely successful in building global connectivity on the carriers' terms, but it marginalized the influence of other stakeholders. In the 1980s, the revolt of TNCs and the spread of new ideas about the necessity of liberalization in a global information economy changed the regime, altered players' incentive structures regarding standards, and catalyzed a decentralization of authority from the ITU toward a growing number of more market-driven fora. The result is an increasingly diverse global standardization architecture that more accurately reflects underlying trends in the industry but that also raises new and unresolved questions about the procedures, policies, and power relations that will shape future global interconnectivity.

References

Besen, S. M., & Farrell, J. (1991). The role of the ITU in standardization: Pre-eminence, impotence or rubber stamp? *Telecommunications Policy, 15*, 311-321.

Drake, W. J. (1988). WATTC-88: Restructuring the International Telecommunication Regulations. *Telecommunications Policy, 12*, 217-233.

Drake, W. J. (1989). The CCITT: Time for reform? In *Reforming the global network: The 1989 ITU Plenipotentiary Conference* (pp. 28-43). London: International Institute of Communications.

Drake, W. J. (in press). Asymmetric deregulation and the transformation of the international telecommunications regime. In E. M. Noam & G. Pogorel (Eds.), *Asymmetric deregulation: The dynamics of telecommunications policies in Europe and the United States*. Norwood, NJ: Ablex.

Drake, W. J., & Nicolaïdis, K. (1992). Ideas, interests and institutionalization: International trade in services and the Uruguay Round. In P. Haas (Ed.), *Knowledge, power, and international policy coordination* (Special issue of *International Organization, 45*, pp. 37-100).

Drake, W. J., & McKnight, L. (1988). Telecommunications standards in the global information economy: The impact of deregulation and commercialization. *Project Promethee Perspectives, 5*, 14-20.

International Telecommunications Union (ITU). (1965). *From semaphore to satellite*. Geneva: ITU.

International Telecommunications Union (ITU). (1991). *Tomorrow's ITU: The challenges of change*. Report of the High Level Committee to review the structure and functioning of the International Telecommunications Union (ITU). Geneva: ITU.

International Telegraph and Telephone Consultative Committee (CCITT). (1964). *Blue book* (Vol. 1: *Third Plenary Assembly, Geneva, 25 May-26 June 1964*). Geneva: ITU.

Irmer, T. (1987). Standardization in the changing world of telecommunications. In Economic Commission for Europe, *The telecommunications industry: Growth and structural change* (pp. 44-47). New York: United Nations.

Irmer, T. (1990, February). *The changing environment in telecommunication standardization: Opportunity or threat for CCITT?* Paper presented at the Interregional Telecommunications Standards Conference, Fredricksburg Virginia.

Krasner, S. D. (1983). Structural causes and regime consequences: Regimes as intervening variables. In S. D. Krasner (Ed.), *International regimes* (pp. 1-21). Ithaca, NY: Cornell University Press.

Rutkowski, A. M. (1985). *Integrated Services Digital Networks*. Norwood, NJ: Ablex.

Savage, J. G. (1989). *The politics of international telecommunications regulation*. Boulder, CO: Westview.

Temple, S. (1991). *ETSI: A revolution in European telecommunications standards making*. Hull, UK: Kingston Public Relations.

Valensi, G. (1965). The development of international telephony: The story of the international telephone consultative committee (CCIF). *Telecommunications Journal, 32*, 9-17.

Wallenstein, G. (1979). *Collaboration without coercion: The ITU as a model for worldwide agreement-making*. (Part 1 of *International Telecommunication Agreements*.) Dobbs Ferry, NY: Oceana.

Wallenstein, G. (1990). *Setting global telecommunication standards: The stakes, the players, and the process*. Norwood, MA: Artech House.

Trade in Telecommunications Services

The European Community and the Uruguay Round Services Trade Negotiations

R. BRIAN WOODROW
PIERRE SAUVÉ

Telecommunications in Europe is moving away from a past dominated by public monopoly provision of virtually all telecommunications services and close protection of domestic markets for equipment and services. The trade in telecommunications services issue, especially as it is evolving within the Uruguay Round services trade negotiations, is one front on which the future of European telecommunications is being forged.

Three prime groups of actors shape the role and position of the European Community on the trade in telecommunications services issue: the Commission of the European Communities, the 12 national governments and their PTTs, and European business and user groups. First and foremost, telecommunications liberalization in Europe since the mid-1980s has been prosecuted principally by the Commission of the European Communities in the context of its efforts to achieve an integrated internal market by the end of 1992 (Ungerer & Costello, 1990). Within the Commission itself, primary responsibility for telecommunications rests with the Directorate General (DG) XIII, supported in different ways by DG IV, in charge of the competition policy of the Community, and by DG I, which exercises the Community's exclusive powers to deal with external relations and trade. It has been DG I that negotiates for all the 12 member states of the Community in the Uruguay Round trade negotiations, on bilateral telecommunications trade issues, and on the ongoing efforts to implement the internal market that have set the broad parameters for the Community position on trade in telecommunications services.[1]

The second key element shaping the EC role and position are the views and interests of the Community's 12 member states. Each individual country within the EC, rather than the Commission or any other Community institution, retains ultimate responsibility for the provision and use of telecommunications networks and services within its territory and internationally. Although all, with the exception of the United Kingdom, maintain PTT monopoly control over voice telephony as a "reserved service," considerable variation remains between and among the 12 concerning how national PTTs operate and how particular telecommunications services should be provided and used as well as on broader policy issues.[2] Indeed, one of the main subtexts to the evolving role and position of the European Community on the trade in telecommunications services issue has been the contrary desire of all the 12 countries and their PTTs to limit the incursion of the EC Commission into the realm of national telecommunications activity (Buhart & Burton, 1989).

Increasingly, there is a third important element bearing on the evolving role and position of the European Community, namely European business and telecommunications user groups. Somewhat belatedly in comparison to their American counterparts, European business interests as well as major user groups such as the International Telecommunications Users Group (INTUG) have begun to lobby strenuously both at the Community and at the national level for telecommunications liberalization and for services trade liberalization (INTUG, 1987; Nicholas, 1990). The role and position of the European Community on the trade in telecommunications services issue have evolved very much as an attempt to balance off the demands of international business and user groups in Europe for increased competition and liberalized access and use against the claims of national governments and their PTTs for continued protection of their exclusive provider status and control over public networks (Mansell & Morgan, 1991).

If three major internal actors have been identified as shaping the European Community's evolving role and position on trade in telecommunications services, there is also one primary player in the Uruguay

Round negotiations against which the Community's objectives and strategy have been primarily directed, namely the United States. Although the EC and the United States agree at a general level on the goals to be pursued in these multilateral negotiations, they have often clashed on the approaches and means whereby these goals might be achieved. Moreover, the United States has chosen, deliberately and much to the consternation of the Community, to mix unilateral and bilateral actions with its overall multilateral strategy in its continuing efforts to open world telecommunications markets through trade and telecommunications liberalization. For example, efforts by the United States to work out bilateral telecommunications agreements such as the International Value-Added Network (IVAN) pact with Japan and even with one EC member state, namely the United Kingdom, is viewed by some within the Community as troublesome (Cowhey, 1990). It is no exaggeration to assert that United States-European Community relations has become the fulcrum on which the trade in telecommunications services issue and the Uruguay Round as a whole has come to rest and will largely determine its outcome.

Until the mid-1980s, telecommunications and trade were viewed as quite separate realms of activity domestically and at the international level—occasionally intersecting with each other but involving fundamentally different tasks and operating in very different ways (Woodrow, 1990a). This began to change as the potential synergy between telecommunications liberalization and trade liberalization was being explored. Increasingly, domestic and international telecommunications in all countries are coming to be regarded as the essential infrastructure for an expanding world trade and commerce across a wide range of services and manufacturing sectors. Telecommunications and the range of network services that it can carry are now widely regarded as the "electronic highways for world trade" (Lanvin, 1989; Robinson et al., 1989). Largely for this reason, telecommunications services has been perhaps the most exposed of any services sector to any multilateral services trade agreement and possible sectoral application that might arise out of the Uruguay Round services trade negotiations (Woodrow, 1990b).

The EC and Telecommunications Services as a Trade Issue

Launched at Punta del Este in 1986 and organized in terms of a Group of Negotiations on Services (GNS), which has operated separately

though in parallel to the mainstream negotiations on goods, their mandate has been nothing less than to develop an overall framework of
principles and rules for international trade in services (what would
constitute virtually an "economic constitution") and to agree on the
application of those principles and rules to as many services sectors and
by as many countries as is reasonably possible (Jackson, 1990). The
services trade negotiations were initiated as the result of a "constructive
compromise" struck among the United States, the EC, and the more
hard-line developing countries—a compromise made possible at the last
moment largely through the deft maneuver and skill of the EC delegation (Nicolaïdes, 1989). Services, Trade-Related Intellectual Property
Rights (TRIPs), Trade-Related Investment Measures (TRIMs), and agriculture would all be included in the new round of multilateral trade
negotiations. However, services would be treated as a separate set of
negotiations, formally unrelated to the mainstream goods negotiations,
though supported by the GATT secretariat and following the same
general procedures.

It was the U.S. government, in part for ideological but even more for
pragmatic reasons of national self-interest, and a determined international business and user lobby that has pressed most strongly and
persistently for a multilateral services trade agreement to cover a wide
range of service sectors including telecommunications. Working through
the late 1970s and up through the mid-1980s, the two were instrumental
in placing trade in services on the agenda of multilateral trade negotiations within the GATT (Feketekuty, 1988).

The EC's initial lukewarm attitude toward services trade liberalization stemmed largely from a lack of awareness about the importance of
trade in services within its overall trade position as well as long-standing concerns about "the Americanization of Europe." With international
business behind the U.S initiative including not only services companies but also firms such as IBM, member states and the Commission
exercised caution before committing themselves to support services
trade negotiations. However, studies conducted by the Commission as
well as by several member states during 1983 and 1984 demonstrated
that one-third of all EC trade was accounted for by services and that
many member states—among them France, the United Kingdom, West
Germany, and The Netherlands—had highly favorable trade balances
in various services trade sectors. Within the Commission and particularly within DG I, the EC began to develop its thinking on how a
multilateral services trade agreement might operate. By way of com-

parison to the U.S. approach, the EC approach was considerably more "evolutionary," emphasizing concepts such as progressive liberalization, appropriate regulation, and levels of development rather than the straightforward and automatic liberalization seemingly advocated by the United States and international business (Richardson, 1987).

During 1987 and 1988, the GNS set about exploring the concepts and parameters of a multilateral agreement, identifying possible principles and rules to be included and investigating the range of services sectors and international agreements and organizations that might be affected. It soon became apparent that no mere extension of the existing GATT agreement and/or its codes was likely to be adequate in handling the conceptual and political problems of dealing with trade in services. At the Montreal midterm review in December 1988, overcoming much disagreement primarily between developed and developing countries, the GNS was able to agree on the essential elements of a draft framework of principles and rules:

- Provisions to promote *transparency* of domestic and international laws, regulations, and administrative practices relating to services
- A commitment to *progressive liberalization* as a general principle and its application in some agreed form to specific services sectors with acknowledgement of the particular difficulties of its application to developing countries
- *National treatment* for services exports and or exporters of signatories vis-à-vis domestic services or services providers in the same market
- Where *market access* is made available, foreign services may be supplied according to the "preferred mode of delivery"
- *Most-Favored-Nation (MFN) treatment/nondiscrimination* should apply in that benefits should be extended to all signatories and apply equally to all covered services
- *Increasing participation of developing countries* should be encouraged through enhanced market access for services exports of developing countries with specific reference to "improved access to distribution channels and information networks" and possible special treatment for the least-developed countries
- *Safeguards/exceptions* are recognized as possibly necessary for dealing with adverse temporary circumstances or for reasons of a more permanent nature
- Acknowledgement of the right of countries to continue to regulate their services sectors, where they feel it appropriate, but recognition that asymmetries exist in the *regulatory situation* of different countries and that any introduction of new regulations should be consistent with country commitments to progressive liberalization under the framework[3]

Much of the "evolutionary" approach advocated by the EC was reflected clearly in this draft framework and the Community's services trade negotiators once again played a key role in mediating conflict between the United States and the more hard-line developing countries.

When it resumed again in April 1989, the GNS for the first time directed its attention squarely to sectoral issues, although still in the context of refining and confirming the outline draft framework arrived at in Montreal. Between June and September, the GNS then undertook a "sectoral testing" exercise wherein each of six important services sectors was examined. Telecommunications services was the first of the sectors to be treated, and the discussion, which drew participation from more than 30 countries and at which ITU participated as an observer, revealed how intellectually and politically challenging it would be to fit that sector within an eventual agreement.

During the fall of 1989, attention turned back once again to the framework and the task of determining the basic negotiating text of an agreement before the end of the year. Several countries submitted full or partial texts, the most detailed and specific of which was submitted by the United States in October. The U.S. draft legal text had a galvanizing impact on the negotiations, not least of all because it included the concept of "special agreements," which might be applied in specific sectors or subsectors and which suggested that the United States might want effectively to exempt certain sectors from full coverage.[4] Conflict between developed and developing countries as well as serious infighting between the United States and the EC concerning the overall structure of an agreement and how initial commitments should be negotiated arose at this point to seriously disrupt the progress of the services negotiations. The proposed negotiating text that resulted in December 1989 (containing some 167 square brackets or alternative texts) was described by the EC services negotiator with considerable understatement as a "disappointment."[5] The large number of square brackets and alternative text was a bit deceptive because many of the more extreme formulations came from only a few developing countries, and the United States, the EC, and other developed countries also made sure that their preferred formulations were also included.

During the first half of 1990, the EC was very much at the center of the action as the Uruguay Round moved toward its scheduled conclusion in Brussels at the end of 1990. In a separately and bilaterally negotiated compromise, the United States and the EC came to seeming agreement on the underlying structure of an eventual agreement in March. Subject to broader acceptance by the parties to the negotiation and instead of the automatic liberalization approach originally intended, an overall agreement would provide for the following:

- A set of provisions of general application applying to all covered services subject to possible sectoral annotations (e.g., transparency, MFN/nondis-crimination, dispute settlement, regional integration arrangements, safe-guards, and the like)
- A further layer of negotiable rather than automatic commitments on market access, national treatment, treatment of monopolies, subsidies, and so on, against which reservations could be lodged on sectors, transactions, or modes of delivery
- A set of commitments to be undertaken in future in order to achieve further liberalization and appropriate balance among signatory countries

Following the earlier lead of the United States, no less than seven countries or groups of countries had by then submitted legal draft frameworks either formally or informally and national negotiating positions were becoming much clearer.

During the first half of 1990, attention also focused again on the sectoral annexes that might be required to tailor application of the framework agreement to particular services sectors. In March, the United States submitted its long-awaited draft of a sectoral annex on telecommunications services, which tended to mix telecommunications as a mode of delivery with the quite specific conditions of network access and use that it would like to see enshrined in multilateral agreement. At its May meeting, the GNS took up the question of sectoral coverage and proceeded to authorize the establishment of sectoral working groups (nine of which were eventually formed) and each proceeded during the summer and fall of 1990 to examine the need for and possible content of sectoral annotations in various services areas. The results from these sectoral working groups were then to be fed into the effort to put together a framework, sectoral annexes, and set of initial commitments that could be presented to trade ministers in Brussels in December 1990.

Evolving an EC Position on Trade in Telecommunications Services

The actual process of formulating an EC position on trade in telecommunications services began in earnest during the fall of 1989 in anticipation of the GNS sectoral testing exercise that took place that summer. Although a preliminary discussion paper on sectoral aspects of a services trade agreement had been circulating as early as the spring of 1988, the Community had not even discussed any formal position prior to that meeting and, at the meeting, the EC services negotiator took a cautious tack, indicating that the community viewed telecommunications services as integral and crucial to any eventual agreement but stating no clear position on any of the key negotiating issues (Sauvé, 1989; Scheele, 1989).

Following that initial examination of six services sectors and given the delicate constitutional and institutional relationships between and within the Commission and member states, DG I chose only to draw "broad conclusions" from those discussions and leave it to member states, each of whom had been present on a nonparticipating basis, to make their own national and sectoral assessments. In general terms, however, DG I reported "no insuperable problems attached to the application of multilateralization concepts to all the sectors, with the possible exception of air transport," although MFN treatment, a standstill on the creation of new regulatory barriers, and controls on monopoly behavior could prove difficult. Further, it concluded that "there is no desire to liberalize basic domestic services, at least for the foreseeable future . . . [but that] . . . there is a need to cover certain issues relating to such basic services because of the issue of access to networks." The issue of access to the network, it suggested, "came out very clearly as one requiring sectoral annotation . . . [and] . . . some of the principles behind ONP/ONA would need codifying at the multilateral level to meet this concern."[6]

The Commission's DG I through its Article 113 Committee attempted to bring together and, to some extent, to broker the views and interests of member states and other parties who might be affected by the trade in telecommunications services issue. In late October, the Senior Officials Group on Telecommunications (SOG-T) considered a discussion paper on trade in telecommunications services. It emphasized that the EC already had considerable experience to draw on in terms of the cross-border liberalization of telecommunications services where member states maintained often quite different domestic regulatory frameworks and that pending Commission directives on Services and Open Network Provision would provide the underlying base for any EC position on trade in services. In addition to the prime importance and likely need for sectoral annotation relating to network access and use, other considerations including the role of international standards versus proprietary protocols, behavior of companies operating in monopoly or dominant positions within telecommunications markets, the continuing role of bilateral IVAN agreements such as those already in existence between the United Kingdom and the United States and the United Kingdom and Japan, and access to information issues including privacy were all identified as matters on which an EC position would need to be developed.[7]

At this point, the evolution of that EC position on trade in telecommunications services came to be related very much to the ongoing development of the Commission's proposed services and Open Network Provision (ONP) directives. The Services Directive, being pressed in particular by DG IV, was intended to open all but "reserved" telecommunications services to competitive supply and to ease restrictions on the use of leased-lines for private data transmission by 1993. It raised particular objections from virtually all member states, including even the more liberal ones such as the United Kingdom, because of the proposed implementation under Article 90 of the Treaty of Rome that allows the Commission to bypass the Council of Ministers and make public monopolies in member states comply with Community competition rules. France, Italy, Spain, and other member states—prompted by their PTTs who felt threatened by these proposals—disagreed in principle with the attempt to open value-added and data transmission to competition as well as with the Commission's use of Article 90. Although the more liberal member states including the United Kingdom, West Germany, Denmark, and The Netherlands supported the content of the Services Directive, they also shared with their more conservative counterparts a clear distaste for the method of implementation chosen by the Commission.

The proposed ONP Directive also raised considerable opposition among member states. Closely linked to the Services Directive, the ONP Directive was intended to establish a framework for the harmonization of network access and usage. It was to be followed by a series of implementation directives on individual telecommunications services including voice, data, leased-lines, and value-added offerings.[8] However, member states disagreed fundamentally on the purpose and application of the proposed directive and divided into the same basic camps on the content of the ONP Directive as on the Services Directive. The more conservative camp saw ONP as a means to ensure interconnection of networks across national borders and some harmonization of telecommunications services offerings across the Community, one that should apply both to "reserved" or monopoly services as well as to those categories of services to be opened to competitive provision. The more liberal camp as well as the Commission itself, however, tended to view the proposed directive more as a liberalization initiative that should apply only to those areas, such as voice telephony and leased-lines where monopolies would still be allowed, and expressly as a means for ensuring that private telecommunications services providers could guarantee their access to public networks.

Member state differences within the Community over the Services and ONP directives came to a head during the fall of 1989, at virtually the same time that the EC position on trade in telecommunications services was being determined. France, in particular, wanted to resolve these issues while it could use its influence as chair of all EC committees, a circumstance that would change at the end of the year. At a special meeting of the EC Telecommunications Ministers early in December, a carefully crafted compromise was reached whereby DG IV agreed that the Services Directive would be modified somewhat if the core elements of the ONP Directive being pressed by more liberal member states were to be approved by the necessary weighted majority and without prejudice to any future European Court of Justice determination of the applicability of Article 90. Basic telecommunications networks and services will not be directly affected, but specific ONP directives for particular telecommunications services would be developed to regulate network access and use. Member states did agree to open value-added and data transmission services to competitive provision by January 1, 1993, except for the poorer Mediterranean countries, which could appeal for an exemption until 1996. Specifically with regard to leased-lines for data transmission, member states may draw up licensing conditions for private operators, as France in particular had pressed for strongly in order to prevent "cream-skimming," but these licensing conditions would also have to be vetted by the Commission in terms of their conformity with the competition provisions of the Treaty of Rome. A "joint position" was formally adopted by the EC Telecommunications Ministers in February of 1990 giving effect to this political compromise that acknowledged liberalization of service provision beyond voice telephony and basic data transmission while also ensuring interconnection and harmonization of technical standards through the progressive implementation of ONP.[9]

From the perspective of the Community, the ongoing battle in Brussels over the ONP and Services Directives went to the heart of the trade in telecommunications services issue, paralleling matters of coverage, market access and national treatment, and MFN treatment as well as the sectoral annex on network access and use then beginning to be developed multilaterally in Geneva. Subsequent to agreement on this "joint position" and premised explicitly on that underlying compromise, the Article 113 Committee took up the matter of sectoral negotiating objectives for telecommunications services within the Uruguay Round.[10] It confirmed that "any agreement on traded services must cover telecommunications"—understood as public networks and services—but that the reserved/competitive services distinction could be used to limit the area of application to competitive services only. In line both with the "joint position" and with the important compromise on structure of an eventual services trade agreement arranged between the United States and the EC only that March, the Committee took the position that reserved services should be subject directly to the general provisions of an eventual agreement (transparency, regulatory situation, controls on dominant position, etc), though not necessarily to the specific obligations on market access and national treatment that would be subject to negotiation. Competitive or value-added services would, however, be subject to the whole of the agreement. Market access and national treatment would then be negotiated on an offer/request basis among GNS participants and included as initial commitments in an eventual services trade agreement. With regard to MFN treatment specifically, the Article 113 Committee made the assumption that basic telecommunications services—as the United States treated it but which approximated the EC notion of "reserved services"—would not be offered or requested. It also expressed concern that any derogations from MFN that any country might seek for existing bilateral agreements should be carefully limited in order to preserve the overall scope and integrity of an eventual agreement.

After deliberation and some revision, the 113 Committee also formalized the Community's negotiating objectives for telecommunications services in the Uruguay Round. These were specifically identified (and can be interpreted) as follows:

- "Equivalent opportunities in third markets for both the provision and utilization of information and communications services," that is, effective intra-sectoral reciprocity
- "Appropriate market access conditions and national treatment," that is, network access and use similar to ONP

- "Promotion of international standards and interoperability," that is, concern about proprietary standards imposed on a mandatory basis
- "Relationships between the Uruguay Round and the ITU," that is, complementarity among institutional arrangements for trade and telecommunications
- "Developing country aspects," that is, recognition of special problems but concern about linking services liberalization to infrastructure funding
- "Considerations regarding access to information," that is, concern that possible limitations on transborder online data access are not adequately addressed
- "Provisions relating to data protection, data privacy, and intellectual property," that is, the absence of any such provisions in the framework or annex
- "Considerations relating to abuse of dominant positions," that is, concern not only about public monopoly behavior but also about private companies operating within the Community and internationally[11]

By late April 1990, the Article 113 Committee had confirmed these broad negotiating objectives for telecommunications services. Further, it agreed to seek early opening of sectoral negotiations in Geneva as well as preparation of the EC's own version of a sectoral annex on telecommunications services, a measure designed to counter the United States proposal for a draft telecommunications services annex that had been released in March.

Through April and May of 1990, the Commission, and in this case particularly DG XIII, set about the task of formulating the Community version of a sectoral annex and guiding it first through SOG-T and then the Article 113 Committee. Once again, the various member states held somewhat different views on the position the Community should adopt on the trade in telecommunications services issue. These differences closely paralleled those held on internal market issues such as the Services and ONP Directives. The United Kingdom had led the more liberal forces on these latter issues and took a similar stance vis-à-vis the trade in telecommunications services issue. It had already privatized British Telecom in 1984 and established OFTEL as the separate regulatory authority in the field; licensed Mercury as a second telecommunications provider; opened up the resale and leased-line market; and entered into bilateral IVAN agreements with both the United States and Japan. Within the United Kingdom, as well, there was a determined business and user group lobby that also pressed for telecommunications and trade liberalization; among all the providers in Europe, British telecommunications service providers were undoubtedly the most liberally inclined.

The United Kingdom has pressed its Community partners for a strong framework and sectoral annex on telecommunications services, supporting the Commission in its efforts to limit the scope of "reserved services" that could remain as monopoly services and that, under the EC position, would not be subject to the full provisions of any Uruguay Round services trade agreement. The United Kingdom also fought strongly to retain its right to enter into bilateral value-added services agreements that might be interpreted as not conforming to MFN principles and viewed CCITT recommendations relating to network access and use as very much out of date. In general, it tended to reinforce liberal tendencies within the Commission, although suspicious of any efforts on its part to use its external relations powers to infringe on member-state jurisdiction over telecommunications, and typically could rely on support from West Germany, The Netherlands, Denmark, and Ireland on the trade in telecommunications issue.

France, by way of contrast, came to be viewed as leader of the more conservative forces on both internal market and trade in telecommunications services issues. In this regard, it tended to be supported by the other six member states, although France's views were always very much a reflection of its own particular interests and circumstances. France holds to a broader specification of what should be considered a "reserved service" than do more liberal forces within the Community and even its other conservative compatriots. Its policy and regulatory framework for telecommunications was in transition during the late 1980s and early 1990s as France Télécom remained a public monopoly but was severed from direct ministerial control while a quasi-independent regulatory authority, the Direction de la Règlementation Général (DRG) within the Ministry, was established to oversee telecommunications in France and in its external dimensions.

France's approach both on internal market and trade issues has been to maintain the public monopoly over voice telephony and basic data transmission, including provision of leased-lines and a ban on resale of transmission services, but to allow for competitive provision of value-added services. This approach has specifically influenced its stance on the trade in telecommunications services issue. It has supported efforts to arrive at a Uruguay Round services trade agreement but with certain clear reservations as to the EC position and any eventual result. In France's view, the principle of monopoly for network infrastructures and voice telephony must be preserved as well as the viability of operators subject to public service constraints. Beyond that, licensing systems for competitive services providers and conditions for access to public networks and services should be based on transparent, objective, and nondiscriminating conditions. And last, the importance of international standards and the continuing role of the ITU and international standardization organizations should be acknowledged.

One important factor bearing on formulation of the EC position on trade in telecommunications services, especially during early 1990, was coincident pressure placed on the Community by possible bilateral measures mandated under U.S. trade legislation. Under the Omnibus Trade Act of 1988, the United States Trade Representative (USTR) was required to investigate countries carrying on unfair telecommunications trade practices and subsequently to negotiate with "priority countries" concerning their removal. The EC was identified as one such "priority country" in early 1989 and the USTR was mandated to report to Congress by mid-February of 1990. At U.S./EC bilateral meetings late in 1989, the USTR pressed the Commission for information and assurances concerning telecommunications procurement and services within the Community. By way of response, the Commission provided a description of recent Community decisions and answers to many of the specific questions posed while also emphasizing its own concerns about legal and other barriers to the U.S. market for the provision of telecommunications equipment and services. In particular, the Commission made clear that both countries should direct their best efforts to achieve success in the Uruguay Round rather than toward possible bilateral retaliation.[12] When USTR reported to Congress in February 1990, it assessed recent EC actions as representing satisfactory progress toward reduction of unfair trade barriers in telecommunications equipment and services.

Finally, after much discussion and fine-tuning within SOG-T and the Article 113 Committee during May and early June of 1990, the EC was able to present its version of a telecommunications services annex. This was submitted as a "nonpaper" at the first meeting of the GNS Working Group on Telecommunications Services in early June and held closely to the delicate compromises reached among member states on the Services and ONP Directives. The EC legal draft of a framework was not submitted until late June and made provision for universal coverage of all services sectors, full MFN treatment, treatment of abuse of dominant position on the part both of public and private sector providers of services, and several other features that continued to bring the Community into conflict with the United States.[13] With these important

Community decisions taken, the EC position had largely been set and further evolution of that position would be determined by broader developments within the GNS negotiations specifically and the Uruguay Round as a whole.

Negotiating the Framework and Sectoral Annex on Telecommunications

Starting in the summer of 1990, the GNS finally undertook to pull all the major threads together and to agree on the basic text of a framework and sectoral annexes on which its remaining work could proceed. This proved unsuccessful, largely because of continuing fundamental disagreement over the question of definition and coverage—specifically, whether or not countries should be able to exempt particular sectors or subsectors from an eventual agreement, as the United States, Japan, and Austria now argued.[14] In its draft framework, the EC had stressed that the general principles agreed to in the framework should apply to all traded services within all services sectors, including basic telecommunications services, and that derogations from MFN and national treatment should be kept to a minimum. What resulted from its July meeting was an incomplete "Chairman's text," packaging together essentially only those elements on which there was general consensus but that also contained a universal coverage provision.[15] These matters of coverage and MFN treatment were to remain crucial points of conflict between the EC and the United States as the GNS negotiations moved toward their scheduled completion at the Brussels Ministerial Meeting in December 1990.

Between June and October, the Working Group on Telecommunications held four formal meetings, spawned numerous more informal contacts among national delegations, and involved ITU officials directly in its discussions. It proved to be the most active and arguably the most crucial of any of the sectoral working groups. Chaired by a telecommunications official (Robert Tritt of the Canadian Ministry of Communications) rather than a trade policy official, but with support from the GNS secretariat and reporting to the Trade Negotiations Committee responsible for the Uruguay Round, the role of the Working Group was a difficult one, namely to examine and report back to the GNS on the content of a possible sectoral annotation on telecommunications services. The Working Group had to be careful not to negotiate coverage and commitments, which was clearly a framework rather than a sectoral task. Participation in its deliberations was extensive and active and with a new element added to the services trade negotiations by the more specialized and technically oriented telecommunications policy officials from the various countries.

There were now a total of six country proposals for possible sectoral annotations for consideration by the Working Group. In addition to the U.S. draft, Japan and South Korea were quick to introduce separately their proposed sectoral annotations, which would be less far-reaching than that of the United States and which reflected very much each country's domestic telecommunications law and regulation. Then, the EC brought forward its carefully crafted proposal, which reflected its ongoing ONP and services directive efforts. Finally, a group of developing countries—India, Cameroon, Egypt, and Nigeria—put forward two proposed sectoral annotations, one dealing with telecommunications as a mode of delivery and a separate one dealing with it as a sector in terms of conditions for network access and use. In so doing, they were clearly attempting to "unbundle" the two elements and gain improvements in the ability of developing countries to manage and utilize their telecommunications services.

At meetings of the Working Group in September and October, the crucial issues were finally joined and the chairman undertook to mediate the differences among and between these various proposals for sectoral annotations. It soon became clear that even a rough consensus could not be put in place around the U.S. draft of a telecom sectoral annex that was viewed by many as too extreme yet also too self-serving. Only a text that started from a more moderate position—such as the EC proposal—could possibly gain broad support within the Working Group. In order to meet the GNS mandate, the chairman and the Working Group sought compromise around this more moderate position while supplementing this by meeting some of the key concerns of Japan and South Korea as well as the developing countries. At this time as well, the U.S. delegation, the Working Group itself, and country trade representatives (including those of the Commission) also came under considerable lobbying pressure from AT&T and other U.S. competitive telecommunications providers concerned that basic services be exempted from the coverage under any agreement as well as about the implications of MFN for entry of foreign telecommunications services providers.

Any sectoral annotation on telecommunications services must deal primarily with matters of network access and use. This was the prime focus of the Working Group and a long list of items was thoroughly discussed. With regard to standards and attachment, there was general consensus that international standards to ensure network integrity and interoperability of public services remained important as well as a concern that standards—whether international or proprietary—not be utilized as discriminatory barriers to competition. On pricing-related matters, an issue receiving considerable media and intergovernmental attention, there was also broad consensus that the pricing of telecommunications services should not discriminate among parties nor result in trade distortions, although more specific provisions on pricing as proposed by the United States proved unacceptable. With regard to conditions of supply and use, there was only limited support for the U.S. position that full resale/shared use or interconnection of private leased-lines to the public telecommunications transport network should be permitted. Finally, there was inconclusive debate over whether information-related matters such as privacy should be treated within the annex.

What emerged from the Working Group on Telecommunications when it reported to the GNS in late October was a considerably watered-down text—when compared to the one originally proposed by the United States earlier in the year—but one that did draw broad support from a range of developed and developing countries. With minor modifications, this was essentially the same text approved by the Trade Negotiations Committee in late November and that went to Brussels for consideration by the world's trade ministers in the first week of December 1990.[16] However, a second telecommunications sectoral annex—advanced at the last moment by the United States, which was obviously concerned about the setbacks it had suffered—proposing in effect that basic telecommunications services be exempted from MFN treatment, was added to the text that went to Brussels making clear that basic telecommunications services would be subject to MFN derogation.[17] And last, on the very eve of that meeting, the EC tabled its conditional offer on telecommunications and other services that it was prepared to bind in terms of market access and national treatment. It was proposed that value-added telecommunications services would be bound as of January 1, 1992, while packet- and circuit-switched data services would be subject to a regulatory standstill until elimination of all but licensing requirements as of January 1, 1996.[18]

Brussels and After

As is well known, what was to have been the final act of the Uruguay Round in Brussels in 1991 foundered primarily on the issue of agricultural trade subsidies rather than on anything to do with the services trade negotiations. In fact, the services trade negotiations in Brussels were just beginning to examine the framework and sectoral annexes including telecommunications when the GATT Director-General suspended the trade negotiations until further efforts could be made to break the deadlock over agriculture. The failure at Brussels to move forward on telecommunications services reflected the continuing disarray within the trade negotiations themselves rather than any determined resistance from the international telecommunications regime or any other services sector. Moreover, although there was considerable lobbying by telecommunications interests both in Geneva and the national capitals, it was not primarily on the part of the monopoly PTTs who were trying to scuttle an agreement but rather from AT&T and the competitive U.S. providers who sought derogation from MFN or custom-designed coverage because of what they regarded as unfair foreign access to the more "liberal" U.S. market.

What is now being said is that "the success in Brussels was that it failed." Rather than agree prematurely to a weak framework and sectoral annex for services trade, there is now a second chance to develop a stronger and more effective liberalizing instrument. In February 1991, all parties agreed to continue with the Uruguay Round negotiations and, in May, the U.S. Congress voted to extend its fast-track approval process for 2 more years. As 1991 moved on and the GNS resumed, there was renewed optimism—confirmed by the end of the year—that a strengthened framework and sectoral annexes were within negotiating reach.

Efforts on the part of the U.S. government and international business and user groups to strengthen the telecommunications services annex have continued. This has placed the EC and other countries under renewed pressure. Following extensive bilateral discussions with all negotiating partners as well as much internal deliberation and consultation with the private sector, the United States moved to revisit the telecommunications services annex. In September, it submitted a modest set of proposed changes and, within the context of the GNS rather than the Working Group on Telecommunications, which was by then defunct, these were considered and decisions taken to assuage some of the key U.S. concerns. In particular, provisions relating to resale and sharing of leased-lines, the use of proprietary as well as international standards, and treatment of intracorporate communications were strengthened, while EC concerns about privacy and the public service responsibilities of the PTT's were acknowledged.[19] By this time, the EC was more in support of these changes—under considerable pressure from European business and user groups— and a revised version of the telecommunications services annex was broadly accepted by all the major participants.

In December 1991, the GATT Director-General intervened to bring about a conclusion to the negotiations by submitting his own version of an overall Uruguay Round agreement.[20] At the same time, the United States also made a possibly significant modification in its position on an MFN derogation for basic telecommunications. As part of its effort to secure a successful conclusion to the Uruguay Round, it offered to extend MFN treatment to both domestic and international long-distance telecommunications services. However, this step would be taken only on the condition that major U.S. trading partners—and the EC first and foremost—would agree to open their own long-distance markets to international competition within 3 years after the entry into force of a final agreement. Under the U.S. proposal, there would be a reasonable transition period for countries currently operating monopolies to make the structural changes necessary for allowing competition in domestic and international long-distance telecommunications but, if and when that condition was met, the basic long-distance telecommunications services market would become subject to MFN treatment and derogations would no longer be permitted. The U.S. proposal presents a clear challenge to the member states of the EC, Japan, Canada, and others, all of whom have pressed Washington for over a year on the MFN issue. It will be interesting to see specifically how this proposal might factor into the exchange of initial commitments among participants in the Uruguay Round services trade negotiations as well as how it might affect the delicate balance of support and reservation that countries are voicing about the Director-General's initiative to finally bring an end to the Round.

Notes

1. Member-state participation in the exercise of those powers is effected through a committee set up according to Article 113 of the Treaty of Rome (Article 113 Committee), which meets on a weekly basis to consider and decide on positions to be taken by DG I.

2. To coordinate the views and interests of member states at the Community level, the Senior Officials Group on Telecommunications (SOG-T) was established in 1984. By way of contrast, each of the 12 member states continues to represent itself individually as a sovereign entity within the International Telecommunication Union (and not always in common agreement with each other on every issue).

3. See MTN.GNS/21. The Uruguay Round has generated a huge amount of documentation. Much of it is nominally restricted but readily available within the trade community in Geneva.

4. See MTN.GNS/W/75. This was interpreted by the EC and many other countries as a means whereby countries could exempt sensitive sectors such as air and maritime transport or even basic telecommunications from full liberalization.

5. See MTN.GNS/28.

6. EC internal document.

7. Personal interviews.

8. Revised Proposal for a Council Directive on the Establishment of the Internal Market for Telecommunications Services Through the Implementation of Open Network Provision, COM(89)325, August 10, 1989.

9. Commission Memo 90/6, February 5, 1990.

10. The basic document for this discussion was a 100-page-plus summary of EC negotiating objectives for all the major services sectors put forward by DG I in March 1990.

11. Ibid., p. 101, as modified by the Article 113 Committee, April 23, 1990.

12. Exchange of correspondence between Carla Hills, USTR, and Filippo Pandolfi, DG XIII, January 23, 1990, and February 7, 1990.

13. The EC version of a trade in services framework is MTN.GNS/W/105, submitted June 18, 1990.

14. See U.S. Trade Representative, "U.S. Telecommunications Services Annex Objectives," Washington, DC, July 1990, mimeo.

15. MTN.GNS/35. The EC and other developed countries were particularly critical of the U.S. position on coverage, which seemed diametrically opposed to their long-standing commitment to wide-ranging services trade liberalization but which clearly stemmed from concern that foreign services providers in certain sectors might gain unfair access to liberalized domestic markets.

16. See MTN.GNS/W/35/Rev 1.

17. Ibid., pp. 369-370; see also MTN.TNC/W/49.

18. MTN.TNC/W/53/Rev.1, dated December 4, 1990.

19. MTN.GNS/W/134.

20. MTN.TNC/W/FA, Annex II, December 20, 1991.

References

Buhart, J., & Burton, D. (1989). *Legal aspects of the Single European Market: A working guide to 1992*. Tonbridge: Euromoney Special Report.

Cowhey, P. (1990). Telecommunications. In G. C. Hufbauer (Ed.), *Europe 1992: An American perspective* (pp. 159-224). Washington, DC: Brookings Institute.

Feketekuty, G. (1988). *International trade in services*. Cambridge, MA: Ballinger.

INTUG. (1987). The INTUG view on the Green Paper. *Telecommunications Policy, 10*, 327-330.

Jackson, J. H. (1990). *The international trading system*. Cambridge: MIT Press.

Lanvin, B. (Ed.). (1989). *Global trade: The revolution beyond the information revolution*. Montpellier: IDATE.

Mansell, R., & Morgan, K. (1991). Evolving telecommunication infrastructures: Organizing the new European Community marketplace. In C. Freeman et. al. (Eds.), *Technology and the future of Europe* (pp. 138-54). London: Pinter.

Nicholas, D. (1990). Global business needs better telecommunications for trade purposes. In R. B. Woodrow (Ed.), *Uruguay Round trade in services perspectives* (pp. 93-96). Geneva: Applied Services Economic Centre.

Nikolaïdis, K. (1989). Learning while negotiating: How services got on the Uruguay Round agenda. In A. Bressand & K. Nicolaïdis (Eds.), *Strategic trends in services* (pp. 161-180). New York: Ballinger.

Richardson, J. (1987). A sub-sectorial approach to services trade theory. In O. Giarini (Ed.), *The emerging services economy* (pp. 59-82). New York: Pergamon.

Robinson, P., Sauvant, K. P., & Govitrikar, V. P. (Eds.). (1989). *Electronic highways to world trade*. Boulder, CO: Westview.

Sauvé, P. (1989). *Telecommunications services and the Uruguay Round: Tentative lessons from the sectoral testing exercise*. Paper Presented at the International Institute of Communications Annual Conference, Paris, September 7.

Scheele, J. (1989). The European Community and the Uruguay Round services negotiations. In B. Lanvin (Ed.), *Global trade: The revolution beyond the communications revolution*. Montpelier: IDATE.

Ungerer, H., & Costello, N. (1990). *Telecommunications in Europe*. Brussels: Office for Official Publications of the European Communities.

Woodrow, R. B. (1990a). Telecommunications and trade in services: Never the twain shall meet? *Transnational Data Report, 13*, 21-25.

Woodrow, R. B. (1990b). A Uruguay Round services trade agreement: Implications for major services sectors and international business. In R. B. Woodrow (Ed.), *Uruguay Round trade in services perspectives* (pp. 19-40). Geneva: Applied Services Economic Centre.

SEVEN

Fostering Telecommunications Development

The Role of the OECD

DIMITRI YPSILANTI
TIM KELLY

The Organization for Economic Cooperation and Development (OECD) was established on 30 September 1961 by an international convention as a successor to the Organization for European Economic Cooperation (OEEC), which had been set up in 1948. Its aims are to promote social and economic welfare throughout the OECD area by assisting its member governments in the formulation of policies designed to this end and by coordinating these policies, and to stimulate and harmonize its members' efforts in favor of developing countries.

Its permanent base is in Paris and its membership comprises 24 of the advanced industrial nations: Australia, Austria, Belgium, Canada, Denmark, Finland, France, Germany, Greece, Iceland, Ireland, Italy, Japan, Luxembourg, The Netherlands, New Zealand, Norway, Portugal, Spain, Sweden, Switzerland, Turkey, the United Kingdom, and the United States. In addition, Yugoslavia participates in the work of the Organization with a special status. In 1991, the Czech and Slovak Republic (CSFR), Hungary, and Poland each signed memoranda of understanding with the OECD under the Partners in Transition (PIT) program, designed to assist them in the transition from a centrally planned to a market economy.

AUTHORS' NOTE: The opinions expressed in this paper are those of the authors and do not necessarily reflect the views of the OECD or its member countries.

The supreme body of the Organization is the Council, composed of one representative for each member country. Decisions and recommendations are adopted by mutual agreement of all members of the Council. The Council is assisted by an Executive Committee composed of 14 members of the Council designated annually by the latter. The major part of the Organization's work is, however, prepared and carried out in numerous specialized committees and working parties of which there exist more than 200. Thus, the Organization comprises Committees for Economic Policy; Economic and Development Review; Development Assistance (DAC); Trade; Capital Movements and Invisible Transactions; Financial Markets; Fiscal Affairs; Competition Law and Policy; Consumer Policy; Tourism; Maritime Transport; International Investment and Multinational Enterprises; Energy; Computer and Communications Policy; Education; Manpower and Social Affairs; Public Management; Environment; Agriculture; Fisheries; and so on.

The various committees and other bodies are, as a rule, composed of civil servants coming either from capitals or from the permanent delegations to OECD that are established as normal diplomatic missions and are headed by ambassadors. They are serviced by an International Secretariat headed by the Secretary-General of the Organization.

The Information, Computer, and Communications Policy Committee

Within the OECD, matters concerning telecommunications are discussed in a number of different fora including the Committees concerned with Trade, Competition Policy, and Development. However, the principal committee concerned with telecommunications is the Information, Computer, and Communications Policy (ICCP) Committee.

The ICCP was established by the Council at its 557th meeting on 1 April 1982 with a mandate to examine policy issues arising from the development and application of technologies in the field of information, computer, and communications systems and services, including the impact of such issues on the economy and society in general, and to strengthen cooperation between the member states in this field. This Committee deals with a number of government concerns related to the economy and international trade, which also have important impacts on society in general.

Telecommunication in the OECD Area

OECD countries account for a high percentage of the global base of installed telephone main lines, having a total of 362 million lines (on average some 43 lines per 100 inhabitants; see Table 7.1 in Appendix). The revenue of public telecommunication operators in the OECD area amounts to some $285 billion or approximately 2% of the gross domestic product of member countries (see Table 7.2 in Appendix). These carriers have been responsible for about 3% of OECD gross fixed capital formation, investing close to $70 billion per annum (see Table 7.3 in Appendix). In terms of traffic volume, 18 of the world's top 20 public telecommunications operators come from OECD countries and account for 60% of total world telecommunication traffic. The OECD area is also the major producer of telecommunications equipment, in particular public switching equipment, and is also the major user of terminal and carrier equipment.

ICCP and Telecommunications Policy: 1982-1988

The work program of the ICCP during its first 6 years was structured under four main headings:

1. Information Technology and the Economy
2. Information Infrastructures and Telecommunications Policy
3. Information Technology and Society
4. International Information Flows

The second and fourth of these were concerned with telecommunications issues.

Studies completed during this period include the areas of value-added network services, videotex systems development policies in selected member countries, and the competition and complementarity between fiber-optic facilities and satellite communications.

During this period, the Committee maintained a Working Party on Transborder Data Flows that addressed policy issues arising from international data flows. This effort led to the adoption of the "OECD Declaration on Transborder Data Flows" at the Council Meeting at Ministerial Level of April 1985, by which governments of member countries expressed their intention to promote access to data and information and related services, and to develop common approaches for dealing with transborder data flow issues. This declaration complemented an earlier set of guidelines, "Guidelines Governing the Protection of Privacy and Transborder Data Flows of Personal Data," which was issued by the OECD Council in 1980.

Current Work in Telecommunications Policy: A Review of the Issues

In its work on telecommunications policy, the OECD works closely with other international organizations such as the ITU, the World Bank, and the GATT, or regional groupings such as the EC, the CEPT, or the European Bank for Recovery and Development (EBRD). The main focus of the Organization's work are issues concerned with economic development. It is possible to recognize four layers of increasing involvement that characterize the OECD approach:

1. The collection of data from member countries, either directly or from secondary sources, and the reworking and presentation of this data in a harmonized format to allow for international comparisons
2. On the basis of this analysis, the conducting of a review of international policies and the identifying of new trends in technology and market structure
3. The making of policy recommendations, especially in those areas where OECD countries have not yet formulated a systematic policy (By its work on international comparisons, the OECD can highlight where a country is out of line with other countries in its policy stance or where reform is necessary to improve its economic performance.)
4. Finally, the use of the OECD as a forum for agreements between member countries

In practice, this fourth stage is reached only rarely; two agreements in 10 years with a third, on information network security, are likely in the near future. The OECD can only go as far as its member countries wish. However, work initiated at the OECD is often taken up by other agreement-making fora, notably the GATT. So although the OECD is only rarely involved in *making* telecommunications policy, it plays a leading role in informing, advising, and guiding the policy making process carried on elsewhere.

Telecommunication Policy Perspectives and Goals

A clear trend towards the liberalization of telecommunication service and equipment markets has emerged over the last few years in the OECD area. Competition in telecommunications, once the exception, is quickly becoming the norm. Differences remain in the rate of change between member countries, but implementation of the European Commission's telecommunication framework as laid out initially in the Green Paper of 1987 and in subsequent directives could lead essentially to half the member countries having a free trade area for telecommunications by 1993. Integration of EFTA countries in this framework could lead to a highly competitive and efficient European telecommunications market. The extension of free trade arrangements that cover telecommunications in the case of Canada and the United States, Australia and New Zealand, and in different bilateral international value-added network service agreements is leading to an opening in international markets. It is in this area where the greatest challenge lies for the next decade. The successful conclusion of a trade in services agreement of the Uruguay Round may facilitate international liberalization. For some countries, such a framework may prove to be too cautious in its initial phase and they may seek greater opportunities for liberalization through extension of existing bilateral agreements.

Certainly the opening of international markets would require, but need not wait for, adjustments in other international frameworks, notably CCITT Recommendations. Furthermore, if the expansion of liberalization internationally in satellite services is foreseen, the framework governing INTELSAT may also need to be reviewed.

The 1990s will see challenges arising from the implementation of ISDN, choices on whether to move toward broadband communications, the implementation of new broadband technologies, and in particular development of new mobile telecommunications services. Policymakers will also need to grapple with the implementation of the opening of international telecommunication markets and the requirements this will pose for changing international rules and frameworks.

Although liberalization of markets can lead to increased competition, the realization of many of these new technologies will call for increased cooperation among public telecommunication operators, between public telecommunication operators and private service providers, among the private service providers themselves, and between service providers and users. New forms of collaboration are already emerging between market participants. Cooperation and competition are not dichotomous but present a means of harnessing and overcoming the complexities of new technologies while gaining from the benefits derived from efficient markets. Nevertheless, the need to monitor conditions of competition remain. As well, the fact that market dynamics are often driven by large users implies that particular attention needs to be given to the requirements of smaller users.

Structural Adjustment

Structural adjustment may be defined as bringing national policy making into line with the economic forces that are changing an industry, notably in terms of market structure, technical change, and shifts in the balance of international trade. As such, effective structural adjustment has been recognized by member countries as a central facet for telecommunication policy development. Analysis has highlighted the importance of modern international telecommunications services to structural adjustment of manufacturing and service industries, the development of global markets, and economic growth and competitiveness. The issue of structural change in telecommunications must not be viewed from a narrow sectoral perspective. Modern telecommunications is the nervous system of emerging industrial and services structures. It is the facilitator and one of the key building blocks for the internationalization of economies (the other being air transport).

The Committee's work has also recognized that the reluctance of many countries to take decisive action to enhance the efficiency of their economic structure and open new opportunities to industries by adjusting telecommunications structures could have detrimental economic effects. Experience has shown that hesitation will in many cases weaken industrial structures and performance, as well as innovative ability, eventually requiring extra efforts to catch up but seldom surpassing major competitors. In addition, catch-up policies are often linked with increased protectionism.

A commitment by member countries to undertake structural reforms of telecommunication market structures is therefore important. This also implies that obstacles to effective competition, such as monopolistic positions or barriers to market entry, need to be reduced, and that regulations and restrictions need to be justified on the basis of clear objectives and should not be excessive relative to the objectives they are aimed at achieving.

The importance of telecommunications for the economy also implies that countries must recognize that telecommunication policy cannot be undertaken in isolation and that there is a need to integrate telecommunication policy into the mainstream of economic policy structures. In many cases this has not yet occurred completely and insufficient consideration has been given to the wider national and international implications of policy initiatives. Work on trade, and in particular the requirement for greater transparency, has highlighted the scope for consultation by other countries in the policy process. One example of this is the type approval process in which policies of accepting manufacturers' self-certification and mutual type recognition are promoting an internationalization of policy (OECD, 1992).

The economic importance of telecommunications also requires that governments provide greater financial autonomy to public telecommunication operators as regards access to financial markets, the level and allocation of investment, and their long-term planning requirements. In this regard, as well, although the principle of cost-related tariffs has been accepted by nearly all governments, operators must have more flexibility in their planning policies. That is, although price constraints directed at improving the efficiency of operators are acceptable, pricing policies aimed solely at managing broader macroeconomic objectives such as reducing inflation invariably end up reducing the efficiency of the operator and introduce market and structural distortions in the economy.

Regulatory Frameworks

Traditionally, especially outside the North American context, telecommunications policy has been internalized within telecommunication administrations. A key element in telecommunications reform has been the need to separate the telecommunications operational functions from regulatory and policy functions. There has been recognition in the ICCP Committee that this is necessary and most countries have completed, or are in the process of undertaking, the required administrative restructuring. OECD countries are also in a position to offer assistance in this matter to the countries of Central and Eastern Europe.

Universal Service

Introducing competition in telecommunications has not been a question of simply eliminating monopoly franchises and allowing market entry. Rather, introducing competition has required the implementation of a number of regulatory frameworks, often detailed and complex. These regulations have been required not only to ensure a transition path from monopoly to competition but to ensure the maintenance of competitive entry possibilities. A cornerstone of telecommunications policy and of regulatory frameworks in all countries is the provision of *universal service*. The concept, which in many cases has not been well-defined in terms of concrete goals, has been used too often in the past as an excuse justifying policy immobility. It has been argued by opponents of liberalization that the universal service principles of nationwide coverage, nondiscriminatory access, and affordability of telecommunications services would be endangered by reducing monopoly power. There has been recognition now that the objectives of introducing competition and the maintenance or achievement of universal service are not mutually exclusive. Nevertheless, the concept does imply that economic efficiency criteria need to be balanced by social considerations and distributive criteria.

In those countries where competition in telecommunications has been introduced, telecommunication service penetration rates have not declined on average, and the overall price adjustments that have emerged as a result of rate balancing appear to have had net benefits to the economy. Rather, the effects of competition and the new regulatory structures that have emerged have been to improve service availabilities, the quality of service, and the performance of the telecommunications operators. Nevertheless, universal service considerations do, and must, remain important. The Telecommunications and Information Services Policy (TISP) Working Party is currently undertaking work to look at cost allocation methodologies used within PTOs. This research should help member countries to assess the real cost to the PTO of meeting community service obligations (such as geographic averaging of tariffs, emergency services, telephone service in remote areas, and public payphones).

Introducing Competition

As markets liberalize, the task of regulation becomes more complex. Although it is important to protect private service providers from unfair competition from state-owned monopolies, it is equally important that these public telecommunication operators are not disadvantaged. What are the costs of providing universal service? Given that charges should be cost-oriented, how can PTOs be compensated for universal service obligations? Are there new services that should be provided on a universal service basis for economic or social reasons? Given existing trends in reducing the coverage of monopolies there may be a need to consider other options to induce the universality of certain services.

A challenge that will face regulators over the next decade will be to decide on the extent of competition in telecommunications. Should there be, for example, competition in the local loop? Technology is now available to put into place a wireless public-switched telephone network. Can mobile services be used to introduce competition to traditional public-switched networks? The advent of intelligent network concepts also raises the issue of whether infrastructure monopolies should be limited only to transmission in the longer term. The increasing difficulty of differentiating between switching functions and terminal equipment raises the issue of where, for regulatory purposes, the monopoly ends, either in general or for specific infrastructures, such as mobile communication networks. Should the infrastructure monopoly be limited only to transmission functions in general or to specific transmission infrastructures?

Countries that have introduced competition to the main telecommunication service provider have found that it has been difficult to reduce the market share of the ex-monopoly services provider because of its existing large customer base and embedded investment. Different solutions to enhance competition are being considered—this issue may become more urgent with the commercialization of integrated services digital networks and the economies of scope they offer. There is a need to consider carefully whether the setting-up of smaller, regional, monopolies is the correct solution to reduce the power of national monopolies or whether it is more effective to facilitate competition, nationally and internationally, throughout the public-switched telecommunications network. What role can new mobile services play in this context?

The proliferation of new services and networks has complicated the task of the regulator. New issues have also arisen such as the question of network security and telecommunication privacy issues. There may need to be new, international fora established to discuss these matters and to formulate codes of practice.

Regional Aspects

The regional dimension of the diffusion of new telecommunication services is important. The tendency is for investment to concentrate in areas where returns are highest, that is, in the heavy traffic routes usually between major cities within a country and between countries. Internationally, investment follows a similar pattern. Within countries the positive effects of liberalization should spill over throughout the geographic area through lower prices, wider customer choice, and more efficient service provision. But a problem still remains on how to provide economically advanced telecommunication services in less developed regions. The ICCP Committee has co-sponsored two seminars in which the regional development dimension of telecommunications has been treated. The issue here is not only a question of liberalization versus monopoly service provision, since even in countries where the latter framework prevails the geographic dispersion of new services is uneven. Often the question is also one of attaining a critical threshold to make it economical for the operator to invest in the required infrastructure to provide a new service. Emerging new technologies are increasingly providing innovative solutions and widening user choice. There is also a question of the diffusion of know-how and the take-up of new services by small and medium enterprises that could benefit from applications of these services.

Where there is a political commitment to the concept of universal service, which covers new services having widespread economic and social benefits, then the regional issue will require a regulatory input. This may take the form of incentives to investment or the encouragement of "lifeline" and other low-volume user support schemes. How can obligations, for example, be imposed on public telecommunication operators to serve peripheral areas when at the same time cost-oriented tariffs are becoming the norm and when PTOs are competing with private service providers? In this context, however, it is important that the costs incurred by operators to service nonprofitable areas are known and calculated by accepted and transparent methodologies.

Pricing

Pricing structures have also posed a challenge to regulation. In a monopoly environment pricing policy was used to pursue a variety of objectives, including subsidizing a certain type of subscriber, service, the post office, or general government revenues. There was no significant pressure from the marketplace and cost of service details were often not known or did not play a role. A commitment has been made by most OECD countries that telecommunication service prices should be cost-oriented. There may be a need to reach greater understanding of the measurement of cost and where prices can deviate from costs so as to implement policy objectives. The pressure to restructure telecommunication rates in preparation for the advent of competition domestically and internationally will ensure that rate rebalancing will enter the policy agenda of most countries as well as internationally.

One of the major focuses of OECD research during 1991 was the system of international accounting rates that are negotiated bilaterally and, it is argued, serve to keep international telephone charges at an unjustifiably high level. OECD work concentrated on examining the applicability of certain guiding principles—transparency, nondiscrimination, and cost-orientation—to the system of accounting rates and settlements. In so doing, the OECD has played a complementary role to that of Study Group III of the CCITT and has added to the pressure for reform.

Performance and Quality of Service

Significant disparities exist between OECD countries in terms of PTO performance, and these disparities appear to be growing rather than diminishing over time. The differences between PTOs are especially evident in the provision, pricing, and quality of newer services such as high speed leased-lines, mobile communications, and packet-switched data communications. This can be explained in part by the constraints imposed by operators—financial, regulatory, or technological—but also by differences in the efficiency of management of the PTO and its ability to respond to technological change. The ICCP recently completed a study that attempted to define a small number of performance indicators for PTOs and a consistent and unbiased methodology to enable comparisons to be carried out between countries. The research focused on four main areas—tariff comparisons, tariff structures, quality of service statistics, and other measures of productivity and efficiency.

In a competitive environment, the monitoring and reporting of performance indicators becomes more important because the user needs reliable information to be able to choose between suppliers. This may require greater transparency in the collection and publication of statistics, especially with regard to quality of service. Working in conjunction with other international fora, the OECD has defined a set of six measures of service quality that could be adopted by PTOs and that allow for international comparisons. These cover waiting time for connection/delivery precision, effective payphone density, call failure rates, fault reports, fault clearance, and response time for operator services.

It is likely that the monitoring and reporting of such indicators will become a regular part of the ICCP's work as policymakers in member countries come to review the effects of the changes in telecommunications policy that took place during the 1980s. For this reason, a new, biennial publication titled *Information Technology and Communications Outlook* will bring together into a single report all the relevant data and performance indicators that the OECD currently publishes.

Competitive Supply of Equipment

The liberalization of the telecommunications service markets has been associated with a deregulation of terminal equipment markets in many OECD countries. It has long been felt that restrictive purchasing agreements, protectionist type approval procedures, and PTO monopolies over the sale, installation, and maintenance of customer premises equipment has kept prices too high and has limited the range of user choices. The Working Party on Telecommunications and Information and Service Policy has been involved in charting markets through its work on trade in telecommunications equipment and on type approval procedures in OECD countries.

The study of trade in telecommunications equipment, originally carried out in 1986 and recently updated, shows that the OECD exports of telecommunication equipment are buoyant, increasing at an average annual rate of 11%. The United States, in particular, continues to have a worsening deficit in telecommunications equipment trade attributable primarily to terminal equipment. Countries with important surpluses include Japan, Germany, and Sweden. The opening of procurement markets by public telecommunication operators has been slow, occurring mainly in countries where infrastructure competition has been allowed and in those countries that are not producers of public switching and transmission equipment.

The study of type approval procedures for telecommunications terminal equipment, originally carried out in 1985 and recently updated, charts the progress toward mutual type recognition and self-certification. The European Commission directive on type approval has set a timetable for implementing the new procedures and it is likely that the EFTA countries will also follow suit. There remains disagreement, however, on the issue of how far type approval requirements should go and whether it is necessary to demonstrate end-to-end interoperability of equipment or merely to avoid harm to the network and personnel. Approval procedures may also need to be modified to take account of the EC directive on electromagnetic compatibility (EMC) of terminal equipment.

Standards

The OECD work has recognized the importance of standards in enhancing open markets, but the work has also noted that flexibility is important in order to avoid choking the dynamics of the industry, given that technology advances much more rapidly than the international standards process. The importance of this international standards setting process is recognized by all countries. As well, it is recognized that there should be equal representation of all interested parties, especially users, in the standards making process. But differences of opinion remain as to the usage of proprietary standards and whether these would affect interoperability. This area requires further reflection, particularly in the context of international value-added network services and trade in telecommunication services issues.

Communications Convergence

Convergence is beginning to blur boundaries between telecommunication and broadcasting technologies. Although technical in nature, this merging will have important regulatory consequences. The two main areas of development for point-to-multipoint and other data distribution techniques involve fixed and specialized satellite services and those services operating in the broadcasting band. These services are making it difficult, for example, to maintain a point-to-multipoint communications (mass media). Policy initiatives are complicated here by the fact that in most countries telecommunications and broadcasting are governed by different regulatory and legal frameworks.

A key issue will be the need to give consideration to allowing cross-sectoral service provision, that is, allowing broadcast cable companies to provide telecommunication services and telecommunications operators to provide broadcasting services. A corollary of this is whether network-sharing should be allowed, either between competitive service providers or between alternative services such as voice telephony and cable TV.

As of the early part of the 1990s, broadband ISDN is technically, and perhaps also commercially, feasible. Investment in broadband needs careful consideration. High investment costs may be offset by integrating broadcasting and telecommunications services in one infrastructure. This may raise issues related to concentration of transmission capacity. However, the nearly unlimited bandwidth supplied by broadband and the potential for freeing scarce spectrum resources may be beneficial. But demand will be a key factor in the decision to invest and, to ensure that this demand is forthcoming, cross-ownership between telecommunications operators and cable operations may be required. An important catalyst, for example, for B-ISDN is high-definition television (HDTV).

In 1992, the convergence project was broadened to consider two areas in which there are already competitive pressures from both telecommunications and broadcasting users, namely the economics of satellite use and frequency allocation.

Satellite communications by their very nature exceed national boundaries. There is already a certain amount of competition in satellite broadcasting: this is likely to continue. However, new satellite broadcasting services are beginning to compete with telecommunications services, which implies that as satellite services are liberalized there will be increasing competitive pressure on telecommunications services, including those on the local loop. One example of this is the proposal for low-earth-orbit satellite systems, among others proposed by Motorola (Iridium) and INMARSAT. These issues are discussed at more length in the OECD's policy review *Convergence Between Communications Technologies* (ICCP 29, 1992).

The Internationalization of Network-Based Services Markets

The ICCP Committee has, through its Working Party on Telecommunications and Information Services Policy, been examining the issue of trade in telecommunications services over several meetings. This analysis has examined the applicability of trade in services concepts to telecommunications. There has been general agreement that trade in services concepts that have been developed by the OECD, and subsequently endorsed by ministers in the midterm review in December 1988, can, to a large extent, be applied to a broad universe of telecommunication network-based services.

However, there has also been agreement that further analytical work is required to consider the issue of access to and use of public telecommunication networks. Preliminary considerations have already been given to concepts that might, in the longer term, lead to a framework of open network conditions aimed at ensuring a more even playing field for the international provision of telecommunications services in the context of a trade in services agreement. The issue of international telecommunication accounting arrangements has also been raised as an area for further consideration, and there has been a preliminary exchange of views in this area.

Trade negotiators will, it is to be hoped, soon complete a general agreement on trade in services. Optimistically, this may lead to a rapid and real liberalization for international value-added network services. Realistically, the process of liberalization, at least outside the OECD area, is likely to be much slower. Yet the general framework to allow for much wider liberalization already exists in the ability to extend more widely existing bilateral agreements and specific provisions relating to telecommunications in wider free trade agreements.

The internationalization of telecommunications also raises the need for adjustment in the international framework for telecommunications as laid out in the International Telecommunication Regulations and more particularly the underlying Recommendations of the CCITT.

Cooperation With European Economies in Transition

Since the dramatic events of 1989 in Eastern Europe and of August 1991 in the former Soviet Union, the OECD has been called to play an increasing role in offering technical assistance to these countries. In 1990, a new Center for Cooperation with European Economies in Transition (CCEET) was established and in 1991 three of these countries—CSFR, Hungary, and Poland—have signed Memoranda of Understanding for closer cooperation with the OECD in recognition of the progress they have made.

The telecommunications network of these countries is generally in a very poor state—much worse than the bare numbers quoted in Tables 7.1-7.3 would indicate. Not only is the penetration of main lines only a quarter of the OECD level, but the quality of service is greatly inferior, with waiting lists of up to 14 years and high rates of call failure. Furthermore, the level of revenue per line in Eastern Europe ($260) is insufficient at present to cost-justify investment in new lines (at around $1,500 per new line) without external funding.

The initial effort of the ICCP Committee in this area was to organize Policy Dialogue seminars on IT (in Vienna in cooperation with the

Austrian government) and on telecommunications development (in The Hague in cooperation with The Netherlands government). The aim of these seminars was to bring together senior officials from Central and Eastern European countries and their counterparts in the OECD countries. As part of the preparation for the seminars, country reviews and other consultant papers were commissioned and these have been published and made available to other organizations working in this field, notably the ITU, the World Bank, and the EBRD. The proceedings of the conference were published by the Telecommunication Policy Division of The Netherlands Ministry of Transport and Public Works (OECD, 1991).

As part of a second round of activities, OECD work has focused on more detailed projects:

- A study of Polish telecommunications tariffs and investment requirements with proposals for reform
- A review of the 3-year plan of the Hungarian Telephone Company
- A proposed seminar to consider ways to attract investment into telecommunications development

Activities in Eastern and Central Europe and the republics of the former Soviet Union will play an increasingly important part of the OECD's work in the coming years.

Future International Cooperation in Telecommunications

Changing telecommunication structures and the emergence of international competition in telecommunications will also have an impact on the respective roles of different international organizations. Clearly there will be a need for better coordination and exchange of information among these organizations. At the same time, there must be recognition that each has its own mandate and areas of competence, and even where there may be some duplication or spillover in their work programs and/or mandates this is often useful by providing analysis from a different perspective and avoids the creation of isolated boxes.

If a general agreement on trade in services emerges successfully from the GATT Uruguay Round, there will be a need for more coordination with the ITU.

This role would reflect the reality of the existing internationalization of telecommunication services. The International Telecommunication Union has a well-established role in the technical and coordinating aspects of the provision of international telecommunication services and in coordinating development assistance. Here there is a need to establish links with the GATT, and with regional associations possessing technical competence, such as ETSI.

The OECD's ICCP Committee and its Working Party on Telecommunications and Information Services Policies can also usefully improve and increase cooperation with these institutions. For example, it has already played a conceptualizing role in the preparation of the Uruguay Round negotiations in its ongoing work on trade in telecommunications services. As a general agreement on trade in services becomes institutionalized and elaborated further over successive negotiating rounds, the OECD provides a useful forum for conceptualizing and examining issues in a context where negotiating positions are still fluid and concrete positions need to be taken. At the same time, however, the possibility exists for agreements to be reached at the OECD when the multilateral process slows down or when possibilities exist to liberalize more rapidly among a number of countries that wish to do so.

OECD also offers a forum where discussion of draft agreements, or other binding or nonbinding international regulatory considerations, could be made subject to a wider audience. For example, the international discussions on HDTV may benefit from analysis of the economic and social implications of different outcomes. Such analysis would complement rather than distract from present discussions.

As well as its economic analysis functions, OECD can also play a role in obtaining greater coherence internationally on indicators and methodologies that may be required for policy analysis or for monitoring purposes. For example, in the analysis of "Performance Indicators for Public Telecommunication Operations," the quality of service indicators that were identified have met with widespread interest among member countries.

In the context of changing economic structures in the Eastern European countries, the ICCP can also play a useful role in analyzing and reviewing policy structures in those countries, advising on strategies for structural adjustment, and providing a forum for an exchange of views between member countries and Eastern European countries. It is likely that the OECD will work closely with the new Center for Eastern European Economies in Transition in offering support and advice to Eastern European countries as they adapt their telecommunications infrastructures toward closer integration with the West. A policy dialogue on telecommunications with Dynamic Asian Economies might also occur.

Conclusion

Rapid changes in the telecommunications industry have cracked its long-standing homogeneity, redesigned traditional industry boundaries, and led to increased product differentiation. New telecommunications services have emerged, characterized by dynamic and complex markets. In turn, these changes have led to increased attention at the international level to telecommunications policy and the need to assess and analyze the international implications of these changes for domestic telecommunications policy.

In an international framework for telecommunications where monopoly market structures were the norm, member countries held a number of common conditions and principles. Lack of symmetry in market structures has reduced this common framework. As telecommunications market structures are transformed from a monopoly framework to a liberalized competitive framework, there is a need again to forge common principles. Some, but not all, of these principles may emerge out of trade in service negotiations. There is also a need for a telecommunications forum where service providers, public and private, users, and policymakers can exchange views. In all these areas there is a major role for the OECD to play in partnership with other international organizations.

Recent ICCP Publications

No. 13. *Trends of change in telecommunications policy.* Paris: OECD, April 1987.
No. 14. *The telecommunications industry. The challenge of structural change.* Paris: OECD, June 1988.
No. 15. *Satellites and fibre optics. Competition and complementarity.* Paris: OECD, June 1988.
No. 16. *New telecommunications services. Videotex development strategies.* Paris: OECD, June 1988.
No. 17. *The internationalisation of software and computer services.* Paris: OECD, March 1989.
No. 18. *Telecommunication network-based services: Policy implications.* Paris: OECD, June 1989.
No. 19. *Information technology and new growth opportunities.* Paris: OECD, June 1989.
No. 20. *Major R&D programmes for information technology.* Paris: OECD, September 1989.
No. 21. *Trade in information, communication and computer services.* Paris: OECD, February 1990.

No. 22. *Performance indicators for public telecommunications operators*. Paris: OECD, September 1990.

No. 23. *Universal services and rate restructuring in telecommunications: Policy problems in OECD countries*. Paris: OECD, February 1991.

No. 24. *Telecommunications equipment: Changing markets and trade structures*. Paris: OECD, September 1991.

No. 25. *Information technology standards: The economic dimension*. Paris: OECD, October 1991.

No. 26. *Software engineering: The policy challenge*. Paris: OECD, October 1991.

No. 27. *Telecommunications type approval: Policies and procedures for market access*. Paris: OECD, January 1992.

No. 28. *Convergence between telecommunications technologies: Case studies from North America and Western Europe*. Paris: OECD, 1992.

No. 29. *Convergence between communications technologies: A policy review*. Paris: OECD, 1992.

Appendix

TABLE 7.1 Telephone Mainlines 1991, Change 1986-1991, and GDP 1990

Country	Mainlines 1/1/1991 (000s)	Mainlines per 100 Inhabitants	CAGR (1986-1991)	GDP per Capita 1990 (US$)
Australia	8,046	47.32	4.13	17,536
Austria	3,233	42.17	3.38	20,816
Belgium	3,990	39.84	5.45	19,449
Canada	14,601[a]	55.01	4.33	21,799
Denmark	2,911	56.65	2.74	25,472
Finland	2,670	53.63	4.04	27,978
France	28,085	49.75	4.05	21,113
Germany	29,981	48.29	3.38	24,005
Greece	3,949	39.30	4.85	6,768
Iceland	126	48.84	4.18	22,093
Ireland	983	28.05	6.93	12,215
Italy	22,350	38.81	5.14	18,912
Japan	54,500	44.13	2.93	23,408
Luxembourg	184	48.68	3.96	23,280
The Netherlands	6,940	46.48	3.57	18,545
New Zealand	1,452[b]	42.63	3.44	12,952
Norway	2,086	49.17	3.48	26,120
Portugal	2,379	22.94	11.18	5,698
Spain	12,603	32.05	6.17	12,488
Sweden	5,849	68.39	2.21	26,918
Switzerland	3,943	58.94	3.77	33,393
Turkey	6,893	12.25	25.12	1,917
United Kingdom	25,404	44.19	3.96	17,021
United States	121,507[b]	48.42	4.48	21,238
OECD	362,306[c]	43.27	4.27	17,148
Bulgaria	1,994	22.18	5.00	2,214
CSFR	2,334	14.89	4.51	2,835
Hungary	966	9.15	5.50	3,117
Poland	3,293	8.67	5.77	1,665
Romania	2,406	10.35	3.82	1,389
Yugoslavia	3,560	14.96	7.36	3,707
Eastern Europe	14,554[c]	12.10	5.47	2,337

SOURCES: ITU, FCC, PTO Annual Reports.
[a]1/1/90 data: 1985-1990 growth
[b]1/1/89 data: 1984-1989 growth
[c]Total Mainlines
CAGR = Compound Annual Growth Rate
GDP = Gross Domestic Product

TABLE 7.2   Telecommunications Revenue, 1989

Country	Telecom 1989 Revenues (US$m)	Revenue per Mainline 1989 (US$)	Revenue per Inhabitant 1989 (US$)	Telecom as Percentage of GDP[a]
Australia	6,305.77	829.43	375.19	2.23
Austria	2,310.96	744.79	303.12	1.82
Belgium	2,140.04	570.99	215.34	1.41
Canada	10,266.65	737.55	391.14	1.88
Denmark	1,946.24	683.37	379.24	1.85
Finland	1,744.40	675.60	351.41	1.52
France	16,316.14	605.59	290.53	1.72
Germany (West)	19,906.76	700.94	321.13	1.66
Greece	992.35	262.08	98.91	1.84
Iceland	78.89	649.97	311.82	1.52
Ireland	967.94	1,071.92	275.37	2.96
Italy	13,901.77	653.72	241.66	1.61
Japan	43,187.50	829.98	350.79	1.54
Luxembourg	120.40	682.69	318.52	1.82
Netherlands	3,969.83	593.31	267.35	1.76
New Zealand	1,369.35	943.28	409.62	3.38
Norway	2,108.21	1,018.34	498.75	2.26
Portugal[b]	940.52	462.15	90.99	2.08
Spain	6,122.85	519.01	157.45	1.63
Sweden	4,028.08	704.70	474.28	2.13
Switzerland	3,670.28	969.82	545.93	2.10
Turkey	1,529.71	260.28	27.68	1.87
United Kingdom	20,819.97	820.88	363.76	2.50
United States	119,763.22	1,053.51	481.41	2.32
OECD	284,507.82[d]	822.52	342.03	1.97
Bulgaria	293.46	147.17	32.72	2.23
CSFR[c]	1,242.23	558.96	79.58	2.07
Hungary[c]	458.21	277.52	43.24	1.23
Poland[c]	519.79	157.87	13.68	0.82
Romania	729.84	337.68	31.82	0.72
Yugoslavia	452.39	127.07	19.14	0.96
Eastern Europe	3,695.92[d]	264.39	32.40	1.19

SOURCES: OECD, from ITU Yearbook, PTO Annual Reports, and OECD Questionnaire.
[a]For Eastern Europe countries, NMP (Net Material Product) is used.
[b]1988 data
[c]1990 data
[d]Total Revenues

TABLE 7.3 Telecommunications Investment, 1989/1990

Country	Investment in 1989 (US$m)	Investment per Inhabitant (US$)	As Percentage of Telecom Revenue 1989	As Percentage of GDP
Australia	1,678.10	99.85	26.61	0.59
Austria	942.55	123.63	40.79	0.70
Belgium	602.60	60.64	28.16	0.40
Canada	3,568.68	135.96	34.76	0.65
Denmark	451.71	88.02	23.21	0.43
Finland	549.91	110.78	31.52	0.48
France	4,364.89	77.72	26.75	0.46
Germany (West)	8,345.96	134.63	41.93	0.70
Greece	276.34	27.54	27.85	0.51
Iceland	10.16	40.17	9.66	0.20
Ireland	215.30	61.25	22.24	0.66
Italy	5,216.52	90.68	37.52	0.60
Japan	11,743.93	95.39	27.19	0.42
Luxembourg	32.87	86.96	27.30	0.50
Netherlands	874.30	58.88	22.02	0.39
New Zealand	333.05	99.63	24.32	0.82
Norway	472.55	111.79	22.41	0.51
Portugal[a]	288.13	27.87	53.46	0.64
Spain	4,403.85	113.24	71.92	1.17
Sweden	997.67	117.47	24.77	0.53
Switzerland	1,340.92	199.45	36.53	0.77
Turkey	384.95	6.97	25.16	0.47
United Kingdom	4,306.06	75.23	20.68	0.52
United States	19,195.25	77.16	16.03	0.37
OECD	70,596.26[c]	84.87	24.85	0.49
Bulgaria	65.66	7.32	22.37	0.34
CSFR[b]	211.08	13.52	16.99	0.37
Hungary[b]	216.99	20.48	47.32	0.43
Poland[b]	77.09	2.03	14.83	0.38
Romania	46.94	2.05	6.43	0.18
Yugoslavia	103.00	4.36	22.77	0.34
Eastern Europe	720.76[c]	6.02	19.50	0.34

SOURCE: OECD, adapted from ITU and PTO Annual Reports.
[a] 1988 data
[b] 1990 data
[c] Total investment

EIGHT

European Telecommunications R&D Systems in Transition

THOMAS SCHNÖRING

In the telecommunications sector, research and development (R&D) activities are an important prerequisite to competing in the world market, particularly for equipment manufacturers. R&D activities in telecommunications have increased significantly during the last decade and it was impossible for any single European country to keep pace with the dynamic development in the United States and in Japan. The R&D systems prevailing in different European countries developed largely in mutual isolation. As a result, different funding mixes and forms of cooperation in R&D have emerged between Public Telecommunications Operators (PTOs), manufacturers, governments, and research bodies (Grupp & Schnöring, 1990, 1991, 1992). Because of the intensifying international competition, the liberalization of the telecommunications markets, and the European Community's policy for a single European market, these different R&D structures came under pressure and started to change. The future of Europe as a location for the most advanced telecommunications R&D activities and the future competitiveness of European telecommunications companies will very much depend on the success of the transformation process of the former isolated national R&D system to an open, world-market-orientated, Europe-wide R&D system.

Past and Present National R&D Systems

The Level of R&D Expenditure

In the six member states of the European Communities surveyed in this study, the level of R&D expenditure varies significantly. To a certain

TABLE 8.1 R&D Expenditures on Telecommunications, 1987

	Germany	France	U.K.	Italy	The Netherlands	Spain
R&D expenditure on telecommunications (in U.S.$ billion)	2.5	2.1	2.1	0.5	0.2	0.11
In the military sphere	0.2	1.0	0.7	NA	0.0	NA
In the civil sphere	2.3	1.1	1.4	NA	0.2	NA
R&D expenditure on telecommunications as a % of total national R&D expenditure	11	13	13	6	5	5

NOTE: Expenditures are estimates, national currencies converted into U.S.$ at purchasing power parities.
NA = Not available

extent this reflects the size of the country's economy. All the countries concerned spend a remarkably large proportion of their total national R&D budget on telecommunications. Since this study shows that spillover effects from the military R&D into civil areas are relatively rare, my discussion will be confined to civil telecommunications.

The Role of PTOs

There are substantial differences between countries in the size of the network operator's R&D budgets and the extent to which their activities in this area are linked with those of manufacturers, universities, and research institutions. PTOs exert substantial influence on industrial R&D via their procurement strategies, equipment standardization policies, and other measures.

As Figure 8.1 indicates, the proportion of R&D funding by the PTOs ranges from about 60% in France to 7% in the Federal Republic of Germany. The funding levels do not correspond to the amount of R&D actually carried out by the network operators themselves. In some countries, a large proportion of their R&D expenditure is dedicated to finance work carried out by manufacturers, universities, and research institutions.

External funding contributions made by PTOs may be regarded as one indicator of the intensity of R&D cooperation or of quasi-vertical integration between PTOs and manufacturers and of the amount of influence the operators have over R&D conducted by other organizations. Nevertheless, the country studies also show that there are many

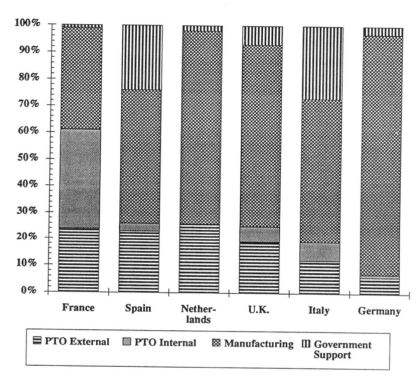

Figure 8.1. The Financing of the R&D Budget in Civil Telecommunications, 1987

ways in which PTOs bring their influence to bear on manufacturers' R&D activities and in which there is close cooperation between the two sides.

Pros and Cons of Vertical Integration

The main arguments put forward in favor of an intensive R&D association between network operators and manufacturers are these (Mowery 1987; Noll & Owen, 1987; Olley, 1982; Wavermann 1990): (a) Vertically integrated systems offer better chances of internalizing the results of R&D, since it is often impossible to predict beforehand whether the R&D activities will be of greater benefit to the manufacturer or to the network operator; (b) in order for new telecommunications systems to be developed, there has to be a permanent, intensive dialogue between manufacturers and network operators; and (c) in view of the pronounced increase in the R&D costs of new systems and the resulting high investment risk, manufacturers need to have relatively secure expectations of future sales.

However, both this and other studies point to the possible problems of vertical integration or too close links between the R&D activities of network operators and manufacturers (Noll, 1991). Such cooperation restrains competition and increases the risk that the development of new systems will be too closely tailored to the demands and specifications of the network operator involved, possibly reducing the export potential of manufacturers. In contrast, the high R&D expenditure required to develop new, large-scale systems makes manufacturers more dependent on sales abroad.

The weight of arguments either in favor of or against close R&D cooperation between network operators and manufacturers varies depending on the type of equipment or system. In the case of end-user equipment, the arguments in favor of close R&D association are weaker since the interfaces with the network itself are generally standardized and the R&D costs involved are relatively low. In the case of exchange and transmission systems, there is a much stronger emphasis on knowledge that is not accessible through interface standards alone, and the sheer amount of R&D expenditure needed is higher, which lends relatively more weight to the arguments for intensive R&D cooperation. The R&D systems within the surveyed countries, in general, exhibit a growing level of national R&D cooperation between network operators and manufacturers related to the growing complexity of systems.

R&D cooperation between network operators and manufacturers takes place in a variety of forms. For example, R&D subsidiaries are jointly owned or specific R&D tasks are contracted out to manufacturers by network operators, and the manufacturers are allowed to exploit the acquired knowledge at no extra charge. In addition, there are joint R&D projects involving both sides facilitating the transfer of know-how and the sharing of R&D expenditure. In some cases, network operators carry out pilot projects together with manufacturers. Finally, in almost all countries there are joint working parties to draw up specifications for new systems, agreements on the exchange of patents, and so on.

Many governments pursue industrial policy objectives (which they believe will benefit the manufacturers concerned) by intervening in the R&D approach of their PTOs without necessarily considering the latter's true future needs. This is relatively easy for them to do, given that PTOs are frequently state-owned or at least state-regulated. Furthermore, monopoly positions occupied by PTOs mean that they usually have the financial means to expand their R&D expenditure beyond what would be the optimum level from the purely entrepreneurial point of view. Such *over*investment in R&D can, with the help of the right transfer mechanisms for know-how, be placed at the disposal of the manufacturers and thus help improve their export opportunities. So far, no large national PTO has been exposed to intensive competition long enough to have developed what could definitely be regarded as competitively determined R&D behavior. Therefore a competitive level of R&D expenditure for PTOs cannot yet be observed.

The French Approach

France's system of R&D shows a particularly pronounced degree of quasi-vertical integration. The national R&D system has been dominated by France Télécom until the recent past. France Télécom has a major influence over all French telecommunications R&D by way of its own considerable R&D activities, joint projects with industry, development contracts awarded to domestic manufacturers, and the funding of research institutions and government research programs. In 1987, about 60% (670 million U.S.$) of the national funds dedicated to telecommunications R&D were controlled by France Télécom, of which about 9% (60 million U.S.$) went to public research bodies, approximately 37% (250 million U.S.$) went to France Télécom's research arm Centre National d'Etudes des Télécommunications (CNET), and the remaining amount went indirectly to private industry. About 430 million U.S.$ were spent by the telecommunications manufacturers. France Télécom has taken upon itself a substantial proportion of the technological and financial risks involved in R&D work, and is therefore also in a position to orient France's R&D system largely to its own needs and objectives. As a government-owned entity, France Télécom is a constituent element and instrument of the French government's industrial policy objectives. The structure of the French telecommunications sector seems to indicate that a share of France Télécom's monopoly rent is used to fund R&D activities for purposes of general technology and industrial policy. With respect to the purely commercial objectives of France Télécom, this situation might constitute a burden on the organization.

The Italian Approach

In Italy, too, the levels of actual and quasi-vertical integration are relatively high. The largest network operator (SIP) and by far the largest manufacturer in the field (Italtel) are both constituent parts of the state-owned IRI/STET group, along with a few other smaller network operators and manufacturers. The group has an R&D subsidiary, CSELT, which conducts a certain amount of research and development work for the other subsidiary companies. R&D activities of network operators and manufacturers are very closely intertwined, and the government, in its role as majority shareholder, is also closely involved. However, R&D activities do not necessarily follow commonly agreed upon objectives. On the contrary, there are substantial amounts of duplication, and it has not yet been possible to convert potential synergies into market success, as evidenced, for example, by Italy's relatively weak position in the world telecommunications equipment market.

The U.K. Approach

In the United Kingdom, the amount of external funding put up by the network operator British Telecom (BT) is now relatively small. However, BT does carry out substantial R&D activities of its own. A few years ago, BT was heavily involved in joint R&D projects with the three large domestic manufacturers GEC, Plessey, and Standard Telephone Company (STC), and BT also used to award development contracts to these companies for equipment items and for systems on a regular basis. A prominent example of such cooperation is the rather checkered career of the development of System X, the British telephone exchange system. BT has now largely moved away from this model of cooperative system development, and the negative experience drawn from the System X project has played a considerable part in this movement. That has also been topped off by the changed regulatory environment in which BT now operates, which encourages it to stick more closely to its own corporate objectives. Thus the close R&D cooperation or indeed quasi-vertical integration between BT and the country's major manufacturers has largely disappeared.

The German Approach

In Germany, both the internal and external contributions to the national R&D budget made by the Deutsche Bundespost (DBP) are particularly low. In 1987, only 7% (161 million U.S.$) of the total funds of approximately 2,300 million U.S.$ for R&D were allocated by German Telekom and only 46 U.S.$ million of these funds went to external R&D. DBP was not involved in any joint development projects nor in any development contracts. In contrast, the private manufacturing industry spent the bulk of 89% of all R&D funds. Despite the low level of direct financing it undertook, the DBP nevertheless exerted a substantial influence on the content of national R&D activities until the end of the 1970s simply by way of its procurement procedures.

In the past, the primary goal was to develop "postal service equipment", and possible sales opportunities on third markets did not play a significant part. To that extent, quasi-vertical integration did exist in the R&D field. At that time, the DBP's influence over the orientation of research and development was well in excess of what was apparent by looking solely at its contribution to R&D funding. In the meantime, new procurement procedures have led to increased competition and to a more pronounced opening of the domestic market to new suppliers from abroad. Since the volume of indirect R&D funding made by the DBP is crucially dependent on the intensity of competition in its procurement markets, the pronounced quasi-vertical integration in R&D activities that used to exist between the DBP and national manufacturers has now fallen back to a low level. Even so, various elements of cooperation between the network operator and manufacturers continue to exist, for example, through pilot projects. In all, the R&D carried out by the country's manufacturers is less geared to the requirements of the DBP than it used to be and is oriented more strongly to foreign markets. As a parallel development, the DBP has now begun to expand its own direct R&D expenditure and its own involvement in the R&D field.

Role of Manufacturers

In all the EC countries surveyed, more than half of the research and development in the field of telecommunications equipment and systems is carried out by manufacturers. They also put up a large portion of the R&D funds. To that extent, manufacturers are very important in all the different types of R&D systems, but there are nevertheless major differences among countries. As Figure 8.1 shows, German manufacturers top the list with a funding share of almost nine tenths. They are followed by The Netherlands and the United Kingdom, where the shares are between three quarters and two thirds, and France, where manufacturers only contribute two fifths of telecommunications R&D funds directly.

Role of Government R&D Support

In most industrial nations, information technology is regarded as an engine of growth. Accordingly, governments generally encourage R&D in that field, including the telecommunications sector. The types of support given differ among countries, rendering international comparisons difficult. The main instruments used are funding of R&D out of the government budget, and the exertion of government influence on the R&D and procurement policies pursued by network operators. (In addition, many countries use other, not industry-specific instruments such as tax exemptions to support R&D, but they will not be dealt with in this survey.)

Figure 8.1 shows the financial contribution by the state to the national R&D budget for civil telecommunications. Some direct financial support is provided in all countries and is particularly large in Italy and Spain. Although one might conclude from this comparison that the manufacturing industry in the first two countries enjoys substantial competitive advantages thanks to government R&D support, there are a number of other aspects, especially the indirect influence of governments, that need to be considered before coming to overall conclusions.

In all, government support for R&D and government influence over the national system of R&D both appear to be especially pronounced in France. Although substantial direct government funding is provided in Italy and Spain, the efficiency of the R&D system as a whole is not regarded as very high. In the case of Germany, and especially of the United Kingdom, government influence is now visibly in decline because of changes in the operating framework and procurement policies of the network operators. In The Netherlands, the state has long since largely refrained from getting involved in support for industrial R&D.

Development Trends

For a number of reasons, the stable relations between the PTOs and the national manufacturing industry started to change in the 1980s. Although these developments do not occur in parallel in all countries, five general trends characterize R&D policies in European telecommunications.

First, R&D expenditure on new telecommunications equipment has increased substantially. Manufacturers therefore need to rely increasingly on being able to market their new systems abroad as well as in their home markets. Especially among the large manufacturers, this has led to increased internationalization, both in their production facilities and in their R&D activities.

In the Federal Republic of Germany, the telecommunication manufacturing industry's R&D intensity, measured as a proportion of turnover, rose from 11% in 1979 to approximately 15% in 1987. That makes the industry one of the most R&D-intensive in the whole economy. The increase in development costs has been especially pronounced in the field of switching systems. Experts estimate that the major manufacturers constantly maintain a team of 3,000 to 5,000 software engineers for this area. In view of the huge increase in development costs, the network operators are now less and less willing to completely reimburse—in one way or another—the basic development costs incurred by their preferred suppliers. This has generated increased pressure on the manufacturers to also sell their systems in other countries.

All large manufacturers are trying to gain access to markets in other industrial countries, chiefly by taking over or buying major shareholdings in established foreign manufacturers. However, there are considerable variations in the amount of progress manufacturers have made along this road so far. Among the largest, the only ones that can truly be considered to have been multinationals for many years are Philips and ITT (which is part of Alcatel NV since 1987). They have long spread their R&D work across a number of countries, yet even then the national subsidiaries generally used to pursue substantially autonomous R&D policies to suit the national markets in which they were operating. AT&T, Siemens, Ericsson, GEC, Plessey, and the Japanese manufacturers NEC and Fujitsu mainly concentrated their R&D capacities in their own home countries until recent years, mostly confining themselves to adaptive development in foreign markets. That picture has changed during the past few years.

At Siemens, for example, the internationalization of R&D has now progressed a long way as part of an expansive foreign strategy oriented especially towards the American market. Of the group's 7,000 R&D staff in its public telecommunications division, 39% were already working at foreign locations in 1990, putting the figure only slightly below the 44% share in the production area. Ericsson is currently establishing a major European R&D center for mobile communications in Aachen, Germany. AT&T is utilizing the development capacity it has gained by purchasing a Philips subsidiary in The Netherlands to adapt its systems to suit the European markets. Similar developments are in progress in other major companies.

The large telecommunications equipment manufacturers are quickly moving along a path where the traditional structure of unilaterally transferring technology from the parent company to affiliates abroad that only adapt delivered technology to local requirements, is becoming increasingly blurred. Multinational companies in other sectors of the economy are experiencing similar changes and some have already moved further along that path toward the creation of a polycentric R&D system located in the different countries (Dörrenbacher & Wortmann, 1991). In that respect, the market structure of the telecommunications equipment industry is adjusting to other oligopolistic high-tech industries with global competition.

Second, the liberalization of the telecommunications network and service markets puts the formerly monopolistic PTOs under growing pressure to shape their procurement and R&D policies according to business criteria. In some countries, this has weakened the close relationships to the supplier industry as well as cooperative R&D efforts with established domestic manufacturers.

These trends are visible, among others, in Germany, the United Kingdom, and the United States. In France, signs emerge that the prevailing R&D system, in which the dominant player France Télécom "guided" the national market leader Alcatel-CIT, is likely to come under pressure after the reorganization of Alcatel NV as an international manufacturing group. With 70% of its turnover now earned outside France, the Alcatel group will need to reorient its R&D activities closer to the demands of foreign markets. That, in turn, would call into question the leading role played by France Télécom and its own research institution, CNET. Both France Télécom and Alcatel need to redefine their R&D strategy in the course of the strong international growth of Alcatel NV.

It has been argued that with the emerging digital paradigm in telecommunications the technological quasi-vertical integration between manufacturers is being replaced by a quasi-vertical integration between manufacturers, software houses and integrated circuit designers, operators, and applications designers (Dang-Nguyen & Blandin, 1991).

Third, increasing imports and exports are signs for a growing internationalization of national equipment markets.

Worldwide, trade in telecommunications equipment is increasing faster than the demand for equipment, and substantial changes in the international trade pattern can be observed. Changes have been most radical in those market segments in which previous trade and production patterns had been distorted the most relative to the pattern of comparative cost advantages. To a large extent, this development was caused by trade with customer premises equipment (Neu & Schnöring, 1989). Between 1981 and 1989, the import ratios for telecommunications equipment increased from 5% to 21% in Germany, from 4% to 22% in the United States, and from 2% to 6% in Japan.[1]

Fourth, telecommunications network and services markets as well as former nationally oriented PTOs (including their R&D activities) are increasingly internationalized.

The liberalization of the network and services markets offers opportunities for international market entry. This is most obvious in the mobile communications and value-added service markets. PTOs redefine their international strategies, becoming competitors in some market segments while cooperating in others. Triggered by the Research and Development in Advanced Communications Technologies for Europe (RACE) program of the EC, and further boosted by the foundation of the European Institute for Research and Strategic Studies in Telecommunications (EURESCOM) in June 1991, the European PTOs are increasing their cross-border cooperation. EURESCOM was founded by 20 PTOs from 16 European countries. The overall objective is to increase the research cooperation of its members and their strategies for the development and the implementation of new Europe-wide networks and services. The work should be pre-competitive and pre-normative. EURESCOM has a small staff for management and coordination located in Heidelberg, Germany, whereas most of the actual research work is carried out decentralized in the existing research labs of the PTOs. The budget and research capacity allocated to EURESCOM for the starting phase 1991/ 1992 was relatively small at about 15 million ECU (approximately 15 million U.S.$).

Fifth, government support for R&D in telecommunications in Europe, spurred on by the Commission of the European Communities, is more and more organized internationally.

The Single European Act of 1986 gave high priority to the creation of a European Research and Technology Community. The overall policy is outlined by the framework program for research and technological development (R&TD), first adopted in September 1987 and renewed in July 1991 (*Bulletin of the European Communities*, 7/8-1991, point 1.2.96). In recognition of the central importance of telecommunica-

TABLE 8.2 Budget of European R&D Programs in Telecommunications and
Information Technologies

	1987-1991	*1990-1994*
Information technologies (ESPRIT)	1,600	1,339
Telecommunications (RACE)	550	484
New services of common interest	125	106[a]
Total	2,275	1,929

SOURCE: Commission of the European Communities.
NOTE: Figures in million ECU; 1 ECU equals approximately 1.2 U.S.$
[a]Estimate

tions, approximately 40% of the total expenditure of the framework
program was allocated to R&D in telecommunications and information
technology (Table 8.2).

The European Strategic Program for Research and Development in
Information Technologies (ESPRIT) was launched in 1984. ESPRIT
supports pre-competitive research projects in the fields of microelectronics, information processing systems and software, advanced business and home systems and peripherals, computer integrated manufacturing, engineering, and basic research. In general, the Community
provides matching funds to proposals submitted by transnational consortia of industrial enterprises, research laboratories, and universities.
In 1990, some 6,000 researchers in more than 1,500 organizations
worked full time in ESPRIT projects (Commission, 1991, p. 136).

The objective of the RACE program is to generate international R&D
cooperation among manufacturers, PTOs, and research institutions within
Europe and, by doing so, to stimulate innovation and competitiveness of
the European industry. In Germany at least, purely domestic R&D support
for telecommunications has been declining in significance since the end of
the 1980s. Partly, it has been substituted by the European R&D programs.
The latest completed phase of the RACE program, running from June 1987
to June 1992, has backed cross-border R&D projects in advanced communications technologies in Europe since 1987 with a financial contribution
of 550 million ECU, representing less than half of the overall project
budgets. More than 300 organizations, equipment manufacturers, PTOs,
and others from EC and EFTA countries, involving about 2,000 people,
participated in 92 projects focusing on pre-competitive and pre-normative
research. The ultimate goal of these efforts is the introduction of Integrated Broadband Communications (IBC) by 1995.

TABLE 8.3 Participation of European Countries in RACE

Country	Participation	Project Leadership
United Kingdom	148	23
Germany	146	27
France	144	10
Italy	60	7
Spain	57	1
Netherlands	49	5
Sweden	39	2
Belgium	37	7
Greece	35	1
Denmark	34	2
Ireland	23	3
Portugal	23	2
Finland	17	1
Norway	14	–
Switzerland	12	1
Austria	4	–
Total	842	92

SOURCES: EC, DG XIII, RACE '91; own calculations.

Table 8.3 shows the distribution of participants (project participation and project leadership) by countries. The three largest EC countries participate the most and their project leadership is even more concentrated. In the beginning, German participation was low but this has changed in the second and third call for tenders (Dang-Nguyen, 1989). Spain has a surprisingly strong participation, which indicates the growing R&D commitment of the country.

The largest group of participants are equipment manufacturers, who constituted 396 of the 842 project participants and took leadership in 53 out of 92 projects. PTOs participated in 189 and assumed leadership in 15 projects, and other participants participated in 257 projects (of which they led 24). Manufacturers are particularly involved in Part Two projects concerning IBC technologies. PTOs are overrepresented in projects concerning the IBC development and implementation strategies, and organizations from other sectors are particularly engaged in pilot applications. Application pilot projects have been started during the second phase of RACE I. They are very important in the context of market opportunities for IBC services. RACE has been criticized as

TABLE 8.4 Participation of Organizations and Companies in RACE

	Participation	Project Leadership
Alcatel	70	15
Philips	30	4
British Telecom	29	6
Swedisch Telecom	25	1
Thomson	23	3
Telefonica	21	
Netherlands PTT	20	
France Télécom	20	
Ericsson	19	3
DBP Telekom	17	4
Bosch Telecom	15	1
GEC[a]	15	
Siemens	14	1
STC	13	3
Plessey	11	3
Telecom Eireann	10	3
Kjobenhavns Telefon	10	
AT&T-NSI	10	
IBM	10	1
Matra	10	1

[a]Including 5 participations of GPT

being not enough market- and too much research-orientated (Dang-Nguyen, 1989).

As Table 8.4 illustrates, Alcatel is a strong leader with 70 participations and 15 project leaderships. This is partly due to the group's numerous subsidiaries scattered all over Europe; it often happens that several of them are present in the same project. But it may be due also to the Europe-oriented business strategy of Alcatel or to the traditionally strong involvement of Alcatel subsidiaries in government-supported R&D programs. Siemens, Alcatel's major European competitor, takes part in only 15 RACE projects and leads just 1 project. It is difficult to draw conclusions from these figures alone, because the participations are not weighted by the financial value of each project.

Philips and Thomson are strongly engaged in RACE although telecommunications is not their main business. Ericsson participates in 19 projects and it is interesting to recognize that both AT&T and Northern Telecom are strongly engaged in RACE through their European subsidiaries

AT&T-NSI and STC. This means that all the world's top equipment manufacturers are directly or indirectly taking part except the Japanese firms NEC and Fujitsu and that all these companies benefit from the RACE program. In a way, the EC is supporting R&D of non-European companies. This is a consequence of the internationalization process of the large telecommunications manufacturing companies and it illustrates the limits of any European R&D policy supporting the competitiveness of European companies.

The third group of European R&D programs in telecommunications supports applications of telecommunications and information technologies. These programs provide financial aid for the pilot phases of new and innovative applications as well as initiatives for the Europe-wide use of information technologies. Major programs in the first ("upstream") category are Advanced Informatics in Medicine in Europe (AIM), Developing European Learning through Technological Advance (DELTA), and Dedicated Road Infrastructure for Vehicle Safety in Europe (DRIVE). Major applications ("downstream") programs include Trade Electronic Data Interchange Systems (TEDIS), aimed at the promotion of the development of Electronic Data Interchange (EDI) systems that meet the needs of small and medium sized business users, and Interinstitutional Integrated Services Information Systems (INSIS) (Ungerer & Costello, 1988, pp. 162).

Problems to Be Solved

As this analysis shows, there are a number of problems that have to be solved by the European telecommunications industry to improve their R&D systems and international competitiveness. These problems are rooted in the fragmentation of the European marketplace and, externally, the structure of the R&D systems in Japan and North America. A major challenge ahead is the establishment of a level playing field within the single European market and the Triade, a difficult question in view of the different market structures and regulations existing in the countries involved.

It is very likely that the major differences among EC countries in R&D funding are distorting competition among manufacturers within Europe. As long as the national markets remained largely protected from import competition, the differences in R&D funding were of minor importance. But with a single European market the situation changes.

Under otherwise equal conditions, a higher share of R&D financing through PTOs or the government means a disadvantage for manufacturers, because they need to recover their cost burdens by charging higher product prices. In reality, one can not restrict the argument to R&D funding. One has to take other factors into account, such as R&D efficiency, costs of market entry, and the whole internationalization process the large manufacturers are pursuing. It is necessary to weigh the various arguments against each other to reach an overall judgment. Given that caveat, it does appear that the differences in the size of financial contributions made by manufacturers in various EC countries, and especially between France and Germany, are severe enough to give rise to substantial distortions to competition in a single European market.

Pros and cons of vertically integrated R&D activities of PTOs and equipment manufacturers have to be assessed in the context of the European market. So far, no market test of the two possible structures can be observed. European manufacturers argue that they have to compete with vertically integrated manufacturers from the Triade and that they need some kind of market protection and/or vertical integration for that reason. From the perspective of this study, the market trends described above are against vertical integration in the European context: The dynamic internationalization of equipment markets and of manufacturing companies reduces the economies of scope in R&D between any single European PTO and its national manufacturers. New products and systems have to be designed to the needs of the world market and not to the needs of just one European PTO. The reference for new products and systems has to be at least the whole European market, if not the world market.

How to ensure a level playing field in the telecommunications equipment market between the Triade (i.e., Europe, the United States, and Japan)? This is essential for the European industry and difficult to reach because their major competitors AT&T, Northern Telecom, NEC, Fujitsu, and the like, are vertically or quasi-vertically integrated with telecommunications operators. These operators either still have monopoly rights or they have market power in the network and services markets. There is a close interrelationship between competition among networks and services (as these are deregulated) on the one hand and competition among different types of telecommunications equipment and systems on the other. The competitive situation applying to network operators (in their own sales markets) is one of the factors that help determine their capabilities of engaging in competition-distorting practices in the equipment and system markets upstream of them, including the R&D field. Empirical inquiries can help to unravel such distortions, thus contributing to the formulation of new economic policy measures. The best insurance against such practices might be the establishment of a competitive framework for the provision of networks and services in all countries.

Note

1. Figures calculated using statistics by U.S. Department of Commerce: U.S. Industrial Outlook; The Telecom Tribune; and Zentralverband der Elektrotechnischen Industrie: Statistische Berichte.

References

Commission of the European Communities. (1991). *XXIVth general report on the activities of the European Communities 1990*. Brussels-Luxembourg: Office for Official Publications of the European Communities.

Dang-Nguyen, G. (1989). *European R&D policy for telecommunications*. Diskussionsbeiträge zur Telekommunikationsforschung Nr. 49. Bad Honnef, Germany: Wissenschaftliches Institut für Kommunikationsdienste.

Dang-Nguyen, G., & Blandin, A. (1991). Between consensus and competition. In Chamoux, J.-P. (Ed.), *Deregulating regulators? Communication policy for the 90's* (pp. 117-142). Amsterdam: IOS Press.

Dörrenbacher, C., & Wortmann, M. (1991, May/June). The internationalization of corporate research and development. *Intereconomies*, pp. 139-144.

Grupp, H., & Schnöring, T. (Eds.). (1990). *Forschung und Entwicklung für die Telekommunikation—Internationaler Vergleich mit zehn Ländern. Band I, USA, Japan, Frankreich und Großbritannien*. Berlin: Springer.

Grupp, H., & Schnöring, T. (Eds.). (1991). *Forschung und Entwicklung für die Telekommunikation—Internationaler Vergleich mit zehn Ländern. Band II, Italien, Spanien, Süd-Korea, Niederlande, Schweden, Bundesrepublik Deutschland und abschließende Bewertung*. Berlin: Springer.

Grupp, H., & Schnöring, T. (1992). Research and development in telecommunications: National R&D systems under pressure. *Telecommunications Policy, 18*, 46-66.

Mowery, D. C. (1987). *Forecasts of the impact of divestiture on Bell Telephone Laboratories: An assessment*. Paper presented at the 15th Telecommunications Policy Research Conference, Airlie House, VA, September 27-30.

Neu, W., & Schnöring, T. (1989). The telecommunications equipment industry: Recent changes in its international trade pattern. *Telecommunications Policy, 15*, 25-39.

Noll, R. G., & Owen, B. M. (1987). *United States v. AT&T—An interim assessment.* Stanford University, Studies in Industry Economics, Discussion Paper No. 139, rev. August 1987.

Noll, M. (1991). The future of AT&T Bell Labs and telecommunications research. *Telecommunications Policy, 17,* 101-105.

Olley, R. E. (1982). The process of technology transfer and application in telecommunications: A case study. In Sahal, D. (Ed.), *The transfer and utilization of technological knowledge* (pp. 175-203). Lexington, MA: Lexington Books.

Ungerer, H., & Costello, N.(1988). *Telecommunications in Europe.* Brussels: Office for Official Publications of the European Communities.

Wavermann, L. (1990). *R&D and preferred supplier relationships: The growth of Northern Telecom.* Paper presented at the 8th International Conference of the International Telecommunications Society in Venice, March.

PART III

Technological Infrastructure, Services, and Applications

NINE

Telecommunication Network-Based Services in Europe

HARRY BOUWMAN
MICHAEL LATZER

Information is a strategic economic resource and telecommunication technologies and their applications can provide business organizations with a competitive edge over their rivals (Keen, 1988). Organizations and businesses are increasingly networked internationally through alliances, contractual arrangements, and other agreements. Telecommunication networks and services enhance the ability of organizations to move and manage information without time and distance constraints, thus contributing to the efficiency and effectiveness of business operations.

In its report *Critical Connections*, the U.S. Office of Technology Assessment (OTA) stated that the impact of new communications technologies on economic activities will not only be due to the inherent nature of technologies themselves but also to the development of two major and interrelated trends: the trend towards a society that is information- or knowledge-based, and the trend towards a global economy (Office of Technology Assessment [OTA], 1990, p. 112). Both trends are also reflected in the development of telecommunication network-based services (TNS) in Europe, which is aiming at the establishment of a single European market facilitated by pan-European services. The single European market and the opening of Eastern European markets are expected to offer unique opportunities for equipment manufacturers

AUTHORS' NOTE: This chapter is based on research projects on VANS and videotex in Europe (Bauer, Latzer, Scheidl, & Sint, in press; Bouwman & Christoffersen, 1992). For comments on an earlier draft of this chapter we want to thank Paul Slaa, Monique Hamers, and Charles Steinfield.

and service providers in Western Europe, improving their position in the triadic competition with the United States and Japan.

The economic significance of telecommunications rests, on the one hand, in its function as a necessary infrastructure for the economy. On the other hand, it is a dynamic economic sector promising high growth and innovation opportunities. Presently, telecommunications contributes approximately 3% to the GDP of the European Communities. Some studies predict an expansion to 7% of GDP by the year 2000. Within the telecommunications sector, the strongest growth is expected in services, especially in the field of data communication and cellular radio (Iwens, 1990, p. 9). Empirical data related to the development of telecommunication network-based services illustrate that the diffusion patterns of various service types differ considerably between single states and regions. Hence, general constraints for the development of telecommunication services are analyzed, and national policies formulated to promote services development.

In this chapter, we discuss trends in the development of Telecommunication Network-Based Services (TNS) in Europe, analyze factors that influence the spread and diffusion of services, and discuss policies of the principal players, including the Commission of the European Communities (CEC), which is supposed to stimulate the TNS development. We begin with a discussion of categorizations of telecommunication services. In the second part, we present empirical data and a short description of trends in the European TNS sector in business services and in two mass market services, videotex and audiotex. In the third part, we provide a brief overview of decisive factors and constraints for the development of TNS in Europe, dealing with technological, political, economic, and social factors and the role of major actors. Special attention is given to the policies of the European Communities regarding the development of a harmonized pan-European telecommunication infrastructure and services market. This provides the context for a comparative analysis of videotex in Europe, offering insight into the different determinants and the role of various players in creating a mass market for telecommunication network-based services.

Toward a Categorization of Telecommunication Services

Categorizations of telecommunication services differ according to the research questions and the purposes they serve, ranging from purely analytical goals to defending vested interests. As a whole, the use of classifications predominantly serves political and economic goals. The importance of these categorizations can be better understood in the light of the economic consequences that market-access regulations, based on such classifications, might have for (potential) service providers. The definitions and interpretations by national regulators, in specifying if services belong to the category of basic, access-restricted services or to the group of liberalized value-added services, determine whether profitable markets can be utilized by others than the PTOs.

Historically, the political motive for categorizations of telecommunication services was the upcoming liberalization of the telecommunication sector. Hence a line had to be drawn between services that should be offered in a competitive environment and services that should remain under monopoly control. This led subsequently to different, periodically changing definitions in various countries. In the United States, where the worldwide liberalization trend began, a distinction between *basic* and *enhanced* services was made in the Computer II decision of the Federal Communications Commission (FCC) in 1976. Enhanced services, which are to be offered on a competitive basis, are conceptualized as a combination of basic services and computer applications, for instance, for the manipulation of information, protocols, and formats for data retrieval. The terms *Value-Added Services (VAS)* and *Value-Added Networks and Services (VANS)* are used more or less synonymously for enhanced services. These concepts were adopted in the United Kingdom in order to help the creation of a competitive environment. More or less comparable is the distinction between *reserved* and *non-reserved* services. These categories point more clearly to the regulatory motive behind the classification efforts, namely to determine services that are to be supplied by the PTOs only. A different solution for the same regulatory problem was found in Japan, where a distinction is made between *Type I Carriers* that own the physical network, and are strictly regulated, and less regulated *Type II Carriers* that do not own but resell capacity on Type I carriers' networks.

Although the wide variety and heterogeneity of services included under such headings as VAS, VANS, and enhanced services do not constitute an economically defined market, these categorizations might still be relevant for economic and regulatory policy questions (Stoetzer, 1991, p. 15). In order to find a common framework for the policy analysis of the services sector, the OECD introduced the concept of *Telecommunication Network-Based Services (TNS)*. These include "all services that combine information production, manipulation, storage and/or distribution, with the use of telecommunication facilities and software functions (OECD, 1989, p. 33). This definition should make the service sectors of various countries comparable. It does not distinguish whether a network represents added value, and it does not depend on what is considered to be added value at a particular moment in time. For example, direct distance dialing, nowadays a common practice, created added value when it was first introduced and required operator assistance (Mansell, 1988, p. 245). For the purposes of this chapter, we use the TNS concept of the OECD, apply functional classifications to analyze specific development in the business sector, and use service concepts such as videotex and audiotex in order to tackle mass market problems.

The Diffusion of TNS in Europe

The various available market research studies use different categorizations of services, vague or no statements regarding the inclusion of services for closed user groups or free services, and different definitions of regions (e.g., Europe with or without Eastern European countries). Furthermore, in most cases little or no methodological information is provided (Stoetzer, 1991, pp. 24). Thus, their results have to be compared with some caution.

According to different sources, estimates of the VAS market in the United States fluctuate between 0.3 billion and 8 billion U.S.$ in 1985. Estimates of the European market are between 1.1 billion and 3.5 billion U.S.$ in 1987 and range from 2.3 to 5 billion US$ in 1989 (Polanen Petel, Bulthuis, & Morsink, 1991, p. 5; Stoetzer, 1991). Although predictions of the VAS market fluctuate significantly, there is no question that this market is growing fast. Should the real value be somewhere in between the highest and lowest value, it would still represent an annual growth rate of over 20%. However, the VAS market is small compared to the market for basic services. According to Northern Business Information, VAS revenues only represent a 3% share of the total telecommunication services market (*Economist*, October 5, 1991, p. 6). Moreover, compared to the United States, the European VAS market is lagging. In 1990, the relative importance of the VAS market for the GNP of the European Communities was considerably lower than in the United States (Stoetzer, 1991, p. 37).

A market research study commissioned by the CEC provides some insights into developments of VAS in EC member states. In this study, a functional classification was used, distinguishing between Online Database Access, Electronic Messaging, Electronic Data Interchange (EDI), Electronic Funds Transfer (EFT), Managed Network Services, Conferencing, and Telemetry (Scicon Networks, 1989, p. 5). The data was obtained in 1989 and extrapolated to 1992; the demand for VAS by private households was not included in the research. According to this study, the largest category of services used by business in the EC member countries was online database access (60%) and the highest growth rates were expected for Electronic Messaging and Electronic Data Interchange (EDI). The largest user was the financial sector, and the highest growth in usage was expected in the industrial sector (EDI). Market concentration was high, with 16 firms in control of 80% of total revenues. American service suppliers, in particular computer companies, had a dominant position on the supply side: 6 out of the 16 principal companies are U.S. owned. However, another trend was the growing importance of network operators in the VAS market. National telecommunication operators (PTOs) are expected to catch up with the private services providers in the VAS sector. Finally, the importance of the markets in small countries within the total EC market was expected to increase (Scicon Networks, 1989).

The European market for online database services directed to the *business* and *professional* user amounted to 365 million US$ and was mainly dominated by the British company Reuters, which is specialized in financial information, and by American companies (for example, Dialog) (Boumans, 1991). As compared to the United States, the European information market is less developed: the revenue for online information services (excluding videotex) in Europe is only one third and the 1120 ASCII database services in Europe are only half of the United States' (Commission, 1991b, p. 6). Commercial businesses are the major producers of databases in the United States, whereas in Europe, libraries, research institutes, and other nonprofit organizations dominate the production of online databases (Boumans, 1991).

In the following section, we concentrate on the diffusion of videotex and audiotex, which are targeted toward the integration of private households in the global telematic marketplace.

The Diffusion of Videotex

General purpose services, such as videotex for the *consumer* market, have developed more rapidly in Europe than in the United States.

Videotex does not fit the above functional classification. It includes all kinds of applications such as information retrieval, ticket reservation, teleshopping, electronic mail, and home banking. With the increasing openness of the system for various transmission speeds (1200/75 bits/sec), data syntax (Prestel, Teletel, and ASCII) and protocols (Prestel Gateway 2.2+, X.29M, and X.29), videotex is becoming a flexible tool that, especially in combination with a PC, offers new possibilities for the user. However, the introduction of videotex in the 1970s and early 1980s, mainly based on the Prestel standard, was not successful. Only in France were the optimistic expectations fulfilled. Nevertheless, in the 1990s a revival of videotex in such countries as Spain, Italy, The Netherlands, and Switzerland seems to be taking place.

Data on the economic value of the videotex markets are hardly available. Based on a number of sources and expert interviews, we estimate the market size in the European Community to be between 600 million U.S.$ and 900 million U.S.$ (services only). The available information with regard to the number of suppliers, users, number of terminals, connection time, and so on, differs from country to country. Comparison between countries is only possible based on (estimates of) a limited amount of criteria (see Table 9.1).

The number of installed terminals in France illustrates the success of the Teletel model. In the other European countries, the percentage of installed terminals does not exceed 3%. The highest growth rates in terms of installed terminals and subscribers can be found in countries that to some degree have copied the French approach, including Portugal, Spain, Italy, and Switzerland (Videotex International, 1991). It is likely that the percentage of households with a videotex terminal or a PC and modem, with which videotex can be used, will increase.

The Diffusion of Audiotex

Another general-purpose service relevant to business and private use is audiotex. Audiotex can be considered the telephone-based alternative to videotex. The common characteristics of audiotex services are that they are accessible through the public-switched telephone network and that telephones are used as terminals. Audiotex comprises interactive and passive services. It includes prerecorded messages, chatlines (telephone conferences for more than two participants), polling services, and sophisticated database services using voice or tone recognition for the input and speech synthesizer for the output of data. For the return path,

TABLE 9.1 Diffusion of Videotex in Selected European Countries

	Number of Service Providers	*Number of Terminals[a] (in 000s)*	*Number of Households (in m)*	*Proportion of Households With Terminal (%)*
Austria	398	12	2.9	.41
Belgium	120	8.5	3.6	.24
Denmark	59	6.5	2.2	.29
France	13,468	5,700	20.5	28.00
Germany	3,107	260	27.8	.94
Ireland	35	.35	1.1	.03
Italy	933	155	18.6	.83
The Netherlands	147	125	6.1	2.05
Portugal	191	4.5	3.5	.13
Spain	1,223	325	11.9	2.73
Sweden	100	30	3.5	.86
Switzerland	551	75	2.3	3.26
United Kingdom	—	100	22	.45

SOURCE: Bouwman & Christoffersen (1992).
NOTE: Figures as of mid-1991
[a]Number of subscribers

voice, fax, or videotex might be used. Audiotex services are charged on the telephone bill and are sometimes categorized as *premium rate services (PRS)* or *kiosk services*. The revenues are split between the information providers and the network operators. For the user, the services might be free of charge (*freephone* services), in which case the receiver of the call covers all the costs. Another option is that the caller pays local call charges only while the rest of the distance-sensitive tariffs are covered by the receiver. Finally, the caller might be charged a premium rate.

Audiotex is rapidly gaining popularity and market shares in the European TNS sector. With a high penetration of audiotex terminals (telephones) already in place, the conditions for the diffusion in private households are much better than for videotex. In the EC countries, audiotex services began to be used on a larger scale in the mid-1980s. Audiotex services for the consumer market, especially "pink" (adult) services, were—as has been the case for videotex—an important factor in the early diffusion. In this respect the responsibility of the network operator for the content of the message has become a point of discussion. In the United Kingdom, for example, new forms of self-regulation developed in the audiotex sector. The market share of pink services—one-third in the United Kingdom in 1989—is expected to decrease substantially. The industry fears that the bad reputation of the "pink" services might harm the future diffusion of business applications.

According to a survey by Electronic Publishing Services (Commission, 1991a), the 1989 professional audiotex services market within the EC was strongly concentrated in the United Kingdom with a remarkable market share of over 80%. In 1990, only five EC countries offered premium rate services. In six other countries audiotex was in a planning stage. In 1989, premium rate services (PRS) represented the biggest mass market for TNS in Europe. France was the only country where videotex exceeded the PRS market (Christoffersen, 1992).

In an international comparison of audiotex market estimates (for which the same definition and methodological problems apply as for the whole VAS market), the high share of audiotex services for the consumer market in the United States and the extremely low diffusion of professional audiotex in Japan is striking (Commission, 1991a).

Decisive Factors and Players in the Development of TNS

The diffusion pattern of telecommunication network-based services is influenced by a set of diverse and interconnected factors. For analytical reasons, these factors might be grouped in four categories: technological, economic, political, and social/cultural. A liberalized telecommunication environment and a modern telecommunication network are not sufficient to guarantee the acceptance of TNS. It is rather the mixture of factors that is important for the final success or failure of TNS. In the following section, several determinants are presented and briefly discussed using the audiotex example. A closer analysis of various factors for videotex will be given in a later part of this chapter.

Technical factors include network development and architecture, the choice of equipment, and standards, which, in turn, have an impact on user friendliness, flexibility, functionality, and compatibility of telecommunication services. In the case of audiotex, the low digitization of the public networks in various countries impedes the provision of premium rate services and freephone services. The low penetration of Dual Tone Multi-Frequency telephones (DTMF) hampers the control of service functions by the user. The incompatibility of national networks and the mutual agreements between PTOs not to deliver foreign audiotex prevent the provision of international audiotex services. These reasons might constitute the main technical barriers for fast diffusion.

Economic factors include investment requirements for the network operators, service providers, and users; maintenance costs; economies of scale, scope, and density; network externalities; tariff structures; demand; marketing; and the average level of disposable income of private households. In the audiotex example, the low flexibility in setting tariffs and in the sharing of revenues between information providers and network operators, and the lack of cost control due to the absence of itemized telephone bills are regarded as diffusion barriers. Obviously, most of these factors are closely linked to technical preconditions.

Political factors embrace technology and industrial policy strategies, including research and development policies, and the regulation of telecommunication on a national and international level. In the case of audiotex, the regulations of pink services and regulatory constraints for private service providers are considered (or have at least been) diffusion barriers.

Finally, *social/cultural* factors include the general attitude of the potential users toward technology and innovations, adoption and implementation strategies, the social acceptability of the services offered, privacy issues, consumer rights, and labor positions. In the audiotex example, the different national approaches to the regulation of pink services that might have an impact on the diffusion of audiotex represent cultural differences in societal tolerance and the regulatory system in general.

The *players* who are more or less consciously manipulating the aforementioned determinants in the TNS sector are public and private network and service providers, the equipment industry, national and international regulators and standardization bodies, and business and private users. Within Europe, the Commission of the European Communities (CEC) has developed from an international regime that reflected national policies of the member states exclusively into a corporate actor with its own goals and strategies in the field of telecommunication (Schneider & Werle, 1990). Other influential international organizations for the European TNS sector are the International Telecommunication Union (ITU), the Organization for Economic Cooperation and Development (OECD), the European Telecommunications Standards Institute (ETSI), and the International Telecommunications Users Group (INTUG).

The member states of EFTA do not follow a common strategy in telecommunication. However, the agreement about the establishment of a European Economic Area (EEA) between the Community and EFTA will extend important telecommunication regulations of the EC to the EFTA countries, thereby forcing some countries to increase their pace of liberalization in the TNS sector and facilitating the provision of international telecommunication network-based services within Europe (Bauer, 1992). Furthermore, bilateral agreements on the liberalization of international value-added network services have been concluded by various states, for example, between the United States and the United Kingdom, the United Kingdom and Japan, France and Japan, as well as Germany and Japan.

On the national level, the regulation of TNS in European countries has not yet been harmonized. Differences in regulations include the resale of leased-lines; their connections to the public network; and the licensing, registration, and notification requirements to the regulatory authority for the provision of TNS. Although the harmonization policy of the CEC gives some discretion to the member countries, an increased unification of the conditions to provide TNS can be expected.

At the corporate level, growing activities in strategic alliances are noticeable. According to Hagedoorn (1991, pp. 13), the worldwide network density for the telecommunication industry, a measure that denotes the linkage between companies, has nearly doubled in the second half of the 1980s, with the German Siemens Company showing the most strategic links in the information industry as a whole. In telecommunications, nearly one third of the alliances in the 1980s were established between European and U.S. companies, followed by intra-European cooperation, which increased strongly in the second half of the 1980s. In general, European telecommunication companies played a leading role in forming alliances with U.S. and Japanese firms. Important motives for alliances are the search for technologically complementary partners, market access, and the high cost of developing new systems (Hagedoorn, 1991). Strategic alliances can be found both in the equipment and service sectors. Examples in the service sector are joint ventures between U.S. West and Intelmatique, the Dutch PTT Telecom and the Swedish Televerket, and France Télécom and Deutsche Bundespost Telekom, which founded the holding company Eucom.

European Policies in the Field of TNS

The policies of the Commission of the European Communities for telecommunication and information technology constitute the dominant framework for the development of the European telecommunication services sector. The policies of the European Community regarding the telecommunication network-based services are mainly developed by DG XIII, the General Directorate responsible for telecommunication, information industries, and innovation. An increase in activities was triggered by rising competitive pressure from the United States and Japan and, in particular, by major events such as the divestiture of AT&T and the rising telecommunication activities of IBM in Europe (Schneider & Werle, 1990). In general, the CEC policies follow two paths. The first is oriented toward the development of a common European regulatory framework, and the second is concerned with research and development in telecommunication (see Bauer & Steinfield, Chapter 4 in this book, for an overview). In this section, we concentrate on activities that are explicitly targeted at telecommunication network-based services.

Regarding regulation, the activities are directed toward the provision and harmonization of services. In that respect, the Green Paper of 1987 on the Development of the Common Market for Telecommunication Services and Equipment constitutes a landmark decision. Regarding services development, the Services and ONP Directives are of crucial importance. These are complemented by the Green Paper of 1990 on Satellite Communications in the European Community. The major proposals of this document, such as the full liberalization of the earth segment, commercial freedom for space segment providers, nondiscriminatory access to space segment capacity, and the harmonization of licensing and type approval procedures can be expected to further Europe-wide services, especially in the case of the integration of Eastern European countries. In the TNS sector, videoconferencing, Very Small Aperture Terminal (VSAT) Networks, and News Gathering Services (NGS) might profit from the harmonized liberalization of the European satellite communication.

The total R&D program of the EC for the period 1987-1991 amounted to 5.4 billion ECU (approximately 6.5 billion US$)—550 million ECU (10%) was allocated to broadband communications (RACE) and only 125 million (2.3%) to new services. The new services program includes pilots of AIM (Advanced Informatics in Medicine), DELTA (Development of Europe Learning through Technological Advances), and DRIVE, which are not directly oriented toward telecommunication services. In the R&D program for the period 1990-1994, 484 million ECU (8.5%) have been reserved for the RACE projects in order to support the introduction of communitywide Integrated Broadband Communication (IBC) by 1995. For the development of telematic services of general interest, 380 million ECU (6.7%) have been allocated. This program is meant to contribute to the development of communitywide telematics services in the fields of administration, health, remote training, libraries, and languages (Iwens, 1990).

Initially, the Commission of the European Communities paid a great deal of attention to information provision for scientific and technical use. In order to stimulate the distribution of information, the Euronet (1975) and Diane data-transmission networks were implemented, basically to link databases, and programs such as Artemis, Docdel, and Impact I and II were started. The Artemis study, aimed at the digitization of documents and their transmission by satellites, was not very successful (Boumans, 1991). Docdel (Document Delivery) was a follow-up on the Artemis study. In the context of this program, 10 projects were selected and partly financed by the EC. The program was directed toward optical storage of documents, electronic delivery of documents, electronic bulletins, and tele-education (Boumans, 1991).

Impact (Information Market Policy Action) was the next step. Impact I (1989-1990) was a 2-year program with a budget of 36 million ECU. In 1988, the CEC decided to support a plan of action aimed at (a) setting up an internal market by the end of 1992, (b) stimulating and reinforcing the competitive capability of European suppliers of information services, (c) promoting the use of advanced information services, and (d) reinforcing joint efforts to achieve Community cohesion with respect to information services policies (Commission, 1991b).

The same goals will be pursued in the follow-up of the Impact program. The results of the first Impact program were that because of the limited duration of the plan of action, the limited budget, and the preparatory nature of the program the initial goals could not be achieved. The new program received a term of 5 years (1991-1995) and has the same general objectives as the original program. The objectives proposed in Impact I and also followed in Impact II focus on (a) improving the understanding of the market, (b) overcoming legal and administrative barriers, (c) increasing the user-friendliness of the services and improving information literacy, and (d) supporting strategic information operations. The costs of the action program are to be shared by public and private sectors. The CEC budget amounts to 100 million ECU (Commission, 1991b, p. 29).

Pilot projects and demonstrations supported on the bases of Impact I were directed toward intelligent interfaces, databases for pictures, information on tourism, licenses, and standards. The multilingual CEC service ECHO (European Community Host Organization), introduced in 1980 to promote information services in the EC and developed further through the Impact program, supports users of information systems with European help desk, electronic directories, low-cost training, and demonstrations. In the audiotex field, experiments with new technologies in a multilingual environment have been carried out. In these experiments, called MAX, voice input and output technologies in three languages have been used (Electronic Publishing Services, 1991). The focus of Impact II is on the removal of technical barriers, the reduction of regional disparities at the level of supply, the use of information services, and encouraging cooperation between information providers (Commission, 1991b, p. 8).

It is clear that the EC policy has concentrated on technological innovations and regulatory harmonization, while services have hardly been stimulated. The EC is preoccupied with the development of technology, as the level of financial support flowing into R&D programs shows. In comparison, the EC gives little support to the development of services. The videotex example, which is discussed in the next section, makes clear that the EC's role regarding the stimulation of services is limited.

Decisive Factors Regarding Videotex

For various reasons, European videotex systems provide an interesting field of research. First, videotex, as a system that connects and integrates private households in the global telematic marketplace, is of strategic importance. Second, the unique success of the French Teletel system, which to some extent rattled even U.S. policymakers, can shed more light on the conditions for success and failure of videotex. Third, it can contribute to a better understanding of the probable impact of videotex on the development of other TNS.

The "videotex saga" began before the EC became an active player in the field of telecommunication. In Europe, no common videotex strategy emerged; rather a number of national initiatives led to extremely different results. However, during the last decade, a convergence of strategies and an improvement in the general diffusion of videotex in Europe can be detected.

In the early days of videotex two dominant models related to the introduction of videotex in Europe could be distinguished—one based on Prestel and the other one on Teletel. The British Prestel concept was initially copied by most countries. The concept was directed toward the adoption of videotex in the consumer market. The consumers had to buy a television set with a special decoder (personal computers, especially with modems, were hardly available at that time) in order to get access to the central videotex database via the public telephone network. The Prestel architecture was very centralized and required subscription. Very soon it became clear that the consumer market was not yet ready for videotex and the predominantly weak marketing efforts of the PTOs were subsequently redirected towards the business sector. A sequencing, niche strategy was followed to penetrate one selected business sector after the other. This strategy did not prove to be successful either. Consequently, the break-even point could not be reached in countries that followed the Prestel concept, which meant that videotex was considered a failure in almost every European country by the mid-1980s.

The French experience alone was totally different. The introduction of videotex was one aspect of French industrial policy (Humphreys, 1990). The first step was the modernization of the telephone network. During the second phase, videotex was introduced in the attempt to generate more traffic on the packet-switched Transpac X.25 network and to create an information service community at the same time. The dedicated Minitel terminals were produced by the domestic industry and were provided free of charge.

The system architecture of Teletel is very simple and radically different from the centralized Prestel concept. The Minitel terminal is connected to the telephone network, which is connected to the packet-switched Transpac network. Up to this point it is similar to other videotex systems. However, in France, external databases of service providers are directly connected to the packet-switched network; consequently, no central host computer is required. This proved to be (cost) efficient for service providers and most of the applications. In combination with the transparent kiosk-billing system, this decentralized approach managed to reach a critical mass of services on the supply side within a short period of time. The marketing of the services was not solely done by France Télécom but mainly by services providers themselves. As the suppliers competed for the same market, many promotional activities were deployed that stimulated the diffusion of applications.

It became quite obvious that the French Teletel model was more successful than the British Prestel system, taking into account the amount of users and the traffic generated on the telecom network. In 1992, technically decentralized videotex systems comparable to the French system could be found all over Europe and even the centralized BTX-system in Germany was gradually changing into a more open and decentralized architecture. The French strategy to supply free terminals was not copied in any other European country. However, the option to use cheap terminals was introduced in Italy, Switzerland, and Spain. As an alternative or additional incentive, the possibility to access videotex with cheap communication-software for personal computers was introduced, for instance, in The Netherlands and Austria. Combined with extensively coordinated marketing efforts by network operators and service providers, these seem to be key factors for a successful diffusion policy.

However, another side of Prestel's failure and Teletel's success should not be neglected. Because of the failure of Prestel, other telecommunication network-based services such as online database services, E-mail, and audiotex became quite popular in the United Kingdom. In France, the development of alternative telecommunication network-based services such as E-mail are developing very slowly. It remains to be seen if Teletel can adapt to technical changes in display standards, transmission speeds, and so on. In the long run, videotex in France may, in fact, be blocking new developments. An open videotex system relying on a number of different standards, protocols, and PC plus modem as a terminal, such as found in the United States, may prove to offer more possibilities within an "open network."

Technical Factors

In general, the introduction of videotex was propagated by technicians of the PTOs. Initially, videotex was considered to be an extension of the television set. When Prestel was introduced, personal computers were not available and dedicated terminals, such as the Austrian Mupid and the French Minitel, had yet to be developed. The hardware for the consumer was expensive and not easy to use. The architecture of Prestel-like systems was very complex, the X.25 networks were not yet available, and standards had to be developed. The United Kingdom, France, and Germany developed the Prestel, Antiope, and BTX standards. After intervention by CEPT, a three-part CEPT standard was agreed on, although not all of the different components were compatible. The technical choices had an effect on the billing systems and the way services were offered. In Denmark, the preoccupation with the technology was so intense that no attention whatsoever was paid to the development of services. In Austria, for example, the ambitious videotex activities were concentrated on the development and production of the intelligent videotex decoder Mupid. Unfortunately the technology policy project failed, which, along with other factors, also harmed the Austrian service development.

Economic Factors

Videotex can be characterized as an example of an innovation driven by technology. After the first experiments with videotex, marketing efforts were stopped or received less attention. The initial orientation on the consumer market appeared to be a failure. The reorientation toward the business market resulted in limited success in certain branches, for example, the travel industry in certain countries. The switch from a generic to a niche marketing approach did not prove to be successful either. Only the French marketing strategy, mainly based on the free supply of terminals and on an easily accessible network for service providers, was successful. Both a critical mass of services and of users could be generated in the limited time slot that is available for the introduction of an innovation (Schnaars, 1989).

The question of whether France's Teletel is also successful in economic terms is difficult to answer. The basic question is whether the cost of the Transpac network should be included. However, Teletel has had a major impact on economic activity in France. The revenues of hard- and software providers and of service providers, the generation of employment, and the benefits for the users should all be taken into consideration when settling accounts.

Political Factors

In the policy arena the dominant position was reserved for the PTOs, especially in those countries where liberalization took a long time. Although the goals of the different actors may have differed in detail, in general the PTOs strived for more traffic on their networks, development of new products and services, and modernization of the infrastructure. Principal competition came from computer and time-sharing firms.

Most of the time the government acted in accordance with the PTOs. In Italy, for example, the PTO suggested how videotex should be organized and regulated. If governments developed their own vision regarding videotex their policy was directed toward the support of domestic industry, especially in the consumer electronics and telecommunication sector.

Initially, media and press participated in experiments with videotex but mainly for defensive reasons. Their role was that of information providers. However, the lack of success of videotex soon demonstrated that videotex would not threaten advertising revenues and they quickly lost interest. In some countries the print media are still marginally involved in videotex as information providers. The position of the press, as service providers, has been taken over by organizations such as mail-order companies, electronic publishers, insurance companies, banks, travel agencies, and software houses.

The dominant players in the videotex game, the governments and PTOs, cooperated at times with other actors. At other times they actively or passively blocked other actors. For instance, the PTT in The Netherlands played a negative role by refusing to cooperate with service providers in the development of videotex systems other than those that were PTT-owned (Viditel) or PTT-supported (Videotex Nederland). Other actors, mostly service providers, had a hard time conquering a position in the policy arena. Yet others were hardly involved at all, most notably representatives of user and consumer organizations. Although the position of the PTOs differed from country to country, the trend toward liberalization in the 1980s weakened their position. However, most PTOs still hold a factual, not a legal, monopoly position because they are the providers of the infrastructure and the dominant actor with whom other actors have to negotiate.

Social Factors

Social factors only played a role in certain European countries, most notably in Germany, Austria, Switzerland, and Sweden. Public discussions regarding social risks of videotex concentrated on labor issues (expected loss of jobs), data privacy, and consumer protection issues. Only Germany passed a specific law on videotex. However, this law deals with the question of whether videotex is a telecommunication service or a broadcast medium. In the first case, videotex would fall under the control of the federal government; in the second case, it would be controlled by the Länder (the state governments). Further regulation in 1983 dealt with privacy questions. The German system is considered to be the most heavily regulated public videotex service in the world.

In most European countries the demand for videotex services has been very low. It is striking that research on user demand is scarce and, when it is available, only plays a marginal role in the marketing of videotex. The field trials were mainly of a purely technical nature and served to legitimate the introduction plans already underway. Social experiments with videotex hardly deserve the label (Qvortrup et al., 1987). These experiments had mainly an agenda-setting function. The public attention the experiments drew was supposed to contribute to the adoption of the new technology. However, on the consumer market with the exception of Teletel, videotex and videotex services became synonymous with high costs, low-quality services (outdated and unreliable information services and pornographic communication services), and limited consumer choice.

In some countries (e.g., The Netherlands and Sweden), codes of conduct were formulated by organizations representing service providers. In Austria the PTT formulated user guidelines as a precursor to a videotex law. However, because of the low acceptance of videotex, the law never passed the draft stage. In Switzerland, the federal government announced a decree that contains some content-oriented regulation. Services and information that are unlawful, that offend moral senses and public authority, and contain hidden advertisements are forbidden.

In summary, a variety of technical, political, economic, and social factors explain the differences in the introduction of videotex in Europe. Although unsuccessful, Prestel was a breakthrough in the field of consumer telematics and in that sense strongly contributed to the development of TNS in the United Kingdom and many other European countries. In contrast, the French Teletel system is one of the most adopted and used systems in the consumer market. More recently, Teletel has been more or less copied in several countries, for example, Sweden (Teleguide), The Netherlands (Videotex Nederland), Denmark (Netplus), Ireland, Italy, and Spain. Intelmatique, the France Télécom subsidiary to market Teletel, is involved in several of these initiatives.

Conclusions

The analysis of the telecommunication services sector in Europe is faced with problems of definition, basically reflecting a mixture of fast technical advancements and regulatory changes that more or less set the tone for such classifications. In any case, the European TNS market is considered to be lagging behind the U.S. TNS development. In the second half of the 1980s, the CEC evolved from an international regime to a corporate actor with growing impact in the European telecommunication policy field. The Community actions that were inspired by the concerns of major member countries are basically aimed toward the harmonization of the telecommunication services sector. Next to general measures, some minor action programs were launched to stimulate service innovation. But the EC is only one player (and often in the role of mediator) out of many on the national and international levels that to some extent are following conflicting micro- and macro-economic and political goals. The videotex example presented shows how these conflicting goals can affect the introduction of TNS.

Liberalization and harmonized infrastructures are no guarantee for a satisfactory TNS development. On the contrary, single actors such as the CEC and single factors such as liberalization have to be regarded as part of a web of determinants that might be grouped in technical, political, economic, and social factors. In general, research on social factors and on the interdependence, interaction, and cumulative effects of factors is not being done. The videotex example shows how some of these factors and actors affect the development of videotex infrastructure and services. Videotex services, like other TNS, should be regarded as "interlocked" innovations. As such, the innovation process presupposes innovations in the field of technology: infrastructure, hard- and software, the supply of services—but also an innovation in the field of user demand. If one of these elements is missing or insufficiently developed the entire chain breaks down and the innovation process is hampered.

After the flop of nearly all European videotex systems, evaluations of the different strategies were carried out with particular attention on France. Some countries seem to have been able to take advantage of the results (Spain, Switzerland, Italy, The Netherlands). However, no country has totally copied the French strategy but only parts of it are diffusing throughout Europe (decentralized architecture, cheap terminals, kiosk system). Hence, more and more multi-standard services are emerging. So far, the French videotex diffusion rate has not been reached in any other country. The learning process continues. In the case of audiotex, a group of services similar in many ways to videotex, it will be interesting to see whether the "old" mistakes regarding technology push, services demand, international strategies, standardization, and so on, can/will be avoided.

References

Bauer, J. M. (1992). *Implications of the creation of a European Economic Area for telecommunications in EFTA countries.* Unpublished manuscript, Department of Telecommunication, Michigan State University, East Lansing.

Bauer, J. M., Latzer, M., Scheidl, R., & Sint, P. (in press). *Telekommunikationsdienste. Österreich im internationalen Kontext.* Vienna: Österreichische Computer Gesellschaft.

Boumans, J. (1991). *Elektronische informatiediensten: Contouren van een nieuwe bedrijfstak* [Electronic Information services: Contours of a new economic sector]. The Hague: Department of Economic Affairs.

Bouwman, H., & Christoffersen, M. (Eds.). (1992). *Relaunching Videotex: Is there a life after death?* Dordrecht, The Netherlands: Kluwer Academic Services.

Christoffersen, M. (1992). Regulating VANS: The case of audiotex services in UK, France, Holland and Denmark. In F. Klaver & P. Slaa (Eds.), *Telecommunication. New signposts to old roads.* Amsterdam: IOS-Press.

Commission of the European Communities. (1991a). *Overview of the audiotex market in 1989 and 1990.* IMO Working Paper 91/1. Luxembourg.

Commission of the European Communities. (1991b). *Proposal for a Council Decision setting up a programme for an information services market.* COM(90)570 final. Brussels: Commission of the European Communities.

Economist. (1991, October 5). *A survey of telecommunications* (special section between pp. 59-60).

Electronic Publishing Services. (1991). *Report on the Audiotex Workshop, 17/18th December 1990.* Luxembourg.

Hagedoorn, J. (1991). *Changing patterns of inter-firm strategic technology alliances in information technologies and telecommunication.* Diskussionsbeiträge Nr. 72. Bad Honnef, Germany: WIK.

Humphreys, P. (1990). The political economy of telecommunication in France; a case study of 'telematics.' In K. Dyson & P. Humphreys (Eds.), *The political economy of communications: International and European dimensions* (pp. 198-228). London: Routledge.

Iwens, J. L. (1990). *Technology assessment in telecommunication in Europe. The state of the art in EC-Countries.* Unpublished Manuscript.

Keen, P. G. (1988). *Competing in time: Using telecommunication for competitive advantage.* Cambridge: Ballinger.

Mansell, R. E. (1988). Telecommunication network-based services: Regulation and market structure in transition. *Telecommunications Policy, 12,* 243-255.

Organization for Economic Cooperation and Development (OECD). (1989). *Telecommunication network-based services: Policy implications.* Paris: OECD.

Office of Technology Assessment (OTA). (1990). *Critical connections: Communications for the future.* Washington, DC: U.S. Government Printing Office.

Polanen Petel, V. van, Bulthuis, R., & Morsink, R. (1991). *Telecommunication services: An economic perspective.* Rotterdam: Nederlands Economisch Instituut.

Qvortrup, L. C., Ancelin, J., Frawley, J., Hartley, F., Pichault, & Pop, P. (1987). *Social experiments with information technology and the challenges of innovation.* Dordrecht, The Netherlands: D. Reidel.

Schnaars, P. (1989). *Megamistakes: Forecasting and the myth of rapid technological change*. New York: The Free Press.

Schneider, V., & Werle, R. (1990). International regime or corporate actor? The European Community in telecommunication policy. In K. Dyson & P. Humphreys (Eds.), *The political economy of communications: International and European dimensions* (pp. 77-106). London: Routledge.

Scicon Networks. (1989). *Analysis of the European market of value added services*. London: Scicon.

Stoetzer, M. W. (1991). *Der Markt für Mehrwertdienste: Ein kritischer Überblick*. Diskussionsbeiträge Nr. 69. Bad Honnef, Germany: WIK.

Videotex International. (1991). Value added services: Regulation and reality in the Federal Republic of Germany. *Telecommunications Policy, 15*, 437-452.

Mobile Communications in Europe

JÜRGEN MÜLLER
SAADET TOKER

The phenomenal market rate of mobile services, like that of facsimile machines, has changed the picture of a steadily moving telephone service market to one in which innovation and competitive strategy are now new buzz words. This chapter looks at some of these issues in the European market for mobile services. After a description of the product and market in the first section, we spell out in greater detail the importance of the different regulatory parameters for this market in the section following. The role of the European Commission, mainly in the regulatory area, summarized in the third section, must be seen against the national developments, that diverge significantly from each other. It seems that in this service market, the Europe of 1992 has still not arrived.

Product Definition and Overview of Mobile Telecommunications

Mobile telecommunications as a substitute and supplement for "wire" or network-based telecommunications services has a long tradition. It started with the *pager* as the most basic product. In its simplest use, a pager alerts the user that someone is trying to get in touch and the user needs to make a return call. The second type of mobile service, the *private mobile radio* (PMR), provides a two-way, mobile service but is usually restricted to a group of users, such as taxi services, company employees, and the like. The third application is *cellular telephones,* which allow the user to make or receive a call while on the move and not accessible to an ordinary wire-based telephone line. A further product recently introduced is the *telepoint* service, which is essentially (in its application up to now) a mobile phone box. Near an appropriate base station the user can make outgoing calls but typically cannot receive incoming calls. The most recent development of *personal communication networks* (PCN) is an attempt to integrate these various capabilities into a hand-held wireless device that will be cheaper than the cellular telephones currently in use (Toker, 1992).

Although pagers and private mobile radio have been in use since the 1950s, their penetration rate was still small in the 1980s. This was due not only to relatively high equipment and user costs but also lower quality (inability to move from one service area into another without redialing) and the limited availability of radio spectrum. However, the technical developments in the areas of microelectronics and digitization, which have influenced the telecommunications service in most areas, have most dramatically affected mobile telecommunications. With the introduction of cellular technology, product quality has been improved and problems of frequency and spectrum limitations have been eliminated through various compression techniques and spectrum re-use of adjacent bandwidths.

This cellular technology (which was developed by Bell Laboratories soon after World War II and commercialized in the 1970s) and the software used to transfer calls between adjacent cells (without redial) have been fundamental technical breakthroughs. As a consequence, the development of cellular radio during the 1980s has seen spectacular growth rates. This has taken mobile telecommunications services from a fringe, specialized market into the mainstream of telecommunications. According to Carrington (1991, p. 1), there are currently over 11 million cellular customers worldwide. The rate of annual new additions is growing at over 60%. Mature cellular markets such as Scandinavia are reaching penetration levels of over 5%, with penetration levels of 20% forecast by the end of the century.

As the service is spreading, economies of scale and learning are leading to lower and lower equipment prices, both for handsets and for network equipment. For instance, based on our estimates, the average price for cellular handsets in the United Kingdom declined from £1,800 in 1985 to £100 in 1991, while the minimum available price fell from £1,400 to zero. In the same time period, the ratio of the average price of a handset relative to annual airtime cost in the United Kingdom fell from 2.14 to .10. The U.K. handset prices were affected by the service providers' ability to subsidize due to network operation incentive payments. TACS and NMT systems handset prices are much lower than other systems. The declining cost of infrastructure and phones have led to the viability of cellular telephones as a bypass option for the local loop.[1]

We can expect in the 1990s that—certainly in the OECD countries—mobile telecommunications will emerge in the forefront of the telecommunications market, in the footsteps of the Walkman or the Camcorder in consumer electronics (Carrington, 1991, p. 2). This will be characterized by a move from high-cost specialized markets into a mass market. Furthermore, given that some countries already allow at least one competitor to the traditional monopoly carrier in mobile service provision, it provides a major entry-point for changing the institutional monopoly structure in telecommunications. Because mobile services are not only important for access to the local loop but also for emerging bypass networks, they fundamentally challenge the concept of a PTT monopoly and the uniform tariff policy that lies behind it.

The Regulatory Framework

The development of European mobile telecommunication markets is to a large extent influenced by the regulatory framework in which the suppliers of services and equipment have to operate. The most important aspects are (a) the administration of the radio spectrum; (b) the licensing and regulation of additional service providers, including the access conditions of additional suppliers in terms of providing a level playing field and the restrictions imposed on them; (c) the standard-setting procedure for the products and services, which is important for interoperability; and (d) the industrial policy considerations underlying these regulatory decisions.

Spectrum Management

Each service provider needs a radio frequency to provide services (essentially a link between the base station and the mobile unit). Effective spectrum management is therefore of basic importance for the development of mobile services. The more spectrum is made available, the lower the development and investment cost for the effective use of the radio spectrum and the cheaper the service.

The European norms for the first generation of digital mobile service (GSM, named after the working group responsible for the standards, Groupe Special Mobile) have set the frequency bands between 890 and 915 MHz (for reception) and 935 and 960 MHz (for transmission) aside. This allows for two times 25 MHz, probably a sufficient initial capacity. A major question is how the frequencies ought to be distributed. Equal distribution, for example, in the case of a duopoly, becomes an operating hindrance if one supplier is more efficient than the other. As a consequence, auctioning of the spectrum has been advocated as a more efficient alternative, as it has in the spectrum competition with other services such as the military, TV and radio, and the like.

How little spectrum there is currently available for cellular services is indicated by a recent study conducted for the Commission by the European Telecommunications Consultancy Organization (ETCO) on the market requirements for radio spectrum. Their detailed analysis of the average distribution of spectrum use in Europe indicates that in the 930-960 MHz range, where all mobile radio is currently allocated, 80% of the spectrum is allocated to broadcast and government (mainly military) use. In the frequency range 960-3000 MHz, where future mobile radio services are expected to reside, over half the spectrum is currently allocated to fixed services (government and civil) (Ungerer, 1991, p. 5). As a result, the Commission created in 1991 the European Radiocommunications Office (ERO) to help coordinate the process of spectrum management.

Competitive Service Provision

Through the licensing of additional non-wireline carriers, extra-competitive influences can be brought to bear on monopoly wireline carriers. This is apparent by the very rapid introduction of mobile cellular services in the United States and the United Kingdom. Competitive service provision provides a trade-off between static efficiency losses and dynamic efficiency benefits. The scarce resource of the radio spectrum is reduced by about 5% (for digital service) to 15% when two suppliers are licensed, because each supplier has to provide for its own reserve capacity (Kruse, 1991, p. 5). Furthermore, uncertainty is increased for each supplier when more competitors are present. The regulatory choice is to decide between one monopoly supplier and limited entry or open entry coupled with the threat of competition. Although there are sufficient economies of scale in the service provision, in dense, high-income regions there is certainly room for more players, especially if access conditions are standardized and a uniform technical system is used.

The additional regulatory issue concerns the rules according to which secondary licenses are issued. One possibility is a competitive bidding and selection process in which the various candidates are chosen according to a number of criteria. In Germany, the conditions were (a) competence in providing such services, (b) previous experience as a service supplier, (c) sufficient financial resources and organizational ability, (d) viability of technical and business plans, and (e) the planned quality level and regional coverage (Kruse, 1991).

An alternative is the U.S. system in which regional lotteries have been used to allocate the second license. This has led to subsequent mergers with the most competitive enterprises buying up other regional operators to reconstruct their own national network areas. As a third alternative, auctioning of licenses for mobile services, especially in connection with the available radio spectrum, is certainly the most appealing idea from an economist's point of view.

Access and Regulatory Conditions: The Basis for a Level Playing Field

Given that most countries now will allow at least a duopoly in mobile service provision, the question of equal access for the non-wireline competitor to the public-switched telephone networks (PSTN) is very important. It provides, after all, the link to where most of the customers are located. Costwise, more than half of the service costs are linked to the access and usage charges of the PSTN. To that extent, it must be ensured that the non-wireline carrier has no cost disadvantage vis-à-vis the wireline carrier.

Some countries have also restricted the extent of vertical integration in which competitive service providers may engage. Equipment suppliers are usually not allowed to provide network service, although they may be active as airtime resellers, such as Motorola in the United Kingdom. Only the United Kingdom has required the introduction of resellers. These are essentially retail firms that buy the terminals and the air time from systems providers, and then sell the cellular services directly to the public. This has encouraged more small- and medium-sized suppliers in the service but has the problem of service interruption if in the competitive process one of these companies disappears. The

United Kingdom is relaxing this vertical integration prohibition in 1993, because with the introduction of PCN services the market is expected to be competitive enough. Another one is the restriction on service suppliers concerning value-added services, again because it is difficult to provide a level playing field. However, if economies of scope exist between two services, alternative solutions should and have been sought.

Standardization

From a public policy point of view, as soon as more than one player is involved, the setting of standards to allow compatibility between various system providers and add-on services has important competitive implications. By not regulating standards, the market may result in fragmented multistandards, with a self-sustained installed base, before one standard becomes dominant. Given the switching costs between standards, subscribers to a minority standard may become stranded with a poorly supported system. The consequences of fragmented standards may be fewer complementary goods and services. Equipment costs may be higher and the minimum efficient production scale may not be realized. This can hold back total market growth. Furthermore, market competition for standards can involve duplicating efforts for development and promotion, which may be quite large. Standardization could reduce this risk and therefore lead to more research and development in the service.

Governments therefore play an important role in standard setting. Farrell and Saloner (1988) have shown that committees may outperform the market as coordinating mechanisms, and hybrid systems (with competition and committees) may be better still. But as we see in regulated industries such as telecommunications particularly in Europe, standard setting is not just performed by some technocratic committee, but by an official authority. It usually has its own policy agenda that goes beyond simple standards coordination. This may interfere with the standardization process and not allow market forces to work efficiently either (Grindley & Toker, 1992a, 1992b).

Regulation is also crucial on the equipment certification side of the market. It is important that it is carried out independently, to provide, again, a level playing field between the wireline carriers and the new competitors, and so that there is a strong enough competitive market in retailing cellular services to potential customers.

Industrial Policy Considerations
Underlying the Regulatory Framework

In the past, the European telephone companies not only had a technocratic mind when regulating the sector but also aimed at the protection of domestic industry and jobs (Foreman-Peck & Müller, 1988). This industrial policy consideration is also to be found in the regulatory framework for mobile services. To the extent that competition in service provision is introduced, the ability to impose industrial policy goals on service providers is limited, unless they are directly ingrained in regulatory roles. The strengthening of European norms coupled with the foundation of the European Telecommunications Standards Institute (ETSI), and the trend to allow at least duopoly service provision, indicates that some check on the industrial policy considerations of the past is being attempted. Instead, the aim is now to utilize the internal market potential of the European common market in the creation of an EEC-wide standard that may help industrial policy considerations, not on a national but on a European regional level.

The Role of the European Commission

Telecommunications policy has traditionally been national. Although the Treaty of Rome provided for the Commission to be active in this area, it was only with the advent of the 1992 campaign (to complete the Single Market) and the EC's Green Book on Telecommunications (Commission, 1987) that the EC really took an initiative. The Commission has since tried to structure the liberalization process on an EC-wide basis concerning both the equipment industry and network services (Müller, 1991). Concerning the issue of mobile communications, standardizing a European-wide mobile service has been a major priority for the Commission. It also agreed on the related question of spectrum allocation in which the standard should be available Europe-wide.

Because there are a number of different national analog systems that are basically incompatible (see Table 10.1), the choice of the Commission was to get at least a uniform standard for the next product generation, digital mobile service. It goes back to a decision of the Council of Ministers of June 25, 1987, with the intention to utilize fully the technical possibilities of second-generation mobile services, to create a compatible Europe-wide mobile telecommunication system, and to reduce the current incompatibility between systems, especially for transborder services. Service based on this standard, the GSM, was first introduced in September 1991 in Sweden, Finland, and Denmark and 3 months later in the United Kingdom by Vodafone. However, the full benefits will only materialize after it is provided Europe-wide.

Because the standard-making bodies were in most cases the national telecommunication authorities or in some cases their European equivalent at the European Conference of Postal and Telecommunications Administrations (CEPT), this involved a much closer collaboration within the CEPT. CEPT started the GSM process in 1983, but this was integrated into the Commission's activities through the creation of ETSI in 1988, which essentially took over the CEPT standard setting group on GSM. The successful completion of the GSM standard can certainly be seen as a major achievement of this process.

The impact of the Commission's mandate behind the activities of ETSI was particularly important for the development of the GSM standard. It first of all gave authority to a normally much slower decision process based on negotiation. Second, it added technical expertise by opening the standard-setting process to non-PTT members such as manufacturers and others, who can also vote (slightly above 300 in October 1992). The fruits of this process are illustrated by the more than 300 standards that have meanwhile been issued by ETSI.

The EC's policy can also be seen as an attempt at having an EC industrial policy: By creating its own European standard, it makes the takeover of other, already existing international standards such as those in the United States or the Nordic countries more difficult. In other words, the trade-creating specialization advantages of a Europe-wide standard must be balanced against the trade-reducing barriers that might affect the long-term dynamic of this market, especially if foreign, non-European suppliers do not gain equal access.

Given the initial success with the GSM standard, the European Telecommunications Standards Institute (ETSI) has also now adopted a Europe-wide paging standard (ERMES) to be introduced from 1993 on. ETSI is also now working on a standard for a Digital European Cordless Telephone (DECT) using a system developed jointly by Ericsson, Philips, and Siemens and the so-called CT-3 cordless proposal. Once the DECT standard is adopted, it should serve both as a standard for private in-house cordless systems (linking telephones to the PABX) and as a public system similar to that known as the *telepoint market*. ETSI also accepted the Telepoint CAI standard as Cordless Digital standard in December 1991 for CT-2 applications. To keep development costs for further applications low, GSM has also been chosen for PCN applications (DCS 1800), and its compatibility with DECT is under consideration (Grindley & Toker, 1992b).

ETSI is currently also working on the third-generation standard (UMTS) of the cellular mobile system (after analog and GSM) to allow broadband applications. Initially, there was even an attempt to work with the Japanese (TTC) and the United States (T1) toward one world-wide standard, but a regionalization of standards seems now more likely.

National Developments

Table 10.1 gives an overview of the European mobile cellular systems, the most important aspect of mobile telecommunications. In terms of absolute numbers, the United Kingdom is certainly the leader, especially if one considers that cellular telephones were introduced there quite late. If one looks at the penetration rates as a source of comparison, it is clear that the Scandinavian countries, who launched their service earlier (in 1981), have achieved the highest penetration rates of between 40 and 60 subscribers per 1,000 population. Iceland and Switzerland are also among the leaders. The cost of using cellular phones, which to a large extent is influenced by the density of the service, after allowing for relative income levels in the countries concerned, shows a clear correlation with penetration rates.

Table 10.1 also sets out the (first-year) cost of using cellular phone service in different countries and shows the relative cost in relation to average incomes in each country. The figures show wide variation from just over 2,000 U.S.$ in the United Kingdom through 3,000 U.S.$ in countries such as Italy, Belgium, and the Netherlands, rising to 6,000-7,000 U.S.$ in France and Germany. Relative to the average annual income, the cost of using cellular phones ranges from less than 10% in Switzerland and Denmark to around 30% in France and Germany. These figures, too, support the view that the lower cost countries also have the highest penetration rates. However, geography is also clearly important. The most sparsely populated Scandinavian countries (Iceland) have higher penetration rates, whereas the reverse is true for the more densely populated Benelux countries.

TABLE 10.1 Country Comparisons Among European Mobile Systems

Country	Relative Cost[a] (first year)	Pene- tration Rate	Absolute Cost in U.S.$[b] (first year)	System Capacity (in 000s)	Technology
1. Switzerland	7.14	20.67	2,417	180	NMT 900
2. Denmark	9.35	30.14	2,382	300	NMT 450/900
3. Norway	10.04	50.19	2,650	350	NMT 450/900
4. Finland	10.45	48.41	2,902	250	NMT 450/900
5. Sweden	10.82	59.73	2,907	500	NMT 450/900
6. Austria	11.82	10.65	2,475	50	NMT 450/TACS
7. United Kingdom	12.32	20.54	2,105	1,400	(E)TACS 900
8. Italy	16.04	6.18	3,033	100	RTMS/TACS 900
9. Belgium	17.18	4.26	3,382	50	NMY 450
10. Netherlands	17.70	6.04	3,290	50	NMT 450/900
11. Iceland	20.19	20.82	2,302	12	NMT 450
12. Ireland	22.74	7.06	2,734	12	(E)TACS 900
13. Luxembourg	27.34	1.24	4,812	NA	NMT 450
14. Germany (W)	29.64	3.98	5,657	600	Net C 450
15. Spain	31.92	1.64	3,991	60	NMT 450/TACS
16. France	32.63	5.52	6,925	160	Radiocom 2000
17. Cyprus	35.57	4.52	2,539	NA	NMT 900
18. Malta	48.89	3.50	2,364	NA	NA TACS
19. Portugal	83.45	0.75	4,715	NA	Net C 450
20. Hungary	195.93	0.85	4,287	NA	NMT 450

SOURCE: *Mobile Communications*, July 18, 1991, PA Management Consultants.
[a]Relative Cost = Absolute cost as a percentage of GDP per capita
[b]Absolute Cost = (Cost of equipment + connection charge) + (12 × [Monthly rental + cost of 5 two-minute peak-time calls per day, 5 days a week, for 1 month])

The high penetration rates and low cost in Scandinavia are probably related to the learning experience as a result of the early set-up of these services, the liberal regulation, and the emerging competitive structure. All four Scandinavian countries from the start applied the same product standard to achieve a large market, bringing in the benefits of inter-country roaming (i.e., moving from one operator's network to another) and achieving economies of scale in the production of the equipment. The U.K. operators have also benefited from these effects, because they used only a slight modification of an already established U.S. analog standard. As a consequence, the number of willing equipment suppliers with ready products was quite large. In contrast, Germany, France, and Portugal (the latter being the only other European country that accepted the Siemens-C standard) had equipment that was very specific to each country and therefore had small production volumes and high prices.

In terms of competitive structure, very few countries already have a duopoly (the United Kingdom, France, and some of the Scandinavian countries). Sweden allowed entry of a private company (Comvik) to compete with the Swedish PTT (Televerket) but not on equal terms. Compared to the 800 channels of Televerket, Comvik was only allowed to operate on 50 channels. Nevertheless, usage price in Sweden is among the lowest. In Finland, there is a de facto duopoly because the state-owned PTT covers only the largest towns and the overland network, whereas the smaller cities are served by over 50 cooperative, municipal, or private networks. Germany is only now in the process of introducing competition in line with the new GSM digital product, so nothing can yet be said on the effect of competition. France also has had limited experience with competition. It started service with its Radio-com 2000, which is not truly a cellular specification because of the lack of a hand-over facility. A private company, Société Française de Radio-diffusion (SFR), started operating only in 1989. SFR has been treated unequally and its limited spectrum availability has constrained its expansion.

Developments in the United Kingdom

Two companies, Cellnet and Vodafone, were licensed to operate cellular networks in 1983. Their service was launched in 1985. With the goal of preventing vertical integration, the United Kingdom prohibited these firms from (a) retailing airtime directly to customers (although they were allowed to own service providers as fully separate subsidiaries), (b) manufacturing equipment, and (c) providing value-added services over their networks. Nevertheless the parent companies were involved in some of these activities but had to deal with them on an arms-length basis. Although the British licensing provisions established a duopoly, one of the companies has a strong vertical link to British Telecom because BT holds a 60% share of Cellnet. Thus Cellnet had no difficulty obtaining a reasonable interconnecting agreement. Given that BT had to act evenhandedly, this also solved the problem of Vodafone. The connections to the PSTN go through BT or Mercury (in the case of Cellnet, only BT is used).[2]

In terms of the universal service requirements, the British cellular network operators were required to cover most of the country and to

TABLE 10.2 Number of Subscribers in the U.K. Cellular Market

	Cellnet	*Vodafone*	*Total*
1985	3.5	2.0	5.5
1986	34.5	27.0	61.5
1987	64.0	79.0	143.0
1988	135.0	158.0	293.0
1989	260.0	288.0	548.0
1990	440.0	500.0	940.0
1991	508.0	656.0	1,164.0

SOURCE: Compiled from issues of *Mobile Communications*.
NOTE: Figures in thousands as of March each year.

introduce inter-system roaming (ISR) by a certain date. Universal coverage was achieved earlier than was required. However, the ISR has been deferred and may not be implemented because both companies cover the same regions and their capacity and subscriber numbers are roughly similar.

The duopoly strategy, coupled with the vertical separation requirement, resulted in an intensive rivalry and thus a very rapid network expansion (see Table 10.2). After 7 years, the total number of subscribers reached over 1.3 million in 1992. The rapid penetration also has to do with the pricing strategy used. Operators set a low markup on the cost of connection to the network (at times, even giving away terminal equipment) and a high markup on the cost of using it. According to Thompson & Toker (1991, p. 6), this policy gives strong incentives to a more rapid product penetration—providing greater product awareness—and is also a popular pricing strategy in the presence of consumer switching costs by "locking-in" the consumers.

At the end of 1991, Vodafone had around 620,000 and Cellnet about 520,000 subscribers, but the pretax profit of Vodafone was more than 3 times that of Cellnet (£75.8 million for Cellnet, and £234.4 million for Vodafone). Thompson and Toker (1991, p. 9) explain this difference partly in their infrastructure costs and their differences in revenue streams. Vodafone subscribers make more use of value-added services than Cellnet users and Vodafone has provided more choice and better schemes for such services.

The U.K. market is also interesting for a different reason. It is the only market in Europe in which fixed links are provided competitively by two private companies. It is also the only country in which vertical separation has been required initially, even though this requirement has been relaxed as of January 1993 (this decision reflects the expected entry of the new PCN networks into the mobile market). The United Kingdom also has a much more active mobile sector than most of the other countries. In addition to the two cellular network operators, which are also licensees for the new digital GSM network, there exist seven national paging networks, two national Private Mobile Radio (PMR) operators, four telepoint operators (although none are active at present), and three PCN licensees with service to be introduced in 1993.

The U.K. experience has shown that allowing entry does not automatically bring about success. Telepoint, where four licenses were granted, proved to be a major failure. Currently, the mobile sector market is dominated by cellular, with 60% of users, followed by pager and PMR users with 25% and 15% market shares, respectively, in terms of the number of subscribers. In terms of market values the importance of the cellular network within the mobile sector is even more pronounced.

Even though more entry is allowed now, the two duopoly operators had 6 years of a protected market. This has allowed them to develop the market and to recoup the investment outlays more than fully.[3] Furthermore, since they have also obtained licenses for the GSM provision, they should have further protection from technologically advanced networks. Their licenses also allow them to provide PCN type services, and Vodafone plans to launch a Microcellular Network (MCN) soon.

France

Although France Télécom has a reputation as a well-managed, innovative player in the telecommunications industry, its lack of success in the mobile area is particularly striking. Already in the 1970s, a transition toward cellular technology was envisaged. The first contracts were signed with French manufacturers in 1979 to install a mobile cellular radio system in the 400 MHz band (Dang-Nguyen, 1990), but given the small bandwidth provided (only for 200-300 channels), the manufacturers were not interested in the market at that time.

In 1981, France Télécom then issued two further tenders for the fixed equipment of an analog digital network. Matra won the first tender for a private network system with her Radiocom 2000 system, and Thomson, the second for a public cellular system with the R-450 system. But as the telecommunications activities of Thomson were sold to Alcatel that year, the tender for the public mobile system was not pursued further by Alcatel.

In 1983, a joint venture between the German Bundespost and the French DGT for the development of a new 900 MHz cellular analog system was founded. This was also part of a French plan to boost European electronics cooperation. The initial schedule was a pilot experiment for 10,000 subscribers in the Paris-Lyon and the Ruhr area in 1986, with a target of 100,000 subscribers by the end of the 1980s. But the subsequent public tender for the joint system was never issued. The German partners instead went for the Siemens technology and the French reverted back to the Radiocom 2000 system of Matra, opening the system officially in December 1985. But as the Radiocom 2000 system was initially conceived for a private network, it had no provisions for hand-overs between adjacent cells. It also suffered from channel limitations, having only 256 channels for nationwide use. In the Paris region the system already reached its saturation point of 8,000 subscribers 1 year after the opening. As a consequence, spectrum originally allocated to the provinces had to be reallocated to Paris and the tariff doubled to keep customers off the network. By the end of 1987, the total capacity in the Paris district was thus raised to 15,000. Finally, by 1989, a hand-over facility was introduced so that the size of the cells could be diminished and the capacity of Radiocom raised to 100,000 subscribers in Paris and 250,000 in France (Dang-Nguyen, 1990, p. 24).

The move to a duopoly was made in July 1987 with a public call for tender to supply the mobile system in the 450 MHz band using a 2.05 MHz bandwidth. The proposal was won by a joint venture between Companie Général des Eaux, Alcatel, and Nokia, offering the standard Scandinavian NMT 450 system. According to the licensing conditions, service had to be introduced by early 1989 with 85% national coverage by 1991, with a capacity of 30,000 subscribers in the Paris region and 100,000 nationwide. The final consortium, which is operating as a second supplier, is Société Française de Radiodiffusion (SFR) in which Général des Eaux (41%) and Crédit Lyonnais (19.9%) are the major shareholders. By the end of 1991, SFR was able to increase its capacity from 100,000 subscribers to 200,000 with extra frequencies provided at 450 MHz. France Télécom also introduced an interim service at 900 MHz before the GSM launch. In mid-1991, SFR had about 70,000 and RC2000 around 260,000 subscribers. Both France Télécom and SFR are to offer the new GSM service.

In sum, we can say that France Télécom never showed much interest in this service, so that the excess demand developed the way it did. The second license has been issued to SFR to change the situation, but the frequencies allocated are such that it seems virtually impossible to recreate the U.K. situation. Prices are sufficiently above those in the United Kingdom and Scandinavia, thereby reducing the attractiveness of the service. In 1991, cellular penetration in France was less than one-tenth the level achieved in Sweden and Norway and barely one-third that achieved in the United Kingdom.

Germany

After the failed agreement toward a joint procurement system with the French in 1989, just as the French at that time opted for one national mobile system, Germany went for the system C of Siemens. This was a highly engineered system, geared to the limited available radio spectrum in Germany. System C was subsequently only adopted in South Africa and Portugal. As a consequence, it could not attain the benefits of economies of scale as the systems in the United Kingdom (relying on the similarity to the U.S. system) and Scandinavian countries had. As a consequence, initial penetration rates were very low and equipment cost very high. By mid-1991 there were 350,000 subscribers on C4.

The move to a competitive service duopoly was actually only possible after the report of the Witte Commission in 1987 and after the separation of the Bundespost into a regulatory and an operating division in 1989. There was considerable interest in the German digital licenses (D1 and D2), which were awarded in the fall of 1989. Ten consortia were looked at in the so-called "beauty contest" by a special evaluating committee that had been set up by the postal ministry. The D2 license was awarded to the Mannesmann Group[4] in February 1990 and Deutsche Telekom received automatically the first license D1.

This duopoly situation for the new GSM digital technology was to be introduced in 1991/1992, and the old C network was expected to continue under exclusive Bundespost direction. Initially, both service providers received 2 times 5 MHz (i.e., 24 channels). In total, there will be a spectrum of 2 times 25 MHz available. The rest of the spectrum will be distributed later. Delays occurred, however, because of the need to develop new terminal equipment for the GSM standard. As a consequence, service was introduced only during 1992.

The German unification in 1990 required additional regulatory decisions. Initially it was thought that a separate mobile GSM license would have to be granted for East Germany. Instead, the license area was extended and therefore automatically awarded to the Mannesmann consortium, with the Bundespost being the other player.

In addition to cellular mobile, the German Ministry of Posts and Telecommunications has also liberalized the market for private mobile radio, allowing it connections to the PSTN. In terms of overall market size, cellular mobile (even before the introduction of the D1 and D2 service) accounts for 90% of value-added service and is thus the most important market, followed by the two paging services, Eurosignal and Citicall (Cityruf). Trunk mobile is only now starting to be developed.

Scandinavia

The Swedish cellular market is shared by three networks; two are operated by the state-owned Televerket and one is provided by an independent company (Comvik). Televerket NMT-450 system and Comvik network (also on 450 MHz band) were both launched in 1981. Comvik was given 26 frequencies to start with; in 1987, 24 more frequencies were allocated. Televerket also launched an NMT-900 network in 1986. Televerket systems provide capacity for 400,000 subscribers and Comvik capacity is stranded at around 25,000 subscribers. By mid-1991, the NMT-450 network had 242,000, the NMT-900 system had 265,000 subscribers, and the Comvik system had 21,000 subscribers. Televerket, just like other Nordic state-telecom operators, was not involved in terminal equipment manufacturing and distribution, which helped in the creation of a downstream market with more than 1,000 dealers and many manufacturers. Comvik's incompatible-standard handsets, however, are provided by two companies and Comvik shares the sales market with dealers almost equally.

The other Nordic countries started their NMT-450 service at the same time. Norway and Denmark also started their NMT-900 networks in 1986, but right away, with full geographical coverage and a large spectrum capacity, just as in the NMT-450 networks, high growth rates were achieved from the beginning. With the high level of demand, portable phone prices were reduced substantially. The GSM networks in these countries will be provided by state telecom operators as well as independent companies. In Sweden, Comvik and Nordik Tel; in Finland, Radiolinja; and in Norway, Netcom are the licensed independent operators to provide this service.

What is interesting about the Scandinavian development is the early product development and early marketing of mobile cellular services and the high penetration rates and product diffusion that were reached with very often near monopoly situations (i.e., without competition in service provision and without any strict regulation on the extent of vertical integration). The services were already launched in 1981, with the ability of transnational operation. Nordic countries demonstrate that achieving international market size and having high per-capita income, which lower the relative costs of using cellular phones, and effective marketing are key to a successful market.

Other Countries

Two other potentially big mobile phone markets are the Italian and Spanish markets. After a slow start the Italian market is currently the fastest growing cellular market. State-owned telephone company SIP provides cellular services on both the RTMS (450 MHz) and TACS-900 networks. RTMS system was launched in 1985 but had a very slow start. The network gained a reputation of having high levels of congestion and a large number of dropped calls. Furthermore, with Italtel—the sister company of SIP within the state holding company STET—being the only handset manufacturer for this system, the terminal equipment prices remained high. In mid-1991 the number of subscribers on the RTMS was only around 100,000. The second analog system—TACS-900—with a capacity for 1 million was launched in 1990 and has been very successful. The distribution of handsets has been opened to competition, with many manufacturers supplying the market; the number of subscribers reached 400,000 by mid-1991.

The Spanish state-owned telephone company Telefónica also launched a TACS-900 system in 1990 in addition to the NMT-450 system that was launched in 1982. But the geographical coverage of the NMT network was limited for a long time. This is also the case with the TACS network. As a consequence, the user numbers were 60,000 and 13,000, respectively, in mid-1991.

In Portugal, two carriers owned by the PTT (CTT and TLP) launched analog cellular services in 1989. Portugal adopted the German Net-C-450 standard with a capacity of 10,000. With its limited coverage geographic area of Lisbon and Oporto, and very high user costs, the number of users was only 9,000 by the end of 1991 although coverage was extended to Algarve in that year. Portugal intends to license a private operator to provide GSM services in competition with the state-owned operator.

In The Netherlands and Luxembourg, state-owned operators launched NMT-450 networks in 1985 and Belgium joined with an identical system in 1987. The Netherlands PTT launched a second network based on the NMT-900 system in 1989. The Luxembourg network had less than 1,000 users, Belgium had around 45,000, and The Netherlands had 30,000 users on NMT-450 and 70,000 on NMT-900 in mid-1991. There is a well-advanced public paging network, named *Semaphone,* that covers all three countries and provided service to more than 400,000 users. GSM services are expected to be provided by the respective PTTs.

Eastern Europe

Cellular mobile services have also become important in Eastern Europe, especially as a shortcut to closing the enormous capacity and technology gap that exists in telecommunication services (Müller & Nyevrikel, 1991). In most of these countries, mobile services have hardly been used except for military and some business applications. Now a number of countries are trying to use the quick introduction of mobile services as one way to alleviate the telephone shortage, especially to aid the development of a private business sector. In 1990, Hungary (within the Budapest area) and (the former) Yugoslavia (for the Zagreb area) opened a modern analog mobile network that was expected to serve 15,000 subscribers by early 1992. In 1991 Ljubljana, Prague, Brno, Bratislava, and Warsaw followed (see Table 10.3). In the next 2 to 3 years, these networks will be extended to the most important business centers in each country. Mobile services therefore become an important access mode to the fiber optic overlay networks that are being constructed at the same time. Such networks are also being built in the CIS and the Baltic Republics. In most of these networks, Western technology and know-how enter in the form of a joint venture but also as a first step in opening up the public monopoly network to competition. A similar trend is expected for analog networks in the 900 MHz range, PCN, and paging networks.

This policy of mobile overlay networks is not only a practical way to solve the technology and capacity shortage in the short term, but it also allows a kind of tariff differentiation, not possible in most of these countries. Given the capacity shortages, access tariffs and usage tariffs should be raised significantly in the traditional networks of Eastern Europe. But instead, it is for these qualitatively better cellular mobile overlay networks that higher charges can be demanded. To some extent

TABLE 10.3   Mobile Radio Projects in Eastern Europe, 1991

Country	System	Operator	Coverage	Start
Hungary	NMT 450 MHz	*Westel*/MTV 51% Hungarian 49% U.S. West Int.	Budapest	October 1990
Hungary	890-898 MHz	HTC 50% Hungarian 50% Contel Cellular	Budapest	Postponed because of license dispute
Yugoslavia	NMT 410 MHz	Croatian PTT	Zagreb	August 1990
Yugoslavia	NMT 410 MHZ	Slovenian PTT	Ljublijana	1991
CSFR	NMT 450 MHz	MPT 51% CSFR 49% U.S. West/Bell Atlantic	Prague, Brno, Bratislava	1991
Poland	NMT 450 MHz	51% Polish PTT France Télécom 49% Ameritech	Warsaw	1991/1992
CIS	NMT 450 MHz	*Delta Telecom* 55% Petersburg City 5% Technical Radio Control 40% U.S. West Int.	Petersburg (50k capacity)	1991
CIS	NMT 450 MHz	*Moscow Cellular Net* 50% Minsviaz 8% Fyodorov's Eye Clinic 22% U.S. West Int. 20% Millicom Int.	Moscow (first of two cellular systems)	1992/1993
CIS	Radiotelephone (no hand-over, only 50 km radios)	AMT Moscow City Telephone Network/Nokia Telecom	Moscow	1990
CIS	MNT 450 MHz	*Byelorussian Cellular Network* 50% Byelorussian MoC 50% Comm Struct Int.	Byelorussia	1992
Lithuania	NMT 450 MHz	*Lithuanian Cellular Net* Lithuanian MoC/Millicom Int.	Vilnius	Planned
Estonia		*Estonian Cellular System* Estonian MoC/Telecom Finland/Swedish Telecom	Tallin	1991

SOURCE: Pyramid Research, 1991; *Communications International*, November 1991; Own research.

this policy may also be the result of a compromise on trying to delay the necessary tariff reform on the regular network. At least, it ensures for business customers' quicker access to modern and qualitatively superior communication products.

Assessment and Outlook

The technical revolution in cellular mobile services has been utilized differently in the various European nations. We have set out how important the regulatory characteristics are in this process. The attempt by the EC to encourage service growth has been essentially limited to its ability to standardize products in the GSM range and for some Europe-wide paging services. Concerning other regulatory issues in terms of ease of access, interconnection agreements, and the like, these are still in the process of being developed. The development of mobile cellular services in Europe must therefore be seen much more as a development of national systems than of Europe-wide systems. As a consequence, the performance of this system is very dispersed and indicators of price-cost margins and attractiveness of mobile services vary widely across Europe. However, regulation is not everything. The take-up of the new system depends also on how well the market for established analog wire systems, the PSTN, is developed, on per capita income, service orientation of the economy, and so on.

The most spectacular market development has been taking place in the Scandinavian countries and in the United Kingdom. The late entry and the rapid development in the United Kingdom provides an example that demonstrates that in the cellular mobile system the duopoly model can operate both practically and competitively. From an economic viewpoint, the question of network duplication does not really seem to matter because service conditions are attractive enough to guarantee a sufficient market size and competition seems to help systems exceed the minimum efficiency scale.

But as can be seen in the United Kingdom and to some extent in the countries where the development has not been successful, regulation plays a key part. It is important not only in securing a level playing field between the traditional wire carrier and the competitor but also in terms of interconnection agreements and the control over cross-subsidies from regulated to monopoly services. Regulation is also playing a crucial role in making decisions on standards, and here the EEC has been more effective than in other areas. It is important that these regulations determine not only the emergence of standards but also that quality is at an acceptable level and that national coverage is provided.

The U.K. model of vertical separation (i.e., competition both in retailing of services and between the network duopolists) seems to have contributed to the rapid expansion of cellular services. This explains both the low prices at which these services are offered in the United Kingdom and the high rates of market penetration that have been achieved. But the United Kingdom also illustrates that competition in servicing and marketing allows some differentiation in services even if both provide the same basic goods at broadly similar prices. In other words, even if the market for cellular services develops into a mass market with intense competition, as we have argued initially, it also provides interesting market niches for certain product specializations. As a consequence, the implementation of technical change will be faster and deeper in terms of market application. But the wide dispersion in national performance shows that only some countries have realized the potential embodied in the new technology.

Notes

1. Callahan (1990, p. 5) cites 1,380 U.S.$ as the cost per cellular line; the cost per line of a U.S. wireline Telco was 1,421 U.S.$; that of a European Telco 2,400 U.S.$.

2. According to the Vodafone agreement with Mercury, Mercury has to pay 20 pence (60% of what the customer pays) a minute to Vodafone for calls initiated on Mercury's network.

3. Between 1985/1986 and 1990/1991 the turnover of Vodafone increased from £10.9 million to £500.5 million and its net revenue from an initial loss of £6.0 million to an operating profit of £245.5 million. Although Cellnet's turnover was lower, it nevertheless was able to generate operating profits.

4. In addition to the 51% of shares owned by Mannesmann, the American company Pacific Telesis holds 26%, the Deutsche Bank 10%, the U.K. participant Cable and Wireless 5%, and the French company Lyonnais des Eaux 2.5%. The remaining 5.5% of shares are still held in trust.

References

Callahan, D. (1990). *Speech at the Funkschau.* Bonn, May 17, 1990.
Carrington, J. C. (1991). *Overlay applications—Economic growth and innovation.* ITU Telecom Forum, Geneva: International Telecommunication Union.

Commission of the European Communities (CEC). (1987). Towards a dynamic European economy—Green Paper on the development of the Common Market for telecommunications services and equipment. COM(87)290 final, Brussels, 30 June 1987.

Dang-Nguyen, G. (1990). *Analyzing the competitive process in a new industry: Mobile telephony.* Unpublished paper, ENST, Bretagne.

Farrell, J., & Saloner, G. (1988). Coordination through committees and markets. *RAND Journal of Economics, 19*(2), 235-252.

Foreman-Peck, J., & Müller, J. (1988). *European telecommunication organisations.* Baden-Baden, Germany: Nomos Verlagsgesellschaft.

Grindley, P., & Toker, S. (1992a) *Regulators, markets & standards coordination: Policy lessons from telepoint.* Working Paper No. 112, Centre for Business Strategy, London Business School, London.

Grindley, P., & Toker, S. (1992b). *Standards strategies for telepoint: The failure of commitment.* Working Paper No. 113, Centre for Business Strategy, London Business School, London.

Kruse, J. (1991). Ordnungspolitische Probleme der Mobilfunk-Liberalisierung. *Hamburger Jahrbuch für Wirtschafts- und Gesellschaftspolitik.* Hamburg, Germany.

Mobile Communications. (1991, July 18). London: Fintech.

Müller, J. (1991) The European internal market for telecommunications. *European Economic Review, 35.*

Müller, J., & Nyevrikel, E. (1991). *Closing the capacity and technology gap in East European telecommunication services.* ITU European Regional Telecommunication Development Conference (EU-RDC), Prague 1991.

Thompson, D., & Toker, S. (1991). *The development of mobile communications in the U.K: Competition and regulation in cellular phones.* Working Paper No. 117, Centre for Business Strategy, London Business School, London.

Toker, S. (1992). *Mobile communications in the 1990s: Opportunities and pitfalls.* Centre for Business Strategy, London Business School, London.

Ungerer, H. (1991). *Mobile communications—A Europe-wide market.* Funkschau Kongreß: Mobile Communications in Germany, May 1991.

ELEVEN

Multinational Organizations and International Private Networks

Opportunities and Constraints

ROBIN MANSELL

The networking strategies of multinational firms are central features of the global economy. Firms whose production facilities and markets span the boundaries of geographical regions and countries now regard networking as an essential component of their technological and business strategies. In the 1990s, the *network firm* is a model toward which companies in Japan, the United States, and the European Community aspire.

The network firm, with its myriad of intra-firm and external organizational linkages, has come to be regarded as an increasingly viable form of industrial organization (Antonelli, 1988; DeBresson & Amesse, 1991). The dynamics of the network relationships that sustain globally trading firms are coming under closer scrutiny in the domains of organizational theory, information economics, and telecommunication (Mansell & Jenkins, 1992). Although these relationships may refer to virtually any form of information exchange and communication among individuals, groups, and institutions, the centrality of telecommunication services as a means of providing the means for more rapid and ever less costly communication has provided a focus for much recent debate as to the future viability of this increasingly predominant form of organization. Firms that are able to integrate the use of advanced telecommunication services within their overall business strategy are

AUTHOR'S NOTE: An extended version of sections of this chapter was presented at the 41st International Communication Association Conference, Chicago, 23-27 May 1991.

widely believed to have a greater likelihood of achieving sustainable competitive advantage in the marketplace.

The ideal network firm requires substantially more than investment in telecommunication (and computer) networks. It involves choices as to the organization of the telecommunication infrastructure to support public and private network development as well as user participation in the policy formulation and changes in the regulatory environment (Bar & Borrus, 1989). Most important, it requires a good match between the company's information requirements and the service applications that are available from internal private networks, public telecommunication operators (PTOs), and a growing number of third-party service suppliers.

This chapter examines the use of advanced business communication services by a sample of multinational firms in Europe. The main focus is on the firms' requirements for high-capacity broadband networks and their applications in the automobile, financial services, and electronics sectors. Variations in demand for advanced networking capability are considered within the context of European Community initiatives to stimulate the growth of public and private network-based services.[1]

Policies for Advanced European Networking

In 1987, the Commission of the European Communities published a Green Paper on Telecommunications (Commission, 1987). This discussion paper set in train a continuing process of restructuring and liberalization of the European telecommunication environment. European Community directives have been put in place to stimulate competition and innovation in terminal and network supply and to encourage the use of advanced service applications. Changes in network access conditions, pricing, standards, and interconnection have raised controversy among the member states of the Community as well as among suppliers and users (Scherer, 1991).

Despite these initiatives, a pan-European telecommunication infrastructure has yet to emerge that is fully responsive to business demand for cross-border advanced telecommunication services. In January 1990, the Council of the European Communities adopted a resolution to the effect that "special priority should be given . . . to the development and interconnection of trans-European networks, . . . in particular the linking of the main Community conurbations by broadband telecommunications networks" (Commission, 1990). In April 1991, the Commission reinforced its belief that telecommunication development is critical to European industrial policy. Among the proposed actions were those directed to increasing demand for computerized telecommunication links and to strengthening production capability in key information technologies.

Computerized telecommunication links between administrations should be set up as quickly as possible and a high level of interoperability of their information systems achieved, . . . projects might relate to the gradual introduction of broadband services networks. . . . Such projects should cover software . . . high-performance computing and telecommunications. (Commission, 1991a)

The momentum for the Commission's continuing attempts to alleviate fragmentation among the Community's telecommunication markets arises partly from the growing gap between the use of advanced services by European and United States firms. Although demand for business data services is growing in Europe at a rate of about 30% per year, public carrier data revenues were estimated only at about 5 billion ECU for 1989. Equivalent revenues reached about 10 billion ECU for private networks and 15 billion for PTOs in the United States in the same year (Commission, 1991b). The data communication market represented a full 20% of U.S. carrier revenues in 1989, but it accounted for only 5% of European PTO revenues in 1989 (Commission, 1991b).

To reduce this gap on the supplier and user side, a number of initiatives are under discussion. For example, the Conference of European Posts and Telecommunications reached preliminary agreement in October 1990 to establish METRAN, a transmission network independent of specific services comprising digital cross-border transmission links. This overlay network could become operational by 1998. In the interim, British Telecom, German Telekom, France Télécom, STET, and Telefonica have announced a 34 Mbit/s fiber backbone called General European Network (GEN), which would provide interim broadband linkages. Another potential provider of a broadband European infrastructure is the Hermes consortium, which includes 11 European railroads, Daimler-Benz, and Compagnie de Suez.

In addition, network management offerings by PTOs increasingly involve the lease of private circuits from other PTOs in order to launch "end-to-end" services. The objective is to compete with services offered by AT&T Istel, U.S. Sprint, Cable and Wireless, Infonet (MCI), IBM, EDS, and GEISCO British Telecom is offering Synchordia, a service that is intended to eliminate user problems in communicating across international boundaries. Like other companies who see themselves as major global players, British Telecom hopes to reach agreements with other operators such as Telekom (Germany), France Télécom, and NTT to enable them to provide seamless "one stop" services.

Although these and other initiatives are being discussed and even implemented, it is not clear that they will effectively stimulate the development of secure, fast, and flexible network systems in Europe. The availability of the technical infrastructure is not a sufficient condition to stimulate the more rapid diffusion of advanced communication services (Leahey & Taylor, 1990). Other preconditions must be met in the telecommunication policy environment. Beyond the scope of this chapter are the difficult issues concerning network interconnection and interoperability, the measurement of relevant costs of network operation and use, and the pricing and terms and conditions of access to the network infrastructure once it is in place. In those telecommunication environments characterized by relatively more liberalized regimes such as the United States and the United Kingdom, the resolution of these issues has come to be recognized as essential to the promotion of incentives for the innovative application of advanced telecommunication service applications.

Communicating Across European Borders

This section examines the opportunities and barriers confronted by multinational firms as they attempt to exploit the potential of new networking technologies in Europe. Although there is little doubt that competitive advantage can be derived from innovative telecommunication strategies, the experiences of some of the world's most sophisticated users suggests that such solutions are complex. To realize the potential of new network applications, firms must integrate telecommunication services with the organization of all facets of the production process.

The willingness of a firm to adopt advanced business communication services is affected by its internal organization, the mix and timing of investment in computing and telecommunication technologies, and the telecommunication supply and regulatory environment (Morgan & Davies, 1990). Telecommunication networking based on a variety of public and private network alternatives is no panacea for weaknesses in technological or business strategy. Nevertheless, firms that are disadvantaged by weaknesses in the telecommunication supply environment will find it increasingly difficult to match the speed and quality of information exchange of their competitors who have located their operations in more supportive environments.

The strategies of multinational firms in the automobile, financial services, and electronics sector provide a glimpse of the linkages between multinational organizational strategies and the use of telecommunication (Mansell & Morgan, 1991). The following analysis of recent trends is based on a multinational survey of the perspectives of some of the largest users of telecommunication services that are based in Europe.[2] In-depth interviews were conducted with company directors, managers, and engineers responsible for telecommunication operations, network services planning, data processing functions, manufacturing automation, and international communication services. In this study, 21 firms in the automobile, electronics, financial services, banking and insurance, aerospace, and petroleum sectors were selected with operations or home offices in France, Germany, The Netherlands, the United Kingdom, and Canada. Firms were selected on the basis of their willingness to cooperate with interviewers over a relatively lengthy period and to provide information subject to publication in the public domain. The following depicts a subset of the results. The sample of firms was selected to provide a snapshot of the strategies of firms in mid-1990. Although no claim can be made to formal representativeness of the sample, the firms are recognized as being among those large actors in Europe for whom international telecommunication must play an increasingly important role.

A structured series of interviews was carried out primarily to ascertain perspectives on the likely short- and medium-term demand for broadband telecommunication capacity.[3] Questions addressed the linkages between corporate competitiveness and advanced communication strategies, the requirements for telecommunication in support of internal organizational functions and links with suppliers and customers, the range of high speed data and digital video applications under development or foreseen within a 5-year period, the growth potential for international broadband capacity, and the nature and severity of obstacles to advanced global business communication.[4]

The Automobile Sector

The predominant trend in the world automobile industry is the emergence of a new production paradigm often referred to as *lean production*.

This production style is being driven by the Japanese automobile firms, for example, Toyota, Nissan, and Honda, and it appears to be superior to traditional mass production strategies. Lean production is associated with radically different ways of organizing the process of production especially with respect to design, manufacturing, procurement, and distribution.

The Japanese lead in the design and development process is considerable. On average, Japanese companies need 43 months to move a product from paper concept to the consumer. Their Western counterparts need an average of 62 months (Womack et al., 1990). Time-economies at the manufacturing stage have been achieved not through massive investment in automation and information technology but by reorganizing the flow of work through the plant, for example, by minimizing downtime. Even without real-time electronic information systems, Japanese companies have created a responsive and flexible manufacturing process.

Although the Japanese *kanban* (ordering) system was late to utilize information technology, it is now adding this to a system that has been tuned to near-perfection. On the distribution side, the retailers are much larger and more sophisticated in Japan than in Europe. They are more interactive both upstream (with the manufacturers) and downstream (with consumers). The Japanese system can deliver customer-specified orders within 10 days, whereas the average for European companies is estimated to be 3 months (Mansell & Morgan, 1991).

Although the Japanese have been late compared to Ford and General Motors in utilizing telecommunication, they have shown that other forms of networking and information flow, such as face-to-face, can deliver enormous advantages. In the future as their operations straddle the globe, they will resort to more sophisticated forms of telecommunication networking.

To counter the strength of Japanese firms in the automobile sector, American-owned firms based in Europe have adopted strategies that rely heavily on private and public networks. For example, *Ford of Europe* aims to reduce design to conception from 60 to 48 months and to improve quality. The company's plants are linked to a private network that enables sharing of design and manufacturing information. Most of the links in the European network operate at 2 Mbit/s. On the supplier and distribution side, the company relies primarily on European Public-Switched Telephone Networks (PSTN), which in 1990 generally did not support 2 Mbit/s speeds across national borders. The company foresees the integration of applications and bandwidth sharing as the path toward optimal use of its networks.

General Motors Europe (GM) depends on its wholly owned subsidiary Electronic Data Systems (EDS) to meet its telecommunication needs. Although GM and EDS Europe believe that improvements to design and manufacturing are crucial to competitiveness, EDS is concentrating on upgrading distribution and service networks. The company is considering the use of two-way satellite communication to meet its bandwidth requirements. The forerunner of this system is the one-way GM Automotive Satellite Television Network that has been implemented in the United States. The system creates a strong demand for sporadic transmission over high-capacity networks. The company has made less headway in the development and use of videoconferencing than its rival, Ford. For example, in 1990, GM Europe had only begun to experiment with a 1.544 Mbit/s link to carry voice and data traffic between its operations in the United Kingdom and Germany. Complementing the company's satellite network for distribution and sales is a plan to establish a 2 Mbit/s network to support design and production.

The Financial Services Sector

One of the most important changes in the financial services sector is the trend towards deregulation. The emergence of a more liberal regulatory regime in the OECD countries is encouraging banks to diversify into securities, insurance, and a wide array of related financial services. This has permitted other financial institutions to take on some of the roles that have traditionally been performed by banks. The main strategic issue with which the banks have had to contend is Third World debt. However, as a result of the tens of billions worth of provisions that have been made over recent years, most banks have overcome this danger.

Two other strategic issues remain to be faced. Deregulation and new technology are threatening to make the financial services sector more contestable than it has been in the past. The European Commission's liberalization program has three main components: to encourage the free flow of capital by removing exchange controls; to promote free trade in financial services; and to encourage greater standardization of banking technology across Europe so as to promote interoperability.

Despite these changes, only modest restructuring has appeared thus far. Many banks expect to see few changes in the corporate and wholesale markets because they are already highly internationalized. Furthermore, few major changes are expected at the opposite end of the market—in retail banking—where the national character of personal banking remains pronounced.

There has been a flurry of transnational activity among smaller banks as they seek partners to expand their geographic reach and to develop jointly marketed products. Within countries such as Italy, Denmark, and The Netherlands, there has been a clear process of concentration. However, the emergence of a pan-European retail bank continues to be an open question because economies of scale that can be exploited by large partnership arrangements may be offset by local knowledge on the part of domestic banks.

The European Commission is moving to establish technical standards to encourage Europe-wide use of automatic teller machines (ATMs) and electronic funds transfer at point of sale (EFTPOS). One of the aims is to tilt the balance of competitive forces toward smaller financial institutions that could have difficulty competing because of the limited reach of their networks. If small institutions can access the ATMs of their larger rivals, this may prevent them from being marginalized by the expansion of electronic banking.

Nevertheless, smaller financial institutions will find it difficult to keep up with developments in computerized communication. In the 1990s, the major players will resort to new technical solutions, including supercomputers, fault-tolerant network systems, and image processing. The aim is to cut the costs of processing information and to develop new differentiated services.

In the financial services sector a different set of telecommunication strategies is emerging. For example, *Citibank/Citicorp,* with its worldwide headquarters in the United States and its European base in the United Kingdom—the most liberalized of the European Community telecommunication markets—provides a basis for judging the extent to which broadband communication is integral to the global and European strategies of financial and related service companies.

Citicorp claims to operate as if there were no frontiers between the European Community countries. The company's network supports internal operations with international fixed-link connections. These are supported by 64 Kbit/s to 256 Kbit/s links. Only within the United Kingdom does the network comprise 2 Mbit/s links.

The availability of higher-capacity links can create conditions for the introduction of advanced services. For example, Citicorp has established "processing factories" that centralize the company's financial operations. Most of these have been located in the United Kingdom because of the liberalized telecommunication market and the relatively attractive tariff structure for leased circuits. For customer services, Citicorp has built a network to support the Citicorp Customer Access Terminal (CAT) and for the volume and speed of traffic generated by the CAT network, 64 Kbit/s lines are considered adequate.

As of the end of 1990, Citicorp had not introduced videoconferencing on a Europe-wide basis but had plans to transfer experience acquired in the United States to the United Kingdom, and later to Germany and Belgium. The company believes that there are no applications that require transborder links at speeds greater than 2 Mbit/s. However, the use of faster links could result from the accumulation of lower bandwidth traffic.

Reuters is one of the world's leading providers of news and information services. It offers real-time information services, transaction products, trading room systems, databases, and media products. In 1989, the information carried on its global networks reached 194,000 terminals in 127 countries. Reuters encourages close links between its telecommunication strategy and its core products. The company is moving toward an Integrated Data Network that will interconnect its previously separate networks.

In Europe, the network is comprised mainly of fixed links running at speeds of 14.4 to 64 Kbit/s. Much faster links have begun to be introduced at speeds up to 1024 Kbit/s, and a few run at 2 Mbit/s. An overlay satellite network runs at speeds up to 168 Kbit/s.

Although, in 1990, Reuters did not foresee an immediate demand for additional broadband links, requirements for higher bandwidth are likely to be driven by services such as Globex (a computer-based system for international electronic trading) and multimedia service delivery. Although the company foresees the development of business television (specialist television services) that could require bandwidth at about 10 Mbit/s, it does not believe the technology is sufficiently developed.

Reuters has been willing to challenge regulatory barriers. For this company, regulation is regarded as one of the least problematic areas in running transnational networks. Nevertheless, Reuters sees an urgent need for better liaison between telecommunication operators to support transnational communication services. The Single European Market is not expected to affect Reuters' business, but the removal of trade barriers could affect the location and pattern of stock market trading and banking. This could result in concentration on a few European exchanges and increased pressures to ensure that PTOs respond to the company's demand for high-speed international links.

The *Amsterdam-Rotterdam (AMRO)* and *NMB Postbank Group* in The Netherlands illustrate variations in the telecommunication strategies that are likely to emerge in different financial market segments. The AMRO bank serves large corporate clients and has moved into treasury management services for its international clients. Despite its highly internationalized profile and its domestic use of telecommunication links at speeds of up to 144 Kbit/s, internationally, the bank's internal Amronet operates at speeds below 2 Mbit/s. Although broadband capacity is needed for connections between data centers, most of this activity is contained within national networks.

Within The Netherlands, AMRO's network supports 64 Kbit/s channels in a 2 Mbit/s backbone. In 1990, treasury as well as telebanking services and the need for increased interbranch communication were expected to lead to increased traffic volumes. Nevertheless, the company maintains that international traffic does not really require broadband capacity. The bank sees one area, merchant banking, as a driver of increased capacity in transnational networks. Even in this area, however, interactive computing between host and distance computers is believed to be served well by 2 Mbit/s connections.

Like the AMRO bank, the NMB Postbank is not overly concerned about the need to stimulate the availability of pan-European broadband communication networks. NMB serves a mix of national private customers and smaller firms and believes that most of its future applications (including digital imaging processing centers) are unlikely to require connections in excess of 2 Mbit/s in the short term. The company believes that it is possible to become a regional bank without high-speed/high-volume data connections. NMB Postbank sees interconnection between international dealing rooms as the main driving force that will lead to pressure to increase speed and bandwidth.

Two banks and an insurance company in Germany have more progressive views as to the timing and application of broadband networks. However, their plans are being developed mainly for the domestic market. The links between internationalization and telecommunication strategy are especially clear in the case of *Colonia Insurance*. German insurers have comparatively little business abroad. Only 5% of the premium income of German insurers stems from foreign countries. In contrast, British insurers raise about 30% of their income in foreign markets and the French, approximately 10%.

Colonia Insurance has been relatively advanced in its development of data networking applications within the German market. As a co-founder of the network service vendor MEGANET, Colonia could be well placed to pursue its strategy of expansion into new local and regional markets. Although the network operates at 64 Kbit/s, 2 Mbit/s connections are planned.

A local or national perspective also prevails in the *Dresdner Bank* and *Commerzbank*. The Dresdner Bank has a strong international orientation and is pursuing a process of forging joint ventures, particularly in France. Dresdner Bank uses SWIFT for transnational transactions and GEISCO in support of international risk management. However, this bank believes that its interbank communication needs are very small. The Commerzbank has operated an international network since 1983, but its branches in the United Kingdom, France, Spain, Luxembourg, The Netherlands, and Belgium are connected by circuits running at 9.6 Kbit/s. The link between Frankfurt and New York operates at 64 Kbit/s.

Both banks regard network security as a paramount aspect of their business strategies. Time and speed of network transmission are secondary considerations. Although neither puts image processing and video-conferencing at the forefront of its plans, both would use broadband connections to support international services if costs were reduced.

The Electronics Sector

The electronics sector embraces five main industries: telecommunications, data processing, semiconductors, capital equipment, and consumer goods. Despite the argument that technological convergence is eroding the boundaries between these industries, their markets continue to reflect their own nuances. As a result, strategies that have sought to exploit convergence (between telecommunications and data processing, for example) have proven rather unsuccessful. Nevertheless, firms in the electronics sector face the common problem of how to deal with the globalization of markets. This problem is most pronounced in telecommunications and capital equipment, as in the defense industry.

In the telecommunications industry, firms are attempting to establish a direct presence in their major markets. The co-location of production and marketing is deemed essential if telecommunications equipment suppliers are to achieve credibility in the eyes of foreign telecommunication operators. This is especially the case in the digital exchange business where close buyer-supplier relations are a necessity. This creates problems with respect to the coordination of R&D, production, and marketing at a transnational level.

Equally challenging is the trend toward shorter product life cycles. This phenomenon is most acute in the data processing industry where the life cycle of some products has declined to as little as 6 months. Firms are being compelled to abbreviate product development cycles, a challenge that Japanese firms have mastered to a greater degree than their Western rivals. Japanese consumer electronics firms are able to bring 2 to 3 times as many products to the market in half the time required by their Western competitors.

Another strategic priority in this sector is the creation of stronger supply chains. The upstream chain linking component suppliers with the electronics manufacturer is being recast to support long-term, high-trust partnerships. The downstream chain between the electronics manufacturer and the final customer is the most critical interface. In the professional electronics markets, software-intensive systems are becoming more important than stand-alone products. Buyers require much more "hand-holding," and logistics systems, such as distribution and the after-sales effort, are growing in importance.

Corporate strategies with respect to globalized markets, product development, and supplier relations are key determinants of success and failure in the electronics sector. Each requires sophisticated communication at both intra-corporate and inter-corporate levels. Within Europe there is a growing trend toward rationalization of capacity. American and Japanese firms appear to be ahead of their European counterparts in achieving a pan-European organizational structure.

In the electronics sector, Siemens and Philips are highly internationalized. Although, Grundig has a less global orientation in the consumer electronics market, these firms have felt the pressure of competition and the need to respond to the challenges of the Single European Market.

Siemens is a pacemaker in high-technology development and boasts a comprehensive product range. Its transnational networking began with the Siekom network in the 1970s. This has evolved into a complex mixture of subnetworks, but in mid-1990 the highest transmission speed was a 2 Mbit/s line that connected Munich and Vienna. Connections between approximately 600 Local Area Networks and internal networks are established only within Germany and many of these support CAD/CAM production "islands." Plans for the 1990s include a Siemens Corporate Network that will interconnect in-house networks using an X.25 packet network running at speeds between 64 Kbit/s and 2 Mbit/s.

Thus, despite the fact that Siemens is a producer of advanced telecommunication technology, it has yet to extend broadband (>2 Mbit/s) links beyond its national boundaries.

The factors that have slowed the development of higher-capacity networks include costs, the unpredictability of tariffs, and the absence of interface standards. Cultural differences in patterns of work and organization are also believed to suppress the international extension of high-capacity in-house applications.

Grundig's use of broadband connections is similar to Siemens', that is, at the end of 1990 it was using capacity running at 1.92 Mbit/s. This was limited to the interconnection of separate operations in the domestic headquarters and Vienna. The company's telecommunication requirements are being driven by the continuing automation of its production, the need to achieve tighter coordination of R&D, production processes, logistics, and increased cooperation with Japanese firms. This is expected to lead to substantially greater use of videoconferencing, high speed fax, and a variety of other applications. Although CAD/CAM will generate a need for transmission at speeds well in excess of 2 Mbit/s, the company has not yet considered establishing linkages between Local Area Networks in different countries.

In The Netherlands, *Philips*' priority is the development of CAD/CAM and Computer Integrated Manufacturing (CIM) using Local Area Networks, and there is a long-term interest in international CAD. Philips is a producer of 2.4 Gbit/s cross-connect switches, but as a user, it has no 2 Mbit/s links in operation between its sites. Several applications are expected to stimulate demand for higher-capacity connections. These include online administrative tasks, funds transfer applications, PC to PC connections, and the need to achieve higher levels of security and to provide internal redundancy.

Business and Telecommunication Strategies

Some of the firms examined in the foregoing section believe it is necessary to move quickly to introduce advanced business communication to support a regional or global business strategy. Others believe that technologies and applications must be developed more fully before they can be implemented.

These different perspectives are influenced by the extent to which competition—or its threat—has stimulated the firms to look to telecommunication as a means of reorganizing their operations. The firms that believe themselves to be least affected by the policy and regulatory environment include those that have operated on a global scale for some time and those that have yet to feel the pressures of transformations stemming from the implementation of the Single European Market. Perspectives also differ as a reflection of the distinctive characteristics of manufacturing operations and services.

Even where traffic growth and new applications are recognized as potential sources of productivity gains, the domestic telecommunication supply structure and the regulatory environment affect perceptions of the optimal rate of network development. For example, firms that have experienced the effects of the U.K. removal of restrictions on the use of leased circuits and the interconnection of private- and public-switched networks have implemented a wider variety of applications than those in other European countries.

In spite of the regulatory differences that continue to exist throughout the European Community, differences in the structure of national telecommunication markets, and sector and firm specific communication requirements, there is considerable commonality in the views of multinational firms on the major barriers to advanced telecommunication networking in Europe.

Multinational firms regard tariffs as a major inhibiting factor. The high cost of increased capacity to support international links prevents them from taking advantage of wider bandwidth unless traffic volumes and applications justify the increased costs. Firms also cite the inflexibility of PTOs and the lack of predictability of tariff structures as major factors that restrain demand.

The absence of coordinated planning by PTOs to provide circuits operating at higher speeds is a concern echoed by many firms. However, there are exceptions among firms that have traditionally operated as global players and have established strong negotiating positions with the PTOs. The absence of one-stop shopping, for example, reciprocal billing arrangements and network management, is often described as a barrier to the extension of international service applications. In addition, restrictions on voice and data integration in several European Community countries frequently prevent integration between public and private networks.

Another factor in the telecommunications environment that limits investment in advanced networks is the availability of appropriate skills. This affects decisions as to whether to develop in-house training schemes or to acquire network management expertise from PTOs or a third-party supplier. Some European firms also regard technical heterogeneity and the absence of standards and gateways for international connections as major barriers.

Network Systems and Organizational Strategy

The networking strategies of multinational firms are linked to information, to organizational processes and the diffusion of advanced telecommunication networks. Telecommunication networks can improve information flow among firms and, depending on their design and exclusivity, they may contribute gains through a strengthened ability to appropriate information. But there is nothing inherent in the hardware and software components of a telecommunication network that produces more productive information exchange. In fact, increased problems for coordination and control often arise alongside the benefits of more flexible networks.

Although the *network firm* is an increasingly accurate description of today's multinational company, the implications for management decision making and internal and external organization are difficult to assess. The primary reason is that telecommunications affect all aspects of the structure and performance of a firm. The benefits and costs of networks can be contradictory and the expected gains in productivity and competitiveness are not always apparent.

The experiences of multinational firms in their home markets must be translated into strategies that successfully weave together cultural, political, economic, and technical conditions. Multinational telecommunication users are concerned with three main issues when they consider their transnational telecommunication needs. First, they expect cost efficiency in infrastructure and services; second, they expect to achieve an optimal organization of internal and external communications; and finally, they expect to be able to manage and control networks by relying on in-house expertise or by opting for third-party supply and the alternatives offered by the PTOs.

The potential of new service applications is not always captured by the individual firm. Experience shows that the evolution of telecommunications strategies involves risk taking and learning to establish a "good fit" between a firm's relationships with its partners, suppliers, and customers; its internal and external information flows; and the technical facets of its network applications.

Within the European Community, representatives of multinational telecommunications users are becoming more influential in shaping policy and regulatory issues that affect the development of public and private networks. The International Telecommunications Users Group (INTUG) includes individuals whose main task is to monitor discussions on the restructuring of telecommunication and equipment markets. These representatives appear regularly in seminars and conferences addressed to these issues and are fully informed about changes in policies and proposed directives at the European Community level. INTUG also works closely with nationally based users groups such as the Telecommunications Managers Association in the United Kingdom.

In addition, as the standards-setting process within Europe under the auspices of the European Telecommunications Standards Institute (ETSI) becomes an increasingly important force in evolution of both private and public networks, larger users are involving themselves in working groups that are tackling problems of interconnection, pricing, billing, and other issues critical to the extension of nationally based networks (Hawkins, 1991). These activities require the commitment of time and resources and it is clear that small- and medium-sized firms are underrepresented in their ability to influence policy and regulatory developments.

Furthermore, the increasing focus on the strengthening of regional telecommunication networks, whether in Europe or in the United States, has led many to question whether sufficient consideration is being given to the development of infrastructure within domestic markets that meets the needs not only of the globally active multinational but also of the smaller firms and residential users of telecommunications. Organizations acting primarily on behalf of residential consumers have contributed to debates on the liberalization of the European telecommunications market, especially in the United Kingdom and at the European Community level.

Conclusion

The multinational firms in Europe are confronting a variety of opportunities as a result of rapid technical change in telecommunication and the liberalization of equipment and service markets. But they are also encountering country-, sector-, and firm-specific barriers. Many of these are a reflection of their competitive positioning in global and regional markets (Imai & Baba, 1989).

For multinationals operating in Europe, the barriers to competitiveness are partly organizational, but these are exacerbated by differences in the telecommunications environment. Nevertheless, telecommunications liberalization and advanced technologies will not by themselves deliver solutions to business communication requirements. Greater attention to the learning processes needed to integrate the use of telecommunications networking with other strategic objectives (Ciborra, 1990) will be required to enable Europe-based firms to catch up with their American counterparts.

Organizational learning is a sequential process and institutional and regulatory conditions differ substantially between Europe and the United States. It is unlikely that increased investment to stimulate the growth of European networking or continued liberalization of European telecommunication markets will, by themselves, stimulate convergence in patterns of telecommunications networking in the two regions. The longer history of experimentation with advanced telecommunication systems in the United States and opportunities to learn through failure, as well as success, have given American firms an edge over their European counterparts. Whether steps taken by the Commission of the European Communities will be sufficient to overcome this disadvantage is an open question. However, the evidence suggests that the Europe-based multinationals are developing innovative ways of coping with a less open and competitive telecommunications environment.

Notes

1. These data are based on estimates provided to the Commission of the European Communities by a consortium of investigators led by Technology Investment Partners, Paris, in a report to the Commission (Commission, 1991b).

2. This section draws substantially on Mansell & Morgan (1991). Supporting case studies were contributed by G. Thomas (Science Policy Research Unit, University of Sussex, United Kingdom), R. van Tulder (University of Amsterdam, The Netherlands), V. Schneider (Max Planck Institut, Germany), and G. Dang-Nguyen (ENST, France) and are reported in detail in the same work.

3. In order to establish a common, if arbitrary, baseline for distinctions to be drawn between *broadband* and *narrowband* telecommunication capacity, circuit capacity capable of supporting 2 Mbit/s or above was treated as broadband—roughly the European E1 circuit and the equivalent North American T1 circuit. More generally, *broadband* was taken to mean the "high end" (in terms of bit rate) portion of the services and also designates the total mix of services to be considered, starting from the "upper end" of ISDN (e.g., including 2 Mbit/s access) and continuing up to what will be required by a

realistic introduction of video (interactive and distributive) services (e.g., 140 Mbit/s) (see Commission, 1989).

4. The analysis and synthesis of a large body of interview material was undertaken by each national investigator (see Note 2) and by the project coordinator at the Science Policy Research Unit, University of Sussex. Results were presented to a public forum sponsored by the Commission of the European Communities and to all firms participating in the study in order to ensure accuracy in the interpretation of the data. All firms participating in the study agreed to publication of the views incorporated in Mansell and Morgan (1991).

References

Antonelli, C. (1988). *New information technology and industrial change*. London: Kluwer.

Bar, F., & Borrus, M. (1989). *Information networks and competitive advantage* (Vol. 1: Issues for government policy and corporate strategy development). Berkeley Roundtable on the International Economy, OECD, CEC/DGXIII, October.

Ciborra, C. U. (1990). *Alliances as learning experiments: Cooperation, competition and change in the high-tech industries*. Paper presented at 8th Conference of the International Telecommunication Society, Venice, March.

Commission of the European Communities. (1987). *Towards a dynamic European economy: Green paper on the development of the common market for telecommunication services and equipment*. COM(87)290 final, Brussels.

Commission of the European Communities. (1989). *Perspectives for advanced communications in Europe: Impact assessment and forecasts related to integrated broadband communications* (Vol. 2: PACE '89). Brussels: Commission of the European Communities, November.

Commission of the European Communities. (1990). *Towards trans-European networks—Proposal for a Community action programme*. COM(90)585 final, Brussels.

Commission of the European Communities. (1991a). *The European electronics and information technology industry: State of play, issues at stake and proposals for action*. SEC(91)565 final, Brussels, 3 April.

Commission of the European Communities. (1991b). *Perspectives on Advanced Communications for Europe, PACE '90* (Vols. 1 and 3). Commission of the European Communities: Brussels, February.

DeBresson, C., & Amesse, F. (1991). Networks of innovators—A review and introduction to the issue. *Research Policy, 20*, 363-79.

Hawkins, R. (1991). *Standards and the art of fortress building: Regional power structures and technical regulations for telecommunication*. Paper presented at the 41st International Communication Association Conference, Chicago, 23-27 May.

Imai, K., & Baba, Y. (1989). *Systemic innovation and cross-border networks*. Paper presented at the OECD International Seminar on Science, Technology and Economic Growth, Paris, 4-8 June.

Leahey, S. G., & Taylor, J. R. (1990). *Telecommunication network-based services and organizational strategy—the TELNETS project*. Report prepared for the Canadian Workplace Automation Research Center (CWARC), Montreal, August.

Mansell, R., & Jenkins, M. (1992). Networks and policy: Interfaces, theories and research. *Communications & Strategies, 5*(1), 31-50.

Mansell, R., & Morgan, K. (1991, February). Communicating across boundaries: The winding road to broadband networking. In Commission of the European Communities (Ed.), *Perspectives on Advanced Communications for Europe, PACE '90* (Vol. 7). Brussels: Commission of the European Communities.

Morgan, K., & Davies, A. (1990). *Seeking advantage from telecommunications: Regulatory innovation and corporate information networks in the UK*. CICT Working Paper No. 10, Science Policy Research Unit, Brighton, July.

Scherer, J. (1991). European telecommunications law. In A. P. Meijboom & C. Prins (Eds.), *The law of information technology in Europe 1992* (pp. 225-242). Deventer-Boston: Kluwer Law and Taxation Publishers.

Womack, J., Jones, D., & Roos, D. (1990). *The machine that changed the world*. New York: Rawson Associates.

ISDN
A European Prospect

JACQUES ARLANDIS

To put into perspective the introduction of ISDN in different European countries is no easy matter. At first glance, some points of convergence in national projects can be detected. A more in-depth look, however, exhibits many different experiences, rationales, and national strategies. Although 26 European parties from 20 countries have signed an ISDN-Memorandum of Understanding (ISDN-MOU) envisioning a widespread, interconnected ISDN across European countries, diversity remains a main feature for the European landscape. In this chapter, I first describe the current situation and then discuss the ISDN policy background for Europe.

Service Concept

According to CCITT terminology, ISDN is a "network originating from the integrated digital phone network (IDN), providing a digital connection from one end to the other in order to supply a large amount of services including voice and data services which the users access through a limited number of standardized and changeable user interfaces." This means that the ISDN supply can be characterized by (a) the end-to-end digital connection; (b) an integrated access to multimedia services; and (c) a limited number of standards accessible in the whole world.

In spite of the CCITT ISDN definition, the real content of ISDN varies from one country to another. These differences are particularly evident in the supply of 64 Kbit/s services without digital continuity; the supply of 384 Kbit/s services, being particularly dedicated to video-communications; the access to packet network services; and the access to leased-lines.

For example, in France it was not possible from the beginning to access the 384 Kbit/s service. In the United Kingdom, there is no link between the packet network and the ISDN. In France, the ISDN is considered as a very highly performing switched network intended to meet public service goals. Such a network should be available on a universal basis to any kind of customer in similar economic conditions, be it a small or big company and independent of the location. In the United Kingdom, ISDN will be much more considered as a new way to transmit data, although it could also be used to transmit images (but to a small extent). In Germany, ISDN is (slowly) being developed in a spirit of universal service, essentially able to transmit voice and data.

Substitute or complementary services do exist for most services ISDN will supply because ISDN is mainly an enhanced network, pro-viding larger facilities to transmit different kinds of input. PSTN, data networks, and private networks will therefore compete with ISDN for the transmission of voice and data. For some types of input, such as still images, however, it is likely that ISDN will prove the most interesting telecommunication medium. Apart from the general options described above, the two main kinds of differences, which will make ISDN look different in the different countries where it is being launched, are the issue of subscriber termination and the use of the D-channel in order to transmit user-to-user signaling.

If ISDN is to be used as an intelligent network, then it is important that access to the D-channel in order to transmit user-to-user signaling be left to operators other than the national carriers, so that they can organize their intelligent network as they like. In countries where competitive market access conditions exist, it is likely that access to this semaphore channel will be authorized. In other countries, national carriers will want to retain the control of this channel, arguing that they are doing so to protect the security and integrity of the network.

As far as the issue of network termination standards is concerned, the separation occurs between the United States and Europe (at the time of this writing, Japan rather shares the European views but could move closer to U.S. interpretations if American pressure mounts up). The digital network termination can be viewed as a "box" linking the T-interface (at the user's premises, on the user side) and the U-interface (at the user's premises, on the public network side). The European carriers want to supply the subscribers up to the T-interface; on the contrary, the U.S. authorities forbade the carriers to supply their subscribers with this T-interface, limiting their role in the provision of the network up to the U-interface, in order to maintain free competition at the level of end-terminals. Such differentiated positions may greatly influence the development of ISDN in some countries (particularly in the United States) but also worldwide.

Entry Strategies

ISDN really started being marketed on a commercial basis in most European countries in 1990, and there is basically the same range of subscribers in these countries. However, ISDN was introduced in different ways in the different countries, and does not supply exactly the same services from one country to the other.

In France, where ISDN has probably been the most strongly promoted by the national carrier, ISDN is intended to replace the PSTN sooner or later and thus supply voice and data. Because France Télécom also wanted to take advantage of the higher sophistication of ISDN, it is also probably one of the national carriers that invested the heaviest in the development of new innovative applications (relying on image transmission, for example). Germany seems to have the same kind of general aim (making ISDN a voice and data transmission service) but is more interested in ISDN as a transition toward broadband networks than in ISDN for its own sake; the Deutsche Bundespost Telekom therefore made fewer efforts to promote the development and marketing of ISDN. In the United Kingdom, ISDN development will essentially depend on British Telecom; however, the former monopoly does not consider ISDN as more than a means of data transmission and wants to let the market decide how much and to what extent it wants ISDN.

France is characterized by the strong will of its national carrier, France Télécom, to introduce ISDN on a broad national basis. This produces aggressive actions: partnerships with organizations willing to subscribe to ISDN, standard promotion, and even the imposition of a supply of services resorting to ISDN. Besides, France Télécom positioned ISDN as a universal network allowing it to transmit voice and data. ISDN is therefore strongly promoted as a service, but this could have damaging consequences for the other networks and services.

France Télécom, being conscious of this danger, wants to gently introduce ISDN into its range of services, in order to cause as little disturbance as possible, and try to present it as a service complementary to the Transfix or Transpac data transmission services.

Three types of markets were considered for ISDN in France: (a) telephony, leading to an integration of voice and data; (b) information technology, with ISDN providing a public switching network with a high capacity and digital continuity; and (c) innovative applications, which could not be carried on traditional networks. The voice market could provide a high number of subscribers. It should basically rely on the extension of PABX facilities for users who were not directly connected to the equipment (for example, a manufacturer will be able to be connected with its distributors and sales agencies). As far as information technology is concerned, ISDN should attract medium-sized customers who cannot afford to pay for more expensive networks to transmit data and customers who will more generally be interested in the answer ISDN provides for applications requiring short connection time and the transmission of important flows of information. The third market is the market of innovative applications, which could not have been developed on the existing networks. France Télécom adopted a voluntarist strategy with regards to these innovative applications, aiming at selling ISDN "through example." It is clear that the partnerships that have been signed so far (more than 100) do not give a realistic representation of the market. But France Télécom will consider them as a worthwhile investment if they succeed in making the possibilities of ISDN well known among the business population, thus maybe initiating some new markets.

At the end of 1989, there were about 3,000 ISDN subscribers in France, very low as compared to the expectations of France of 20,000 subscribers by the end of 1990, 150,000 by the end of 1992, and 500,000 in 1995. ISDN will only be accessible to the residential sector in 1995. At the moment, France Télécom's expected market only consists of the business sector. However, small companies only represent 10% of the subscribers so far, and it has to be noticed that 70% of the small companies (under 100 employees) did not intend to subscribe to ISDN; however, 83% of the interviewed companies with more than 5,000 employees intended to subscribe to ISDN.

In Germany the development of ISDN will be impeded by the lack of digitization of the network and the fact that long-term options are more geared towards Integrated Broadband Communications Networks (IBCN).

Besides, the recent regulatory evolution in Germany is likely to modify the supply of services. It is therefore likely that Telekom will not have a very discretionary position to spread ISDN, apart from the pilot experiments that have been launched quite early. So far, ISDN is developing rather slowly. It was launched on a commercial basis in March 1989; in November of the same year, 1,200 basic and 100 primary access subscribers were connected. The eight main towns (Hamburg, Stuttgart, Berlin, Frankfurt, Hannover, München, Düsseldorf, Nürnberg) each had access available for 1,000 subscribers, with more than 2,000 ISDN circuits per town. It is estimated that in early 1992 the number of subscribers ranged between 2,000 and 5,000. As in France, few of these subscribers are small companies so far (according to the Bavarian Center of Communication, 42% of the German small companies did not even know the meaning of ISDN).

Research performed during the pilot experiment in Mannheim and Stuttgart showed that even potential subscribers were not all that interested in ISDN (at least in this experiment) and 36% of the users had a low level of acceptance of ISDN. Although this may be due to the way the pilot studies were conducted (delays, problems of equipment, etc.), it does not especially encourage the Deutsche Bundespost Telekom to invest heavily in the marketing of ISDN on a very large scale.

In the United Kingdom, British Telecom does not intend to have too arbitrary an approach as far as ISDN is concerned. ISDN (at European standards) is launched in a progressive way. In a first step during 1990, the telecommunications equipment manufacturers were allowed to test their equipment and subsequently ISDN was introduced on a commercial basis. ISDN will remain positioned as a very high technology network, but it is clear that it will essentially be used to transmit data. ISDN should allow British Telecom to increase its supply of enhanced services, particularly those associated with the Centrex service. But British Telecom will not heavily promote ISDN, since this is not the kind of service from which short-term benefits are to be gained. However, Mercury does not seem to be willing to heavily invest in ISDN, either. The number of primary accesses is estimated at approximately 500 in the United Kingdom, 300 being served so far by Mercury and 200 by British Telecom, which have launched basic ISDN during 1990. The first ISDN services are essentially facsimile, data transmission, and call transfer.

In countries where deregulation did occur, ISDN was often considered as a possibility to supply enhanced services, either by new carriers willing to attract big companies (for example, Mercury supplies at the moment more primary accesses than British Telecom) or by the former monopolies trying to retain these big companies while providing high technology networks that they can more easily afford to invest in than new carriers (this is the case of NTT, for example). Therefore, ISDN could be considered as a means to position oneself in front of competitors. However, on the whole, it cannot really be considered that ISDN played such a role. In fact, ISDN does not represent a crucial stake in the relationships between the new carriers and the former monopolies, each organization generally preferring to concentrate on shorter-term businesses and to invest in projects likely to improve their situation toward their competitors more quickly. This competitive situation in some countries may impede the development of ISDN, preventing the carriers from investing sufficiently in this new network or investing in a coordinated way.

It is also interesting to study the relationships between the PABX manufacturers and the carriers, for the former still have national visions of their markets and tend to integrate and to react to the different developments of the ISDN networks in the different countries. PABX manufacturers are at the moment trying to keep their systems as closed as possible, so as to retain their customers. This means that they do not want to develop common ISDN interfaces and are trying on the contrary to develop ISDN interfaces that would be specific to their equipment. The risk behind such a strategy is that there probably exists different sets of subscribers who cannot communicate with each other. The development of phone applications of ISDN would be all the more impeded if PABX manufacturers do not come to an agreement. Facing this problem, the national carriers have different strategies. France Télécom tries to impose a common standard as much as possible. British Telecom can only suggest that manufacturers produce open systems, but its pressures seem to have been in vain, so far. The computer manufacturers follow a wait-and-see approach. In fact, important computer manufacturers only deal with international markets and do not intend to manufacture separate national systems for each market.

Key Issues and Policy Background

ISDN

In the Beginning

From a techno-economic point of view, ISDN is carried by the digitization of public networks. The trend toward generalization was developed throughout the 1980s. However, when ISDN strategies were fixed in the late 1980s, national situations were rather different from that perspective. If the trend toward relative homogeneity is real, national disparities are still very much in existence and will determine the very perception of ISDN, country by country.

The value of a network being worth the value of its weakest link, some operators are (or will be) in a situation all the more favorable for putting ISDN on a switched network, because the degree of digitization is homogeneous. France Télécom is a good example. With a high level of digitized local switches, it can rapidly afford the national coverage for local access to a "universal" ISDN service.

Others, who have not had this experience, are getting ready to manage jointly public network development and ISDN development. Such is the case with Telefónica in Spain, which unveiled its ISDN objectives when the general telecommunications plan was made public in late 1992. Some, who are not making digitization a precondition to a more widespread use of ISDN, are getting ready to offer a limited ISDN based on "CCITT" recommendations. Such is the trend that is visible in the United Kingdom and Sweden.

Network or Networks?

Because of the emphasis being put on digitization, European operators must now answer a question that is more strategic than technical: Which definition should be retained for the nature of the ISDN network? The first option consists in constructing a new network (identified as a particular product), a new value-added network, placed side by side with other networks managed by the operator. The second option consists in the creation of a meta-network, having overall responsibility for and linking all the different networks, switched networks, packet networks, and leased-lines. The furthest reaching option consists in making ISDN *the* telecommunications network, that is, the outcome of a universal network logic and the substitute for all the dedicated networks.

The choice of one of these three options is closely linked to the culture of the telecommunications operator and technical developments, in particular the speed of digitization that was mentioned above. International standardization, from the subscriber terminal to the switch, passing through transmission, signals, and security, enables ISDN to be treated homogeneously and leaves open every opportunity to place oneself on one of these three dimensions: value-added network, meta-network, or universal network.

Thus, British Telecom seems to have opted for the first definition, Deutsche Bundespost Telekom wishes to position ISDN on a meta-network dimension, and France Télécom has chosen the third definition as a starting point. However, it should not be assumed that this choice rests on easily obtained national consensus. The debate, more public in Germany, more muffled and internalized in France and Italy, did really exist and in many respects still does. At this stage, the European comparison, clear in its principles, remains confused in its methods.

Introduction of ISDN

By and large, the network operators in Europe have an organizational culture dominated by technical issues. The emergence of a managerial or marketing culture is more recent. The ISDN dossier, like all new dossiers, is an internal test as to how the two logics coincide: for the engineers, ISDN is a super "mecano" or a toy; for the salespeople, it is a product or a service.

The management of an internal consensus is, it seems, at the base of ISDN introduction strategies; the step-by-step approach is similar in all countries. The first step of this strategy is the pilot project. The United Kingdom, France, Italy, Germany, and the majority of European operators have carried out or are soon to carry out this step. On closer inspection, it seems that these pilot projects have always had an ambiguous status. They are, at the same time, technical test beds, social experiments, test markets, and lobbying tools. Without really being able to be one or the other, their definition is often a compromise. However, and in all likelihood, this is their main interest. For a long time, presented as an ISDN experiment, the Renan operation was assimilated, toward the end of 1987, in the commercial opening of ISDN. The pilot project of British Telecom, IDA (Integrated Digital Access), launched in 1985, was mainly a technical test bed in the beginning; but, in fact, it had a limited impact on the strategic options defined by the new British Telecom.

The Constraints of an ISDN Strategy

A supply policy for ISDN imposes the need for its European promoters to make a certain number of economic choices. Two questions will be raised: (a) What services should be promoted, and (b) what tariff structure should be retained? If the questions are easy to formulate, the answers are obviously more difficult to elaborate. The European authorities have tried this exercise (see in particular the Council resolution of 18 July 1989 on the strengthening of the coordination for the introduction of ISDN in the European Communities). But the solutions they have proposed are sufficiently vague so that each country is left to define its own options.

The Choice of Services

The typology of ISDN services and their definition have been fixed by international authorities in the International Telecommunication Union. Their contents in Europe have been set by a certain number of committees placed under the aegis of the European Commission—particularly the Analysis and Forecasting Group (GAP), a subgroup of the Senior Officials Group on Telecommunications (SOG-T), as well as the European Conference of Postal and Telecommunications Administrations (CEPT). All the ISDN promoters in Europe are thus called on to refer explicitly to bearer services (e.g., transmission capacity, packet switching), teleservices (services offered to users, such as telephony, telefax, videotex, videotelephony), and supplementary services (e.g., caller identification, direct dialing-in, terminal portability).

But what terms should potential ISDN clients use? Is ISDN a super telephone (supplementary services), a value-added service (teleservices), or a value-added network (bearer service)? When ISDN was introduced in Europe, choices made by the national operators did not clearly indicate the service positioning. Perhaps we should even speak of voluntary ambiguity: ISDN, as a universal network, is not fortunate enough to correspond, like the telephone network, to one service only.

Tariff Policy

In the tariff policy, all the contradictions of a project converge and must be resolved, and all the compromises that have resulted will become visible. Thus, it crystallizes all the strategic options that have been retained. The choice of tariff policy reflects the way each carrier considers ISDN and on which kinds of services it intends to focus its ISDN supply. For British Telecom, the ISDN price will be the price of data transmission; for the Deutsche Bundespost Telekom, the price will be that of voice transmission. France Télécom differentiates between data and voice (the price of data transmission being 1.8 times that of voice transmission). However, Japan does not make any difference between voice and data but tariffs are different between the business and residential sector. In the United States, local carriers' ISDN tariffs vary widely, and long distance carriers are offering private network ISDN access, often via custom tariffs that are not published.

The French position is clearly linked with France Télécom's ambition to eventually replace the PSTN with ISDN. It is therefore important that the network includes elements of voice transmission. However, ISDN should also play an essential role in data transmission. The same kind of motivation can be found in the German method of tariffication, although it is likely that Telekom considers ISDN more as a transition to more powerful networks than as an aim in itself. For the United Kingdom, however, ISDN is not meant to do anything other than data transmission, and any voice communication will therefore be more expensive on ISDN than on PSTN. Japan remains in between these two positions, favoring first the data transmission but intending to reduce the weight of the distance factor in the telecommunication price, thus making this network more interesting for long-distance voice calls (and thus attracting big companies, which consume more long-distance calls than any other organization).

Pending Issues

The lack of clarity and consistency of ISDN strategies in Europe is partly based in the uncertainty over service definition and the failure to properly segment markets, but the exclusion of users and potential customers from strategic analysis has not helped. Arguably, these issues will become more important than in the past for a number of reasons.

First, the market structure is rapidly moving from a restricted number of European public network operators to multi-vendors and a multi-service supplier environment. This could result in greater emphasis than before on services whose requirements will determine network architectures. Moreover, the telecommunications market will become more fragmented and will provide opportunities for a wide range of service providers. Competition could intensify, many prices will be lower (although niches will exist for premium services), and customer choices will be more complex. In the meantime, the regulation process will have produced a conceptual framework in Europe in which openness is encouraging the use of telecommunication facilities at different (economic) layers. Finally, new strategic customer requirements such as flexibility and control will encourage a specific emphasis on service issues. ISDN—which is potentially the last network to have been set up by a highly concentrated PTT structure—has found real difficulties in its promotion phase and a resulting slow level of take-up, possibly due in part to a lack of understanding about how user services should be defined and provided.

In fact, the CCITT approach to services (which was established for ISDN purposes and is still alive in research on broadband technologies) is of limited value in relation to user needs. This is partly a function of the distinction between bearer- and tele-services, which are purely technical rather than user or business concepts.

Toward a European Policy?

The European authorities, and especially the Commission of the European Communities, have supported the development of ISDN in Europe (see chapter Appendix for major initiatives). But up to now, the basis of such a policy is limited by the type of consensus that European countries and their national operators are willing to find.

The lowest point of convergence, what I will call the highest common factor, rests in the validation of the CCITT's standards. This first level of consensus is perhaps the easiest to bring about. The highest point of the project's convergence is discourse. The lowest common multiple corresponds, indeed, to creating an ISDN mythology carried by the European network operators, relayed by industry and more timidly by the European authorities. Between these two "limits," types of fixed points in the ISDN "arena," the Commission has launched the basis for a European policy that has been drafted in the Green Paper of 1987 on Telecommunications. It is relying on three elements: (a) the support of the Memorandum of Understanding on the coordinated introduction of ISDN, (b) the application of open network provision principles to the field of ISDN, and (c) the support of the European ISDN forum. These may be seen as the instruments of a "Euro-policy" on ISDN. However, this framework does not bind the players to a single scenario.

A case in point is the tariff issue. In its Recommendation 86/659 on ISDN, the Council of the European Communities recommends a tariff policy less dependent on distance, in coherence with conventional telephone tariffing in order to further the rapid adoption of the digital service in Europe. Actually, this was not highly compulsory. An ambitious (and compulsory) European policy is difficult to set up. The borderline between voluntarism and laissez-faire, especially regarding market forces, has always been a subject of internal discussions in the EC. It is clear that this is actually the case for European ISDN policies.

Conclusion

As I indicated previously, ISDN as a service is subject to multiple definitions. It is (a) a universal service whose value relies on network externalities—the more numerous the users are, the more useful the service is (in this context, entry strategy is more concerned with establishing the conditions for access and subscription than with identifying high value applications); (b) a value-added network, potentially an overlay, used mainly for data communications; and (c) a value-added service supporting a wide range of innovative applications.

Market evaluation has been oversimplistic. Many authorities have simply quantified the market in terms of the percentage of subscriber lines that are ISDN. This approach, which homogenizes user requirements and assumes that ISDN is a substitute for existing services, makes traffic forecasting and estimation difficult and limits the scope for market segmentation.

Public network operators have shown some hesitation about and inconsistency in their entry strategies and have not given unanimous or clear answers to such questions as these: Does ISDN introduction require a collaborative process among suppliers or not? How should fixed technical standards (2B and 30B+D) and service integration be managed?

The preceding analysis suggests that there will be many faces to ISDN in Europe. Although the major public telecommunications operators and the European Commission still appear to share a vision of an interconnecteded, pan European ISDN, the very different national trajectories described here cast doubts on their ability to reach such a goal in the near future.

Appendix: Key European Community Actions on ISDN

- *Council Recommendation of 22 December 1986 on the Coordinated Introduction of the Integrated Services Digital Network (ISDN) in the European Community* (86/659/EEC). OJ L 382/36, 31 December 1986.

- *First Annual Progress Report on ISDN from the Commission to the European Parliament.* COM(88)589 final, Brussels, 31 October 1988.
- *Council Resolution of 18 July 1989 on the Strengthening of the Coordination for the Introduction of the ISDN in the European Community up to 1992* (89/C 196/04). OJ C 191/5, 1 August 1989.
- *Progress Report 1989 Concerning the Coordinated Introduction of the Integrated Services Digital Network (ISDN) in the European Community.* COM(90)123 final, Brussels, 23 March 1990.
- *Council Directive of 28 June 1990 on the Establishment of the Internal Market for Telecommunications Services Through the Implementation of Open Network Provision* (90/387/EEC). OJ L 192/1, 24 July 1990.
- *Commission Proposal for a Council Directive Concerning the Protection of Personal Data and Privacy in the Context of Public Digital Telecommunications Networks, in Particular the Integrated Services Digital Networks (ISDN) and Public Digital Mobile Networks* (90/C 277/04). OJ C 277/12, 5 November 1990.

THIRTEEN

Broadband Services in Europe

STEPHEN CONNELL

This chapter is concerned primarily with the potential for radical change in the design, provision, marketing, and use of telecommunications. The emphasis is on Europe, although many of the issues raised are just as relevant elsewhere. Higher bandwidths and data rates are important issues, but they are not the prime reasons why everybody in the tele-communications industry will have to rethink some of their most basic assumptions if end-users, at home or at work, are to gain the full benefit of broadband communications. The integrating aspects of broadband communications offer the prospect of so much change: The potential for integration of the telecommunications, broadcasting, and cable industries; the integration of media (speech, other sounds, motion video, still images, and data); and the resulting need for newly designed regulatory and commercial structures are the reasons why the subject of this chapter is likely to become increasingly important.

These issues are covered by a review of the status quo, an examination of European initiatives in development of strategies for the development and exploitation of broadband communications technologies, discussion of obstacles to service development, and a brief account of some empirical analysis of potential applications for IBC. The implications of these issues for service provision and demand creation are then considered.

The Concept of Broadband Communications

Broadband is a term that can have several meanings, but it is most usually used to identify digital telecommunications services with data rates above 2 Mbit/s (or in the North American context, 1.5 Mbit/s—the T1 rate). At present, broadband networks are little used in any country, but they could become the basis for a future generation of business and residential services, carrying interactive telecommunications and TV broadcasts at data rates of 140 Mbit/s or more.

Broadband technology could radically change our ideas about telecommunications services. The operating systems of powerful computers and workstations could interconnect in real time, large CAD files and high-resolution still images (e.g., X-rays) could be transmitted in a matter of seconds, and the concept of multimedia could be exported from the computer industry to telecommunications services. In business or at home, users would have instant access to motion video images, real-time videotelephony, high-speed data communications, and a variety of intelligent network features.

In the residential market, this technology could radically affect the entertainment industry (TV viewing and program selection would become a truly interactive process rather than a choice from a limited menu) and would extend the concepts of computer-assisted learning to interactive access to wide-area multimedia facilities, thus creating a revolution in patterns of studying and distance learning. A whole new range of home-shopping and transaction services, based on the transmission and display of high-resolution still and moving images, would come into service.

In business or professional markets, broadband communications could be used for direct local area network (LAN) interconnection (without the loss of speed that is increasingly being encountered when LANs operating at Mbit/s speed are interconnected on wide-area networks at Kbit/s rates) and for a whole new set of multimedia applications in remote training, collaborative design, remote meetings, and database access.

In a highly competitive world economy, the impacts of IBC deployment and usage, by businesses and households, are potentially enormous. New electronic publishing, software, and telecommunications service industries would be created, presenting both a threat and an opportunity to all the established players. But the main economic impacts would come from the leverage that new products and services would create for companies in other industries. If manufacturing companies can design products and bring them to market more quickly, they save money and create competitive advantage. If financial services or travel companies can find ways of more effectively customizing their products and of explaining them more easily to their clients, revenue per sales office can be dramatically increased.

Visions of this kind, however, beg the questions of whether there really is a market for advanced communications services and of the choice of optimum entry and evolutionary strategies. As this chapter will show, the European industry is, in many ways, uncertain about how it should develop, promote, and use broadband communications; and it is clear that the European market for broadband telecommunications services will change dramatically before the end of the 20th century, although the manner and direction of these changes is, at this point, very difficult to predict. Data, presented below, from the analysis of potential applications for broadband networks suggests that many of the traditional concepts in telecommunications service design will have to be overturned or modified if broadband infrastructures are to be properly exploited.

Although this chapter is focused on Europe and presents data collected in European studies, much of the argument is strongly relevant to conditions elsewhere.

National Trials

At the end of the 1980s, most European countries had no broadband services or local infrastructure. Broadband circuits were exclusively used for trunk communications or interconnection of local exchanges. At that time, European telecommunications networks were a varying combination of digital and analog; ISDN and all-digital public networks were on the way and analog CATV networks provided households with a wide choice of TV programming in the areas in which they operated. France Télécom and Mercury Communications in the United Kingdom offered 8 Mbit/s private circuits and the Deutsche Bundespost Telekom operated an experimental broadband network in Berlin (the Berkom network) and a public trunk network—the Forerunner Broadband Network.

Most European PTTs are now proceeding with the creation of all-digital trunking and switching in their networks and with the rollout of narrowband ISDN infrastructure, but provision for the construction of broadband services is at a generally low and uncoordinated level. Although Germany appears to have made an early start in broadband development—both Berkom and the Forerunner Broadband Network operate at 140 Mbit/s—these services are not commercial. Berkom is only for scientific use and application development and is not tariffed. The Forerunner Broadband Network has principally been used, without commercial success, for broadband videoconferencing and for some experiments in access to supercomputers; but it is not a public service for general use.

Most PTTs are conducting trials of broadband fiber optic loops, but, as in the United States, these are largely assessment of basic design, construction, operational, and maintenance issues and are not concerned with application or service development. Although the architectures vary—and include Telephony on a Passive Optical Network (TPON) and star and mini-star configurations—the services carried are Plain Old Telephone Service (POTS) and broadcast TV.

There is some promise of novel service developments in the development of Metropolitan Area Networks (MANs), which are under construction in such cities as Copenhagen, Munich, Stuttgart, the Hague, Zurich, and Vienna. These MANs will be similar to the SMDS (Switched Multimegabit Data Services) that are currently being tested by the Regional Bell Operating Companies and Telecom Australia and will offer asynchronous communications at data rates up to 45 Mbit/s.[1] The position of France Télécom is not clear: It pioneered the installation of fiber optics in the local loop (for analog services). Work began in Biarritz in 1980, but it has not announced any plans for digital broadband services. BT is reported to be preparing for a MAN pilot in London, but at the time of writing had given no details of the choice of technology.

International Trials

European telecommunications administrations have been involved in several collaborative attempts to build advanced transnational telecommunications. The Managed European Transmission Network (METRAN) is intended as a pan-European broadband backbone network, developed by 14 PTOs. It will use the SDH (Synchronous Digital Hierarchy) transmission standard to link national networks at speeds up to 155 Mbit/s. Although this could represent a tremendous advance in the provision of broadband linkages for multinational applications, there is some doubt about the willingness of METRAN's PTO members to allow the provision of broadband private circuits internationally or as local tails.

A predecessor initiative—the European Broadband Interconnection Trial (EBIT)—came to grief. EBIT was launched in 1989 as a way of providing the application pilot projects of the RACE program (which is discussed below) with a switched 2 Mbit/s network. It was withdrawn after PTOs failed to agree on tariffing issues.

A more recent but equally controversial initiative is Hermes, a proposed pan-European data network that will be carried by fiber optic cables laid alongside Europe's railway lines. The Hermes consortium includes Nynex, Daimler-Benz AG, Sprint International, and a number of European financial and industrial groups. Initially the service will carry X.25 services, but it could be upgraded to carry broadband communications. Hermes can utilize the rights of way of the railway companies but will have to negotiate third-party access with local public telecommunications operators. If successfully launched, it could provide a source of innovation in the development of novel communications applications.

A more specifically broadband proposal is the Commission of the European Community's European Nervous System. This will be, if it goes ahead, a private broadband network to support pilot intergovernmental communications applications (e.g., in linkages between member states and the Commission, cargo movements, collaboration between police forces, international trade, joint development of technical standards). A call for proposals for application pilots was made in the summer of 1991, but the Commission has not yet announced the results of its negotiations with PTOs over the provision of leased private circuits and the conditions of use.

To summarize the European position, a number of attempts are being made to improve the supply of broadband communications at national and local levels, but their effect hitherto has been negligible. Prospects for an improvement in this situation are uncertain.

Next Steps

The piecemeal development and pilot testing of technologies is no basis for the development of a coherent strategy for the deployment and utilization of broadband communications. Such a strategy is clearly needed, for a number of reasons:

- Widespread utilization of broadband communications, by households as well as businesses, will require the refurbishing of almost all local loops.

If every street is to be dug up (most of the cost of building broadband local loops lies in civil engineering and labor rather than in electronics), it is important that the design of the network is optimized for the full range of new services that are likely to be needed.

- The need for economies of scale mandates the use of generic and consistent designs and components across Europe—individual national solutions will become increasingly impractical.

- Development of a single infrastructure that will carry both telecommunications and broadcasting services brings together, often in conflict, regulatory concepts and political interests that have hitherto been separate. If the cause of broadband is to be advanced, a general framework for collaboration rather than confrontation is needed. This framework must provide for the interworking of a variety of commercial interests and harmonize regulations as well as deal with technical issues (e.g., network architecture).

- The technical choices made in the design of a new telecommunications infrastructure must allow flexibility of use and application or service development, while providing the equipment manufacturers with the opportunity of developing products whose specification meets the needs of wider markets, outside Europe.

This context has provided much of the impetus for RACE (Research and Development for Advanced Communications Technologies in Europe), a collaborative R&D program initiated by the Commission of the European Communities.

RACE

The main phase of RACE (after some exploratory work) began in 1988 and will continue to 1994. RACE consists of collaborative projects (more than 70 in the first phase) that involve most of the major players in the European telecommunications industry—PTTs and carriers, equipment vendors (Alcatel, Siemens, Ericsson, GPT, etc.), and a number of major users (e.g., Ford Motor Company, Commercial Union Assurance [Britain], Banque Nationale de Paris, Scandinavian Airline System). The Phase 1 budget, including contributions from participating organizations (the CEC normally only funds 50% of the project's costs) is just under 1 billion ECU.

RACE is organized in three main areas: Part I is Consensus Formation and Development and Implementation Strategies; Part II is Technologies (networks and switching, optical communications, software and network management, customer systems and usability engineering); and Part III is Application Pilots and Verification. The program's goal is to develop common views and strategies for Integrated Broadband Communications and to develop momentum in the development and utilization of its technologies. Contributions to ETSI, CCITT, and other standards bodies are an important part of RACE outputs.

The concept of Integrated Broadband Communications goes beyond the mere provision of bandwidth. IBC is a goal for RACE that embodies a number of key concepts:

- The provision of high data rates, to households and businesses, at rates measured in hundreds of Mbit/s.
- The use of a single infrastructure to carry distributive, messaging, and conversational services (telecommunications and broadcasting services will use the same access network).
- The availability, during a single call or session, of multiple modes of interaction (e.g., switching from conversational to messaging) and of media (data, voice, high quality sound or TV, still images).
- Flexibility of the control of calls with users being able to allocate or de-allocate channels, media, and types of interaction as a communication session proceeds.
- The features of an intelligent network.
- Terminal and transmission costs equivalent to those of today's narrowband services.
- Ease of constructing and providing a variety of narrowband services.
- Provision of roaming and personal mobility functions.

In practice, these represent long-term rather than immediately achievable goals, but the development of Asynchronous Transfer Mode (ATM) offers the promise of technical feasibility. RACE projects are each concerned with some aspects of IBC: service definition, reference models for network design, ATM technology, the role of satellites, the design of user interfaces, applications for people with special needs, and so on.

Application pilots are an important part of the RACE program. In Part I, there are 17 of these projects, in such fields as medicine, publishing, banking, motor design and manufacture, and aircraft maintenance. These projects study user needs, develop and test prototype versions of advanced communications, and provide input (on user needs) to the functional specification and consensus formation parts of the program.

TABLE 13.1   Priority Areas and Budget of RACE-II

Area	Budgeted Community Contribution (in millions of ECUs)
Integrated broadband communications R&D	111
Intelligence in networks/Flexible resource management	43
Mobile and personal communications	53
Image and data communications	68
Integrated service technologies	39
Information security techniques	29
Advanced communication experiments	121
Test infrastructure and interworking	20
Total	484

NOTE: On average, in 1991, 1 ECU approximately equaled 1.2 U.S.$.

RACE-II

The new RACE program commenced in January 1992 and is focused on eight priority areas (see Table 13.1). As in RACE-I, broadband is a key issue but only in the context of the integration of services and functions. RACE-II is intended by the Commission of the European Communities to provide a much more practical and less theoretical approach to the development of a European broadband strategy and market. If RACE-I was concerned with reference modeling and technology development, RACE-II is focused on application development, testbed creation, and priming of the broadband market pump. RACE is, however, not empowered to deal with two issues that are likely to be potential obstacles to the development of IBC: tariff policy and the convergence of telecommunications and broadcasting.

Obstacles to the Deployment of Broadband Technologies

Tariff policy is likely to be a major barrier to the full utilization of IBC, and not just in Europe. This is partly due to the difficulty of pricing a network that can support services ranging from 32 Kbits/s (voice telephony) or even lower (e.g., for credit card verification) up to hundreds of Mbit/s (for TV, either in current PAL/NTSC/SECAM form or in whatever emerges from the PAL plus/D2 or E-MAC/HDTV nexus). Traditional per-bit-kilometer rates would render video-on-demand hideously and impractically expensive, and discounts for economies of scale would open the doors to cream-skimming and arbitrage on a massive scale. To take an extreme example, if the price of transmitting a movie for a video-on-demand service is, say, 4 ECU for two hours (about the cost of renting a videotape), a reseller of that transmission capacity (which cannot necessarily be reserved only for that application) could price 64 Kbits/s services at rates well below those of the local telephone company and still make money. Already, fear of these effects has meant that European PTTs offer private circuits less willingly and at generally higher costs than their North American equivalents. British Telecom has promoted and marketed leased circuits more aggressively than any of its continental counterparts but refuses to market private circuits at datarates above 2 Mbit/s.

Even if data rate and tariff tiers could be constructed in a way that encourages users to optimize their use at each level, how are flexible calls or sessions to be tariffed? To give an example, a user might start a database search with a travel company (conversational slow speed data), gain access to a video database that shows films of locations and resorts (high bandwidth video retrieval), and then start a videophone call with a holiday consultant, before choosing a holiday and returning to the transaction database. This user will only begin this sequence of events if he is sure that the telecommunications are both affordable and what he regards as reasonable.

Ideally, tariffs should encourage flexibility of use and should minimize the cost of varying the parameters of a call while it is in progress. If this cannot be done or if per-bit pricing is used, IBC becomes BC—the integration (I) is lost.

At present, RACE has no answer to the question of how tariffs can be constructed that offer network operators the promise of a fair return and users the promise of affordable, flexible, and integrated services. These answers, when they come (from whatever source), must take into account the likely existence of a regulatory regime that reflects ONP principles and thus encourages multiple levels of service provision.

A single local broadband loop, operated by a national or local monopoly, should be capable of carrying basic telecommunications services, advanced and flexible communications services (e.g., complex forms of videotelephony), and a variety of broadcast services. This resource could be an upgraded CATV network, which offers telephony and a variety of interactive services, or a new PTT/local telephone company network.

Merger of broadcasting and telecommunications technologies will, however, bring the regulatory regimes of both industries into conflict. The telecommunications industry is now accepting the principles of recursive service design and modularity (e.g., an EDI service operated by a VAN supplier utilizes and adds value at varying levels to leased circuits, computer bureaus, and the PSTN). In RACE, it is working on the assumption that the user may access more than one service (or service provider) in a single call or session. For example, somebody in a tele-shopping application may need to interact with a retailer through one on-screen window and with a bank through another, using the services of more than one communications service vendor.

The telecommunications industry also accepts the common carrier principle but cable TV broadcasters, in contrast, do not work on this basis, nor are they prepared to give up their local monopolies and become just one of the service providers using a common infrastructure.

The extent of this difficulty is likely to vary in Europe by country. In Germany, the Deutsche Bundespost Telekom owns and constructs all telecommunications networks (even those operated by local cable TV companies); in France, France Télécom has shareholdings in most CATV networks; but elsewhere, a separation has grown up between the cable industry and the telephone companies.

Another regulatory issue that could slow the adoption of IBC technology in Europe is control over advertising. A number of studies have suggested that a key source of revenue for new broadband entertainment services is advertising. McKinsey and Co. (Wenner, 1989) estimated that in the United States $35-$72 billion in advertising revenues could be found for the financing of a new local telecommunications infrastructure, over 15 years; this income would represent 46%-58% of the sales of broadband home information and entertainment services. The other sources of income would be end-user tariffs for information or entertainment consumed (less than 30%) and plain markups on transaction services (21%-27%). The 1990 PACE (Perspectives for Advanced Communications in Europe) study commissioned by the Commission of the European Communities (CEC; Commission, 1990) prorated these estimates by economic indicators and estimated that these three sources of funding for broadband networks might yield 10-30 billion ECU in Western Europe.

European countries vary widely in their attitudes to the provision of television advertising and the amount that is permitted. For instance, advertising by political parties is prohibited in the United Kingdom,

Spain, and Denmark, whereas it is allowed in France and Italy. The advertising of medical services is prohibited in Denmark, restricted in The Netherlands and Italy, but liberalized in France, the United Kingdom, and Spain.

The issue will be complicated by the development of new types of programming and information services that mix product information (e.g., on motor cars) with entertainment (e.g., motor racing TV footage or games) and transaction services (e.g., remote purchasing of motor accessories). How all of this is to be regulated has hardly been studied, but the absence of an appropriate framework could deny network operators a valuable and much needed additional source of revenue.

Applications

In these circumstances, with uncertainty about the timing and pattern of vendor initiatives and about the extent to which networks for IBC services will be constructed, questions about the nature of potential demand are difficult to pose and, for residential and organizational customers, difficult to answer.

One approach to this dilemma—of how to identify applications and uses for a new communications technology—is that of RACE project R.1071, Applications Analysis, which analyzed communications problems in 127 organizations or workgroups and proposed solutions, on the assumption that a mature IBC network was available and affordable.[2] The result is a set of application domains defined by user functions and mapped to a context of service provision—the service domain.

Five application domains have been identified:

1. Transactional database
2. Database access and file exchange
3. Computer-assisted communications
4. Multimedia collaborative work
5. Interpersonal image and video communications

Each of these application domains has between 3 and 5 user functions that are mandatory and up to 15 that are optional, whose relevance depends on the precise usage context (task goals, user familiarity with communications technology, budget, etc). Application domains are, it should be stressed, statistical entities rather than concepts elaborated as part of a theoretically based taxonomy and so do not correspond neatly to traditional ideas of telecommunications services. The traditional distinctions between messaging, distribution, and conversational modes of communication do not emerge as being critical in this empirical classification of telecommunications applications.

Of the applications, 21% can be classified as being messaging, distribution, point-to-point, or point-to-multipoint interaction; 35% require 2 such modes; and 42% require 3 or more (2% could not be classified). The frequency of double counting, of needing more than one mode of communication (or of requiring multiple media), explains why a statistical view of communications applications for an integrated broadband communications provides untidy (for the telecommunications standards writer) bundles of communications functions.

This database strongly suggests that the telecommunications industry will have to develop a view of future applications and services that respects the inherently flexible and unpredictable nature of human communications and that offers a less constricting set of communication channels than current telecommunications options, which tend to limit the modes of communication (conversational voice only, voice plus synchronized motion video, broadcast data only, etc.), and often require the user to have a dedicated terminal (and perhaps connection or line) for each service.

It should be remembered, however, that this novel view of applications depends on assumptions about the principal features of IBC: If it is assumed that the network can support complex and flexible applications, then most potential contexts of use will require such facilities; but a more limited and more pessimistic view of the outcome of the RACE program might have identified simpler communications requirements.

Service definition is, therefore, indissolubly linked to tariffs and to the context of supply.

Service Provision

Telecommunications services are an interaction between the application (the required set of communications or user functions, in a usage context) and the way services are provided. The way an application, say, for interpersonal conversation that requires moving images of co-locutors to be transmitted (videotelephony) is served by a PTT may be quite different from the service offered by a local cable TV company. Jacques Arlandis (1990) has developed the concept of service domain—a way of describing the organization of telecommunication service provision—and distinguishes among three possible industrial and commercial structures for the provision of broadband communications in Europe (or anywhere else):

1. *Mass video* is focused on the development of low-cost and easy-to-use products and services suitable for consumption by the general public and the simultaneous provision of telecommunications functions and their content (e.g., for pay-per-view or home-shopping).
2. *Integrated broadband network* is, in contrast, based on common carrier principles and on the provision of ubiquitous public networks optimized for conversational and transactional applications, offering a variety of intelligent network functions and trade-offs between network speed and bandwidth.
3. *Intelligent broadband system* is driven by the interests of very sophisticated users of telecommunications and closed user groups and is strongly oriented around high-bandwidth applications (e.g., distributed collaborative design). Carriers will participate as providers of private circuits or bearer services to which corporate users and their hardware and software vendors add value.

In Europe, the second and third of these service domains are most likely to be responsible for broadband service development, although prospects for the mass video scenario vary considerably from country to country, depending on the strength of the local cable TV industry (cable TV penetration in European countries varies from almost 100% in Belgium to less than 5% of households in several countries, including Spain, Italy, and the United Kingdom). The PTTs can be expected to fight against the IBS approach—although much depends here on how vigorously the CEC prosecutes the enforcement of its Open Network Provision (ONP) regulations.

The R.1071 project matched its five application domains to the three service domain concepts of Arlandis and identified 11 services:

- Two services—transactional entertainment (e.g., pay-per-view) and general tele-shopping—are in the mass video domain.
- Five services—simple and enhanced videotelephony, simple exchange of high-quality images and data, flexible exchange of multimedia files, and

mobile access to databases—are in the intelligent broadband network (IBN) domain.

- • Four services—high-speed bearer communications, remote database access, multimedia collaborative work, and secure computer-aided work—are in the integrated broadband system domain.

On this evidence, the advanced communications services most likely to be developed in Europe in the 1990s are those of the IBN or PTT-led sphere of influence. The R.1071 project shows a potential market for the others, but the development of residential services (in the mass video service domain) depends on the prior provision, over a wide area, of appropriate infrastructure. This investment will not occur until the regulatory obstacles (discussed above) have been cleared; whereas, as has been noted, the PTTs can be relied on to obstruct the development of the integrated broadband system concepts.

The Future of Broadband in Europe

A number of forces will affect the ways national and international carriers, equipment suppliers, user organizations, and governments develop and implement strategies and policies for broadband communication infrastructures and services. These include the following:

■ *The extent of eventual success or failure of direct-to-home satellite television services.* DBS is potentially important to the development of broadband services in several ways. It could preempt demand for cable TV programming services or play a more collaborative role by providing broadcast, pay-per-view or narrowcast services that are redistributed by CATV networks as well as being purchased direct.

■ *The pace at which ISDN infrastructure is rolled out and, as important, the vigor with which it is marketed, as a service in itself or as the basis for a variety of novel value-added services (VANs).* It could be argued that successful utilization of ISDN will satisfy enough of the demand for advanced communication services to deny developers of broadband services the markets and revenues they will need. But another possibility is that ISDN should be regarded as being the first testbed and stimulus for the development and use of multimedia communication services that will come to maturity with integrated broadband communications.

- *Continuing liberalization of the supply of telecommunications products and services, as foreseen in the Commission of the European Communities Green Papers on telecommunications policy and the associated implementation of Open Network Provision.* It is clear that the challenge of developing new applications and service concepts, and the associated terminals and customer premises equipment, cannot be adequately met by a narrowly defined telecommunications industry, and it is also clear that there should be scope for multiple value-added layers in IBC services. A heterogeneous and rapidly growing telecommunications service industry that is selling to end-users, and to its own members, needs an appropriate regulatory climate and the freedom to buy and sell resources with few artificial restrictions on what can and cannot be done with each type of network resource.
- *The creation of demand for an entirely new and state-of-the-art telecommunications infrastructure in the countries of Eastern Europe.* Developments in the state of what was East Germany will have a critical role in the provision of a proving ground and in the creation of economies of scale for new technologies.
- *Experience and product development in other markets, most notably Japan and North America.* Already, Europe takes much of her computing and electronics equipment from these markets (and runs a negative balance of trade in information technology) and could, if it fails to develop the products and services that users require, become increasingly dependent on imported telecommunications concepts and products.

At present, PTTs have little real motive to invest in the full-scale deployment of advanced broadband communications. The technology is not fully mature, the markets and applications are not defined, and there are a number of regulatory barriers, most notably the prohibition that most of them face on the provision of broadcast services.

Once some of the uncertainties are removed—as technologies become cheaper, as regulatory conditions become easier—developers of business cases will need to consider how the economics of network construction can be justified by the carriage of familiar services such as the PSTN and broadcast TV and the extent to which they depend on estimates of demand for novel services of the kind described above. Either way, full exploitation of the potential of broadband—for users and vendors of services—depends on new ways of defining and providing telecommunications services. This issue will come to the fore if new service revenue is needed to justify new network development and if the potential of broadband networks constructed for POTS and television is to be fully realized.

Notes

1. These MANs will be used primarily for LAN interconnection, using the Dual Queue Dual Bus (DQDB) technology that is the basis of the IEEE standard 802.6. DQDB is the basis of the European Telecommunications Standards Institute's (ETSI) standard for Connectionless Broadband Service.

2. This project was carried out by IFC Research Ltd. (1991), IDATE (Montpellier), Institut Cerda (Barcelona), and the Fraunhofer Institute ISI (Karlsruhe).

References

Arlandis, J. (1990). *Broadband scenarios: Strategic options and techno-economic developments*. Paper presented at the International Telecommunications Society Conference, Venice, March.

Commission of the European Communities. (1990). *Perspectives on advanced communications for Europe, Vol. II: Issue analyses*. Report prepared for the CEC by a team of consultants led by Technology Investment Partners, Paris.

IFC Research Ltd., IDATE, Institut Cerda, & Fraunhofer Institut ISI. (1991). *IBC applications analysis: The final report of RACE contract R.1071*. A report presented to DG XIII/F of the Commission of the European Communities. August.

Wenner, D. L. (1989, May 22). Are you ready for residential broadband? *Telephony,* pp. 84-103.

Selected Addtional Readings

CIT Research Ltd. (1991). *Media map*. London.

Commission of the European Communities. (1991a). Provisional Text of the Council Decision Adopting a Specific Program of Research and Technological Development in the Field of Communications Technologies (1990-1994). June.

Commission of the European Communities. (1991b). Provisional Text of the Council Decision Adopting a Specific Program of Research and Technological Development in the Field of Telematic Systems of General Interest (1990-1994). June.

Commission of the European Communities. (1991c). *Research and development in advanced communications technologies in Europe: RACE '91*. Brussels: CEC.

Saffo, P., & Johansen, R. (1988). *Believable broadband for business: Five scenarios*. Institute for the Future, Menlo Park, California. Mimeograph.

Solomon, R. J. (1990). *New paradigms for standards*. Paper presented at the IDATE 12th International Conference, Montpellier, France, November.

PART IV

Emerging Trends
and Global Strategies

Telecommunications in Central and Eastern Europe

JOHANNES M. BAUER
JOSEPH D. STRAUBHAAR

The radical changes in the former Communist bloc are often simplified by Western observers as the definitive triumph of democracy over dictatorial regimes and as final proof of the superiority of market organization over planned economies. Not surprisingly then, much of the debate focuses on the opening of new export markets for stagnant Western industries. The failed coup of conservative forces in the Soviet Union in August 1991 or the burgeoning nationalism in large parts of Eastern Europe are warning signals reminiscent of the complexities and possible drawbacks of this transition process to a new form of social and economic organization. The development of a new and stable institutional framework for more democratic, more market-oriented economies in these countries cannot be accomplished by simply freeing prices and introducing private ownership of capital but needs more encompassing institutional reforms (Blanchard, Dornbusch, Krugman, Layard, & Summers, 1991; Clague & Rausser, 1992; Murrell, 1991).

The specific strategies and problems in the development of telecommunications are intertwined with these other processes of societal transformation. The far-reaching political developments in Eastern Europe and the former realm of the Soviet Union over the past few years have also moved telecommunications into the center of attention. Whereas these countries, and especially the former Soviet Union, have developed elaborate systems of broadcasting, telecommunications did not enjoy a

AUTHORS' NOTE: The authors wish to thank Thomas Muth for helpful comments on an earlier draft of this chapter.

high priority in the national investment plans. Deliberately starved by earlier regimes, telecommunications is now increasingly perceived as a pivotal infrastructure for economic and social development. The conditions under which the institutional status quo ante can be replaced by a new policy are influenced by the historical, political, and economic context of each country, the global regime of technology transfer, as well as the economic and political relationships between East and West.

Historical and Political Background

Outside the U.S.S.R., telecommunications in Central and Eastern Europe developed in diverse ways before World War II. In some countries, facilities were owned by foreign companies, such as ITT and Ericsson. In other cases, telecommunications were provided by state-operated Postal Telephone and Telegraph administrations (PTTs). The reorganization of interest spheres after World War II, established at the meetings of Yalta and Potsdam in 1945, expanded the Soviet approach of socialist central control and ownership to the Central and Eastern European countries. Subsidiaries of foreign telecommunications providers, such as those of ITT, were nationalized, and centralized, PTT-like structures were created.

Within the national investment plans, telecommunications did not enjoy the same high priority as, for instance, investment in the transportation infrastructure. In part, this might be due to the Marxist-Leninist view of material production as being the only source of economic welfare and growth. In this theoretical concept, most services were seen as belonging to the consumption, or "unproductive," area of economic activity. Given this approach and the enormous competing investment needs faced by the governments, residential telephone service was not regarded as a necessity of life. When it was created at all, service was developed primarily in urban areas leading to a substantial gap in the availability of telecommunications between rural and urban areas.

In contrast, during the extensive debate on the possibility of effective centralized economic planning of the late 1950s and 1960s, considerable hope was placed in the use of computing and information technology to solve the huge optimization and coordination problems. As a consequence, users in the manufacturing sector and government institutions (as well as members of the political elite) were, in general, better supplied with telecommunications services than residential users. Still, they did not have access to the latest technologies and services.

Two more factors help explain the overall slow and unbalanced development of telecommunications in Central and Eastern Europe. One key historical *political* issue has been a perceived need by leadership elites to control information flow. Dizard and Svensrud (1987) have seen this as imperative stemming from a highly centralized and control-oriented Soviet system and its Eastern European partners. Political leaders have in fact frequently seen (individualized) telecommunications as a threat, as when Polish authorities shut down intercity and international direct dialing to keep Solidarity union leaders from communicating with each other and with outside media.

The results of the emerging Cold War between the Soviet bloc and the Western world led governments in the Central and Eastern European countries to pursue an industrial strategy of a comprehensive autarchy and import substitution, thus voluntarily isolating the Eastern European telecommunications industries. In Poland, Hungary, and Czechoslovakia, equipment manufacturing for telecommunications was continued after World War II and even developed somewhat further, to supply both domestic and Soviet markets. Nevertheless, the technological level of even the most sophisticated manufacturers, such as in Hungary, lagged behind their Western equivalents (Jakab, 1991, p. 55).

The same spirit led Western nations to impose tight export restrictions for "sensitive" technology regarded to be a possible military safety risk. Led by the United States, above a dozen industrialized nations joined in the Coordinating Committee for Multilateral Export Controls (COCOM) severely curtailing, among other things, the East's ability to buy advanced telecommunications technology from the West. Although these restrictions have been relaxed in 1989 and again in 1990, key telecommunications equipment and software, such as high-capacity optical fiber or Signalling System 7 (SS7), still fall under its ban.

Change germinated first in Hungary, which attempted a greater degree of economic modernization and integration with the West earlier than the other Central and Eastern European nations. For instance, international direct distance dialing (DDD) was introduced in the early 1970s and access to international data bases as well as the use of SWIFT in the early 1980s (Jakab, 1991, p. 60). By the mid-1980s, perceptions of the role of the telecommunications infrastructure in economic development were changing in Hungary and beginning to change elsewhere. Political change toward more democratic systems accelerated rapidly in 1989, beginning in Poland but eventually touching all regimes. As will be seen in greater detail below, relatively sweeping reforms have been initiated in all countries. There is a perceived need by nearly all the new regimes to create infrastructure for economic growth. Not least, change is due to the perceived inefficiencies of the existing organizational structures and their ties to the former centralized Communist structures.

There is a growing perception that economic efficiency, particularly market-oriented reforms, requires a more extensive and more horizontally open, less centrally controlled telecommunications infrastructure. Malik (1984) wondered, "Can the Soviet Union Survive Information Technology?" Dizard and Svensrud (1987) speculated that the need to more efficiently use information and telecommunication technology to help the Soviet economy keep up with the rapidly changing West may have been a principal motive behind the policies of *glasnost* and *perestroika*. These trends evolved faster in Eastern Europe than in the Soviet Union, as first Poland and then others gathered more independence from the U.S.S.R. in 1989-1990. By 1990, East Germany had been absorbed into the Federal Republic of Germany after a plebescite, and all of the others had changed regimes at least formally away from the former Communist governments.

The current political issues seem to revolve around just how much change to introduce into the organization and structure of telecommunications. Major topics in this debate are (a) the degree of independence from communications ministries granted to the telecommunications entities, (b) the permission and role of competition by private entities, (c) the role of foreign companies, and (d) the extent of cooperation with the rapidly evolving regime of telecommunications promoted by the European Communities (EC) in Western Europe.

Present Situation and Challenges Ahead

The saying of a Hungarian telecommunications official that "half of Hungary is waiting for a telephone; the other half is waiting for a dial tone" (Advisory Committee, 1990, p. 29) seems equally representative for the dismal status of telecommunications across large parts of Central and Eastern Europe. Several studies have shown a distinct correlation between the GDP per capita of a country and the telephone penetration rate (e.g., Siemens, 1987). Against this background, most Eastern and Central European countries show a lower average telephone penetration than would correspond to their state of economic development. Al-

TABLE 14.1 Central and Eastern European Telecommunications as of January 1, 1991

	GDP/ Capita[a]	Popu- lation (m)	Main- lines per 100 Persons	Telex Lines per 10,000 Persons	Data Conn. per 10,000 Persons	Telecom Investment as % of GDP
Bulgaria	26	8.9	22.2	6.7	NA	0.34
CSFR[b]	35	15.7	14.3	7.5	1.4	0.37
Hungary	30	10.6	8.6	13.7	1.3	0.43
Poland	25	37.8	8.2	8.9	NA	0.38
Romania	19	23.3	9.4	5.6	NA	0.18
CIS and Baltics[c]	31	290.9	13.0	4.0	NA	0.23
Yugoslavia	24	23.8	15.1	6.3	NA	.34

SOURCES: ITU country data; Murrell (1991); Ypsilanti & Kelly, Chapter 7 in this book.

[a]In percentage of U.S. GDP/capita (U.S. = 100); converted according to purchasing power.

[b]Czech and Slovak Federative Republic.

[c]Commonwealth of Independent States (of the former U.S.S.R.). The average of 13 mainlines per 100 persons conceals the variability within this group. The ITU reports the following figures for the former Soviet republics in 1991: Armenia, 6.5 mainlines per 100; Azerbaijan, 9.0; Belarus, 16.4; Estonia, 21.0; Georgia, 12.3; Kazakhstan, 11.4; Kyrgyzstan, 5.6; Latvia, 24.0; Lithuania, 21.8; Moldova, 11.4; Russia, 14.3; Tajikistan, 4.9; Turkmenistan, 6.5; Ukraine, 15.6; and Uzbekistan, 7.2.

though a great variability exists (see Table 14.1), telephone availability is more comparable to industrializing Third World countries such as Brazil than to lower- or middle-income Western European countries such as Spain, whose telephone penetration amounts to slightly above 30% of the population. The only exceptions are Bulgaria, which pursued a program of accelerated telecommunications investment during the 1970s and early 1980s, and the Baltic republics of Estonia, Latvia, and Lithuania.

However, these average figures do not reveal the full severity of the telecommunications infrastructure problem of Central and Eastern Europe. Most of the equipment in place is technologically antiquated. For instance, in 1990, 54% of local area exchanges in Czechoslovakia were still equipped with crossbar switches, 43% with step-by-step selectors, and only 3% used computer-controlled and -integrated digital systems (NTIA, 1990c, p. 21).

This quantitatively and qualitatively underdeveloped infrastructure has led to substantial excess demand by both business and residential customers. At present, Muscovites face waiting times of about 4 years for plain telephone service and, with a waiting list of about 10 million people, waiting times in rural areas of the former U.S.S.R. exceed 1 decade (Ponomarev, 1991). The situation is quite similar in other Central and Eastern European countries. Hungary reports a list of about 500,000 (Jakab, 1991, p. 57) waiting for a telephone line, Czechoslovakia 350,000, and Poland a 2 million queue. These figures do not include the unknown potential demand by those who are discouraged from even applying for a telephone.

Closing the capacity and technology gap in Central and Eastern Europe will be a major challenge for the years to come. To elevate the availability of telecommunications services to the level of middle-income Western European countries, Eastern European countries, and the former U.S.S.R. would have to install about 100 million new access lines and, at the same time, upgrade the existing facilities. Depending on the specific technological solution, this implies an aggregate investment volume of about $150-$300 billion. To accomplish this goal, the past annual investment efforts into telecommunications networks and services would have to increase substantially (Müller & Nyevrikel, 1990, p. 14).

Given the need to construct other infrastructures and manufacturing capacity, this investment poses an enormous financing burden on the national economies, especially under the conditions of limited internal sources of finance as well as limited convertible currency for technology imports. But the challenge reaches beyond the financing aspects of telecommunications development.

The fast build-up of a sophisticated telecommunications infrastructure also calls for appropriate organizational solutions for the sector. Most Western European countries developed their telecommunications systems in a monopoly environment that enabled their telecommunications operators to generate various forms of cross-subsidies to construct local and rural facilities. In Central and Eastern Europe, state-run monopolies bear the legacy of the former Communist regimes and do not seem to be a feasible mechanism to be the exclusive developers of a modernized telecommunications infrastructure. However, no sufficient or adequate alternative planning and coordination mechanisms seem to be developed yet to facilitate such a task. A strategy of privatization and increased competition might serve to overcome immediate bottlenecks. However, under the specific conditions of the telecommunications sector with possible significant positive and negative externalities (Antonelli, 1991; Bauer, Chapter 2 in this book), the efficiency gains of private, more competitive production have to be weighted against possible inefficiencies due to these specific sectoral conditions. For instance, private service suppliers may use their market position to charge (near) monopoly prices and cause substantial wealth transfers without contributing to the infrastructure build-up. In the light of the tasks ahead, the creation of a regulatory and planning environment seems to be an even greater challenge than the financing problem.

Organizational and Regulatory Framework

Most Central and Eastern European countries as well as the republics of the former Soviet Union are either engaged in or planning major organizational, legal, and regulatory reform. Perhaps with the exception of Hungary, the overall strategy of reform seems to follow more the Green Paper of the EEC than, for instance, the U.S. strategy of deregulation. This is not surprising given the common PTT-tradition in Eastern and Western Europe as well as the intention of Eastern European countries to establish closer ties with the EEC. Telecommunications functions are separated from the postal service and operational from regulatory functions. This reorganization is in most cases accompanied by a "corporatization" of the entities to enhance the internal efficiency of production. It seems as if most countries will maintain a monopoly on basic services, but some, such as Poland, do allow private operators into some basic network operations. Most nations will allow relatively open terminal equipment competition, again along the lines suggested by the EEC, and seem inclined to allow more competitive market structures in value-added services and networks.

Hungary has led this reform movement by relocating the regulatory functions from the PTT to the Ministry of Transport, Communication, and Construction in 1989. Telecommunications operations were separated from postal and broadcasting operations as of January 1, 1990. Hungarian authorities transformed the new telecommunications company (Matav) into a limited liability in 1992, thus enabling it to enter partnerships with foreign companies. Matav has entered a three-way joint venture agreement with Helsinki Telephone Co. of Finland and the private Hungarian company Kontrax Telekom RT to develop local infrastructure in the Pest section of Budapest. The Hungarian government has delayed the enactment of a new telecommunications law that will define the extent of monopoly privileges for Matav and lay ground rules for the partial privatization of Matav as well as two cellular GSM licenses.

Poland enacted a new Telecommunications Act, which took effect in January 1991. Major provisions separate operation from regulation, allow for competition in a number of services, and permit foreign investments. Although independent operators can now provide local services, none is in operation yet, leaving Telekomunikacja Polska SA (TPSA) in a dominant de facto monopoly position. Other countries are also proceeding fairly quickly to reform telecommunications organization statutes and laws governing changes in market structures. In the former U.S.S.R., one of the main problems is the creation of new republic-level structures to replace the former national monopoly PTT organization and to work out details of a privatization program (Kuznetsova & Filimonova, 1992).

Important measures in this overall reorganization process are various forms of privatization. In a wide interpretation, *privatization* goes beyond the divestiture of ownership from the public sector and can denote more general strategies of "entry and/or participation of nongovernment parties" (Nulty, 1991, p. 97) as well as a reorganization of telecommunications operators along lines characteristic of private enterprises (corporatization). A vast spectrum of possibilities exists to implement such measures. They include joint ventures, the sale of stock, the exclusive or competitive licensing of alternative providers, the contracting-out of specific services, and the general liberalization of market entry.

Whereas these organizational reforms constitute important steps in the overall reform strategy, a new and effective regulatory regime still needs to be implemented in Central and Eastern European countries. Like their Western European counterparts, these countries lack a tradition of explicit industry regulation such as the United States has. The dynamics of the entire telecommunications sector is vitally influenced by the regulatory framework established for interconnection of facilities, the use of common property resources such as the radio spectrum, the control of anti-competitive practices such as predatory pricing, and the conditions governing the quality of service requirements.

In these areas, the interests of the major telecommunications actors (incumbent operators, new market entrants, domestic and foreign investors, different groups of users) often conflict and are part of strategic games. For instance, new entrants have an interest to pay minimum prices for interconnection. However, a marginal cost price strategy may impede the overall strategy of network expansion and modernization. Nulty (1991, p. 106) mentions the demand of new entrants for tax privileges and protected markets such as exclusive franchises, which could be detrimental to efficiency. Effective regulation will have to mediate these conflicting interests. Such a "social contract" between the different interest groups cannot be established as a once for all blueprint but needs continuous evolution.

A major exception in these reform processes is the former East Germany. In the unification with the Federal Republic of Germany in October 1990, most of the West German policies were extended to the five East German states. The development of the telecommunications infrastructure is financially and technically backed by German Bundespost Telekom and the German government. To relieve short-run capacity shortages, a number of licenses for the operation of cellular and satellite-based services were granted by the German Bundespost. These licenses expire in 1997 but might well be renewed by then.

Financing

Financing the targeted expansion and modernization of telecommunications in Central and Eastern Europe will be a challenging task. To accomplish a telephone penetration rate of about 30 access lines per 100 inhabitants, the annual investment budget will have to rise from currently 0.2%-0.4% of GDP to 1.5%-2.0% of GDP (Müller & Nyevrikel, 1990; Nulty, 1991). Because of the need to improve other infrastructures and to modernize production facilities, this volume will be hard to accomplish and requires a strategy of mixed financing from all available sources. These include internal, revenue-generated funds by the major telecommunications operators as well as domestic and foreign outside financing in the form of debt or equity financing.

A continuation of the past policy of relatively low tariffs, frequently even below costs (Martelanc, 1991), does not allow the accumulation of sufficient internal funds to finance this expansion. Under the conditions of large excess capacity, charges could be revised to contribute to the modernization of the networks and services. These measures include an increase in the general tariff level as well as the introduction of concepts of peak-load pricing, which, properly enacted, would enhance allocative efficiency. According to calculations by the World Bank, internal funds could contribute up to 50% of the necessary investment volume in the short run and 85%-90% in the medium and long run (Nulty, 1991, p. 104). However, such a policy of tariff realignment and increases might interfere with the goal of supporting economic growth in general and constitute a source of unwanted inflation.

In most Central and Eastern European countries, an institutional framework for domestic capital markets is not yet developed. The possibility of raising domestic equity capital or loans is, therefore, seriously limited. Some Eastern European telecommunications operators have experimented in the past with innovative forms of financing. Network expansion in Bulgaria was accomplished with the financial help of municipalities, agricultural cooperatives, and enterprises that helped construct the local networks. After completion, the local facilities and the associated real estate became property of the PTT, but the local user community had the advantage of early access to improved telephone service (Müller & Nyevrikel, 1990, pp. 3).

Beginning in 1986, Hungary also started to establish forms of cooperation with municipalities and experimented with different forms of subscriber financing such as subscriber bonds or "subscriber-subscriptions" (Nulty, 1991, p. 104). In these cases, a subscriber gains a preferred place in the waiting list for connections by the purchase of a financial asset. Subscriptions or deposits may or may not be repaid by discounting the monthly bill after connection. Subscriber bonds may or may not be transferable. Magyar Posta, the former Hungarian PTT, raised about 8% of the total value of capital expenditure during the 1986-1989 period in the form of subscriber deposits, another 8% by subscriber bonds, and 9% through municipal partnerships (Nulty, 1991, p. 104). If a country considers the full or partial privatization of the telecommunications operator, this concept of subscriber financing could be extended to equity instruments granting the subscriber ownership in the newly formed enterprise.

The third possible source of funds is foreign (outside) finance. The perceived high degree of uncertainty, the unclear macroeconomic perspectives, and the lack of an established institutional framework in the Central and Eastern European countries have caused considerable hesitation by the Western financial community to provide funds for Eastern Europe. Some funding has been provided by the World Bank, the European Investment Bank, and the European Bank for Reconstruction and Development. However, Nulty (1991, p. 104) estimates that in the foreseeable future these institutions will not provide more than 40%-50% of the total foreign funds required to accomplish the telecommunications investment programs.

Direct foreign investment, which could bring equity capital and management expertise, faces a number of obstacles and seems likely to develop much slower than originally expected. Given the importance of telecommunications, governments in Eastern Europe, like governments in the rest of the world, are hesitant to turn over control of telecommunications networks to foreign investors. Hungary, for instance, has repeatedly postponed the partial privatization of its PTT. After the postal services were split off from the telecommunications divisions of the Czech and Slovak PTTs, it was planned to privatize up to 45% of Czech Telecom via the voucher method (*Communications Week International*, 5 October 1992, p. 14). The regulatory frameworks governing franchises, service obligations, frequency allocation, interconnection, and tariffs are established only slowly, creating some insecurity for foreign investors. Under these circumstances, *joint ventures*[1] between foreign and domestic companies emerge as a primary model for telecommunications development. These models reduce market insecurity for foreign investors and, inter alia, facilitate the transfer of technology and know-how.

Development of Networks and Services

Faced with the high excess demand for telecommunications services, most Central and Eastern European countries have embarked on a mixed strategy of short- and long-term measures. The short-term goals of relieving bottlenecks for commercial and residential users as well as a technological upgrade of services are complemented by long-run goals of constructing universal service telecommunications infrastructures.

From an economic point of view, these strategies should attempt to maximize the net improvement of welfare. In the telecommunications sector, as in other infrastructure sectors, it is difficult to operationalize abstract concepts of welfare into decision-guiding tools (Diewert, 1986). The prevalence of externalities can lead to a substantial divergence between the private and the social benefits of investment and innovation in telecommunications. An overall rational telecommunications development strategy should try to incorporate these tangible and intangible effects (Bauer, 1992). Besides the imperfections of the telecommunications market, this goal usually requires some form of explicit government coordination or oversight. Such coordination can assume the form of planning, tax-subsidy policies, government regulation with specific incentives, or also be pursued using the existing public enterprise structures.

Despite the difficulty of measuring the proper cost and benefits of telecommunications infrastructures, fundamental decisions have to be made quickly. At the heart of any development strategy is the choice of technological concepts. The most efficient strategy is not self-evident. Should investment concepts follow the introduction strategies of the Western world countries or maybe leapfrog generations of technology? Could low-cost versions of technology be used to accomplish the giant infrastructure development task with the available financial means (Kudriavtzev & Varakin, 1990)? What would a proper mix of urban/rural development be? And so on. The particular framework of telecommunications development in the Central and Eastern European countries puts considerable strain on the designs of such "first-best" strategies. Given the status quo ante and the time pressure to accomplish reforms, it seems more appropriate to look for feasible, if maybe "second-best," solutions.

Basic Network Expansion

A fundamental problem is to find a balanced strategy of expansion of the basic network, particularly for residential and rural service, and, at the same time, to provide more advanced services for the business community. Demand for both is high. Countries that want to expand their economies rapidly are receiving very strong pressure from both domestic and foreign business to focus on their needs first. They are also under strong domestic political pressure to serve average residential users as well (Nulty, 1991). As of 1991, the Polish PTT wanted to add 1.6 million access lines over the next 3-4 years, if financing could be found. In addition, other network operators were licensed to build 175,000 access lines (Radziminski, 1991). In the Czech and Slovak Republics, the priorities are first, to install service for all locations; second, to construct and upgrade data networks; and third, to invest in new services (NTIA, 1990a, p. 4). Hungary is also following a strategy of constructing overlay networks to alleviate bottlenecks while maintaining wide geographical availability. In Poland, Komertel, launched on a small scale in 1991, plans to expand to a capacity of 10,000 lines of which 500 are configured for ISDN use. One reason many countries are investing in cellular telephone services is to seek a lower cost and faster means of expanding the reach of the basic telephone system, thus serving both business and private users (Nulty, 1991; Radziminski, 1991).

With the exception of Czechoslovakia and Hungary, most Central and Eastern European countries had rather poor and limited long distance and international service. In this area, too, cooperative joint ventures with foreign companies are sought to overcome immediate problems. Among others, a joint venture was formed between AT&T, PTT of Netherlands, S.V., and the Ukrainian State Communication Committee to expand network capacity and manufacture telecommunications equipment. Similarly, Nokia of Finland, Ericsson of Sweden, the Belgacom and U.S. Sprint have made their inroads into Russia (see Thimm, 1992 for a discussion of corporate strategies).

Network Digitization and Upgrade

Most of the countries are attempting to upgrade their networks and switching systems to digital technology rapidly but only have limited experience with it. For example, Poland's network is 90% analog. For business users, most countries are also planning to install digital overlay networks in key cities, create digital international connections, install digital equipment as soon as possible (both installing new equipment and replacing old equipment), and install packet-switched networks to meet business data transmission demands (Nulty, 1991; Radziminski, 1991).

Almost no digital switching has existed previously. The replacement is being done by various major European and U.S. equipment manufacturers. In some cases, such as in Poland, outside manufacturers are acquiring or building local manufacturing capabilities to make switches in the country. In most cases, new switches are just being imported, but the major countries in Eastern Europe would like to build them, if they could. Poland, with three domestic manufacturers, ZWUT, Telettra, and PZT (with foreign partners), and Hungary, negotiating in 1991 with Northern Telecom, had the most advanced manufacturing capability for supplying Russia and other Central and Eastern European markets, so they are the most likely candidates for building digital equipment eventually. In the former U.S.S.R., a major issue is arranging for transfer of military technology to civilian uses. That could accelerate digitization of civilian networks.

Digital overlay networks are being constructed in major cities in some countries. The advantages for business users include cleaner data transmission, clean voice, and automatic dialing, which is itself still a relatively new idea in some areas. In Warsaw, the Komertel network had about 2,000 digital lines as of 1991, primarily serving business, banks, and hotels. The installation fee for lines was priced at about $1,000 (Radziminski, 1991), approximately 4 times the cost of a regular phone line. A similar system has been built in Moscow. In Hungary, U.S. West has built a microwave system, largely as backup for its cellular system, but it can also be used as an overlay network for other purposes. Czechoslovakia plans an overlay system, as do most other countries in the region. Specialized networks are also being constructed. A banking-oriented network has been built in Warsaw. Hungary and the Soviet Union have small science- and research-oriented packet-switched networks.

Cellular Networks

Analog cellular networks exist or are being built in several of the Eastern European countries. Because of its cost characteristics, cellular is particularly suited to relieve bottlenecks and improve coverage of telecommunications services. To speed up the installation of services, Central and Eastern European governments have issued a number of cellular franchises to foreign companies, partly as joint ventures with the domestic telecommunications operators. Examples include the joint venture of U.S. West with Matav; the license to L.M. Ericsson of Sweden to construct a cellular system based on the NMT 450 technology in Budapest, Hungary; and the activities of Bell Atlantic in Czechoslovakia, Moscow, and Leningrad (St. Petersburg). The new cellular service built by the joint venture with U.S. West was already in service in Budapest, some other major cities, and main connecting routes in Hungary by 1991 and is expanding for nationwide coverage. The Russian Republic had at least two systems underway in 1991. The Moscow system was functional but not yet being offered for service, since accounting and other issues also had to be resolved, and the system was under construction in St. Petersburg (see Müller & Toker, Chapter 10 in this book, for a more detailed discussion).

Very Small Aperture Satellite Terminals (VSATs)

Proposals are being made to initiate VSAT service in a number of countries. VSAT services are already being used in East Germany to remedy basic infrastructure problems. In Poland, VSAT services are seen as a way of meeting demand for data services by banks and companies. As with cellular telephony, a problem for VSAT usage is that the Polish government radio frequency inspectorate has not been ready to respond to the need to allocate frequencies used or reserved by the military.

Satellite and Optical Fiber Infrastructure

Particularly in the former U.S.S.R., there is some useful experience and infrastructure in communication satellites. The U.S.S.R. had satellite facilities, both civilian and military. Through the Intersputnik consortium, a Soviet-dominated alternative to INTELSAT, both the former U.S.S.R. and most of the rest of Eastern Europe has developed satellite facilities and experience. Intersputnik interconnection has been proposed by AT&T, to increase the number of circuits to the former U.S.S.R.

Russia is relying heavily on the use of satellites to overcome immediate bottlenecks. For instance, Sovam Teleport began to offer international data links in the 1980s; Combellga offers voice connections and leased-lines via a satellite link to Belgium; and Sovintel, a GTE joint venture, also offers voice services via satellite (*Communications Week International*, 5 October 1992, pp. 20). In another cooperative effort with Western companies, a trans-Siberia optical fiber link was proposed as a joint venture with U.S. West and European and Japanese PTTs, as a $500 million project for the mid-1990s. It would link Japan with Europe and provide domestic facilities for the former U.S.S.R. However, it was vetoed by the United States because of some U.S. government concern as to the sophistication of technology involved. U.S. West participation was not allowed, although the Soviets assured that the project would be nonmilitary and they would allow inspection. As developments in the former U.S.S.R. proceed, such policy restrictions may change.

Conclusions

Telecommunications in the Central and Eastern European countries evolves in a complex web of domestic and international political and economic conditions. Several countries, such as Hungary, Czechoslovakia, and Poland, have indicated their intention to apply for membership in or at least an association with the European Economic Community. Although a full membership in each case will require a long negotiating process, it is possible that a multilateral agreement will be found establishing a European Free Trading Zone comprised of the EEC, EFTA, and the Central and Eastern European countries. If such an integrated trading zone is modeled after the European Economic Area agreement between the EEC and the EFTA countries, it will probably extend most of the EEC regulations to such an enlarged association. In telecommunications, the organizational reforms visible in Central and Eastern European countries conform by and large with these requirements. Participation in a European trading zone would provide companies in the former Communist bloc access to European industrial policy and research and development programs and should provide an additional impetus for the development of the telecommunications sector.

Note

1. Joint ventures can take various forms. A usually relatively loose form is the cooperation between organizationally and financially independent firms to accomplish goals such as the development of specific technologies. Other joint ventures reach beyond this model and lead to a mutual financial and/or organizational integration of existing firms. Last, but not least, they can involve the joint creation of new entities.

References

Advisory Committee on International Communications and Information Policy. (1990). *Eastern Europe: Please stand by*. Washington, DC: U.S. Department of State.

Antonelli, C. (Ed.). (1991). *The economics of information networks*. New York: Elsevier Science.

Bauer, J. M. (1992). *Measuring the costs and benefits of telecommunications infrastructure*. Unpublished manuscript. East Lansing: Michigan State University, Department of Telecommunication.

Blanchard, O., Dornbusch, R., Krugman, P., Layard, R., & Summers, L. (1991). *Reform in Eastern Europe*. Cambridge: MIT Press.

Clague, C., & Rausser, G. C. (1992). *The emergence of market economies in Eastern Europe*. Cambridge, MA: Blackwell.

Diewert, W. E. (1986). *Measurement of the economic benefits of infrastructure services*. Berlin: Springer.

Dizard, W., & Svensrud, S. B. (1987). *Gorbachev's information revolution—Controlling Glasnost in a new electronic era* (Significant Issue Series IX:8). Washington, DC: Center for Strategic and International Studies.

Jakab, Z. (1991). Hungary's evolving telecommunications policies. In H. Mowlana & N. Levinson (Eds.), *Telecommunications and international relations: An East-West perspective* (pp. 53-64). Washington, DC: International Communications Program, School of International Service, The American University.

Kudriavtzev, G. G., & Varakin, L. E. (1990). Economic aspects of telephone network development. *Telecommunications Policy, 13*, 7-14.

Kuznetsova, O. K., & Filimonova, G. A. (1992). *Deregulation of telecommunications in the Russian Federation.* Paper presented at the 9th Conference of the International Telecommunications Society, 14-17 June 1992, Sophia-Antipolis, France.

Malik, R. (1984). Communism vs. the computer: Can the Soviet Union survive information technology? *Intermedia, 12*, 10-23.

Martelanc, T. (1991). Yugoslavia, the European Community and the information revolution. In H. Mowlana & N. Levinson (Eds.), *Telecommunications and international relations: An East-West perspective* (pp. 39-52). Washington, DC: International Service, The American University.

Müller, J., & Nyevrikel, E. (1990). *Closing the capacity and technology gap in East European telecommunications.* Paper presented at the 18th Telecommunications Policy Research Conference, Arlington, VA, September 1990.

Murrell, P. (1991). Can neoclassical economics underpin the reform of centrally planned economies? *Journal of Economic Perspectives, 5*, 59-76.

NTIA. (1990a). *Telecommunications in Czechoslovakia.* Document PB90-214321. Washington, DC: U.S. Department of Commerce/National Technical Information Service.

NTIA. (1990b). *Telecommunications in the GDR.* Document PB90-214339. Washington, DC: U.S. Department of Commerce/National Technical Information Service.

NTIA. (1990c). *Telecommunications markets in Eastern Europe: Country summaries.* Document PB90-213943. Washington, DC: U.S. Department of Commerce/National Technical Information Service.

Nulty, T. E. (1991). *Using privatization as a development tool in the telecommunications—The Central and East European situation.* Paper presented at the Economic Symposium, 6th World Telecom Forum, Geneva, October 13-15, 1991.

Ponomarev, V. V. (1991). A Soviet perspective on telecommunications and trade. In H. Mowlana & N. Levinson (Eds.), *Telecommunications and international relations: An East-West perspective* (pp. 33-38). Washington, DC: International Communications Program, School of International Service, The American University.

Radziminski, A. (1991, 17 November). Personal communication. President/CEO of RP Telekom, Ltd., Poland.

Siemens AG. (1987). *Internationale Fernsprechstatistik.* München, Germany.

Thimm, A. L. (1992). *New strategies for changing structures. The complex nature of Eastern European telecommunications systems.* Paper presented at the 9th Conference of the International Telecommunications Society, 14-17 June 1992, Sophia-Antipolis, France.

FIFTEEN

Telecommunications Strategies in the Developed World

A Hundred Flowers Blooming or Old Wine in New Bottles?

ELI M. NOAM
RICHARD A. KRAMER

The process of providing telecommunications services and equipment in developed countries has traditionally involved a closely knit community of interest groups. Until the late 1980s, most countries combined postal and telecommunications functions under the same roof. These civil service PTTs (Post, Telegraph, and Telephone Administrations) go back to the age of European absolutism when postal monopolies were first established (Noam, 1992) and have since spread to most of the world. The PTTs' operations were typically controlled and operated through state institutions such as ministries of post and communications. They held a monopoly over all mail and telecommunications services and were closely allied with domestic manufacturers of telecommunications equipment. Internationally, they collaborated through various cartel-like organizations and coordinating agencies. Additional support groups in this "postal-industrial complex" were labor unions and rural populations.

After a century of institutional stability, the PTTs underwent a metamorphosis in the 1980s. They were separated from postal functions, and in some cases from direct civil service status, and renamed themselves Public Telecommunications Operators (PTOs). They followed different institutional and legal models and pursued varied strategies. Yet the question is raised: Did the new strategies and structures herald real change and diversity, a blooming of a hundred flowers in the telecommunications field, or were they largely the old wine of PTT control in new bottles? This chapter argues that for all of the diversity of institutional arrangements the new PTOs have emerged from a turbulent decade with greater power than before. However, this condition is temporary. In time, corrective forces will emerge. What we are witnessing today, therefore, is the golden age of traditional telecommunications organizations.

Reform of the Old PTT System

For most developed countries, the trend of economic history had been toward increased public control. Joseph Schumpeter described capitalism as a no-win situation. Its economic success and creative processes undermined the foundations of the private sector. Yet in the 1980s this trend appeared to be reversed. Now, public enterprises around the world were the ones being challenged.

In telecommunications, one route was laid out by the United Kingdom, where the conservative government of Prime Minister Thatcher created and privatized British Telecom. Japan pursued a similar strategy, privatizing the domestic carrier NTT, inviting competitors into the market, and permitting new international carriers as rivals to the traditional KDD. The United States, in particular, forged ahead with competition, introducing it first into long distance and then into local service. It dismembered the private near-monopoly giant of telecommunications, AT&T.

In contrast, France in the 1980s took a more traditional statist approach and increased the role of government. The Socialist government made high-technology a national priority and nationalized much of the French electronics and telecommunications equipment industry to meet this goal. The effect was that the French actually created, for a time, a state-owned analog of the old AT&T system: a vertically integrated complex of equipment manufacturing coupled with a telecommunications transmission monopoly and an R&D laboratory. Conservatives, returning briefly to power in 1985, re-privatized several of the equipment firms, and the telephone administration was gradually made more independent. But the state and its affiliated institutions remained in charge, continuing the French tradition of industrial policy for the telecommunications and electronics sectors.

In most of the developed world, telecommunications strategies were somewhere in between the U.S., British, and Japanese market ideology and the French statist policies. The classic model was set in The Netherlands, where the traditional PTT was split into postal and tele-communications bodies under the managerial autonomy of a public corporation. This model was eventually followed in most European countries, where the initial resistance of PTTs gave way to increasing support.

Other countries instituted hybrid strategies. Spain partly privatized its monopoly operator Telefónica. Italy, Portugal, and Denmark attempted to consolidate separate service providers. Finland strengthened its inde-pendent local companies. Sweden opened its market to new entrants. Australia privatized its national carriers along service segments, and New Zealand, in perhaps the most farthest reaching reorganization, totally deregulated telecommunications, selling its traditional monopoly carrier Telecom New Zealand to U.S. firms, abolishing the formal regulatory body, and permitting others to enter as competitors in all telecommunica-tions services. Singapore aggressively used telecommunications to de-velop other sectors of its economy. Many Latin American countries privatized their monopoly operators in debt-equity swaps to improve creditworthiness, and for some, the infusion of foreign capital allowed dramatic improvements in service. And in Eastern Europe, where networks had been developed sparingly as a form of political control under the old regimes, rapid expansion and restructuring of telecommunications as part of democratization was considered.

The Policy Portfolio: A Hundred Flowers?

In this policy Tower of Babel, can one distinguish some basic struc-tures and strategies? We will identify 11 fundamental building blocks of national strategies for telecommunications. The first 4 strategies pertain to the structure and form of telecommunications markets. They are *liberalization*, *devolution*, *consolidation*, and *deregulation*. In vari-ous combinations, they provide the materials for the new structures that were built in the 1980s. They are concerned with the status of a single unified PTT monopoly. Two other strategies, *corporatization* and *pri-vatization*, deal with the question of ownership and control and do not require a challenge to monopoly. A third set of strategies are those of international collaboration: *transnationalization*, *international alliances*, and *harmonization*. A final set of strategies are those of high technological development: *vertical integration* and *industrial policy*. These approaches are now examined in greater detail.

Market Structure Strategies

Liberalization

Liberalization means the introduction of competition into monopolized markets. For equipment, it may involve adoption of standards that do not favor any group of suppliers, simple procedures for type approvals, nondiscriminatory rules for public procurement, and the absence of protective quotas. On the services side, liberalization may involve licensing entrants to provide a particular service, such as cellular telephony or long distance. Liberalization policies often require government scrutiny to prevent anticompetitive behavior by the former monopoly. In some cases, governments create or support firms to compete with the monopoly operator.

In the services sector. the most common liberalization strategy is to license new entrants to compete in specific markets. The European Commission in Brussels encouraged liberalization of value-added services and cellular markets. In the United States, the FCC developed policies for long-distance, cellular, and local competition, the latter with some of the state commissions. In Japan, the government licensed facilities-based carriers and service providers (Type I and II carriers). South Korea introduced two new carriers to compete with the existing PTO. In Britain, Mercury was licensed as a rival long-distance carrier. A more radical liberalization strategy is to open every market segment to unlimited competition. This was done in New Zealand.

Liberalization should not be confused with deregulation. Deregulation is a reduction in government-imposed constraints on the behavior of PTOs. One may, for example, have a deregulated monopoly or a tightly regulated multicarrier system. The experiences in the United States and the United Kingdom, two of the most liberalized markets, reveal that more rather than less regulation is often needed in the early stages after markets have been opened. For example, interconnection arrangements may have to be set. A "level playing field" among competitors may have to be ensured through the application of antitrust laws, or, conversely, some competitors may receive preferential treatment in order to protect competition in its infancy. Thus the experience of liberalization has shown that the introduction of competition into the market often leads to a period of regulatory scrutiny.

Devolution

Devolution is a policy of dismantling a single monolithic structure into several units. On one level, this has occurred wherever the postal and the telecommunications authorities were split. Another more important level is the devolution within telecommunications organizations, along lines of functional operations or geography.

The prime example of devolution is the divestiture of AT&T in America into local and long-distance operations. So far, no other country has pursued devolution, but it is under consideration in Japan and Britain. Devolution is not a necessary condition for either liberalization or privatization, although it addresses the problems of competitive barriers to new entrants. Devolution serves the long-term policy objective of isolating market segments that may at some point be subject to competition. Devolution can also be part of liberalization, where some segments of the market are opened up to competitors and others are not. If a differentiated regulatory treatment of carriers active in both open and restricted markets is sought, a policy of devolution may be chosen.

For example, in the United Kingdom, portions of BT face competition, such as in VANs and long-distance service. Other market segments remain monopolistic, in particular, the critical local loop access, despite regulation efforts to introduce competition. Hence an AT&T-style divestiture of BT has been proposed by the Labour Party (Garnham, 1990).

However, devolution does not necessarily lessen monopoly power, because it may substitute a shared monopoly for an end-to-end national one. In Italy, the public network is segmented along functional lines among several organizations (local, domestic long distance, satellite service, international service, telex), but each operator is monopolistic in its service segment. Similarly, Portugal and Finland have regional or local monopoly carriers. In Canada, mostly private firms hold regional monopolies in local service and jointly control long-distance services.

Consolidation

The opposite strategy to devolution is consolidation. Consolidation has occurred where a country's telecommunications were divided for various historical reasons along geographic or functional lines. The rationale for consolidation is to capture the economies of scale and scope of a single monopolist, which are important to competition in global markets.

In Denmark, the country's four regional service providers were merged with the national PTT that provided long-distance service to create a single operator, TeleDenmark. Similar plans to create national integrated "super-carriers" were advanced in Italy and Portugal but have met stiff political resistance. The East German network was absorbed into the West German Deutsche Bundespost Telekom system after unification.

Consolidation has also been a major trend in the equipment industry. With the rising costs of research and development, especially for digital switch software, the number of major manufacturers has been shrinking through mergers and acquisitions. The French company Alcatel acquired ITT's far-flung telecommunications manufacturing operations as well as Italy's Telettra. Siemens took a stake in the U.K. telecommunications firm GPT and acquired the American firms Stromberg-Carlsson and Rolm and the German computer firm Nixdorf. Canada's Northern Telecom bought the U.K. manufacturer STC. AT&T forged alliances with Italtel, the leading Italian manufacturer, and for a while with Philips and Olivetti. Smaller national companies offered products of the larger international firms, such as in Switzerland, Portugal, Austria, and Turkey.

Deregulation

Deregulation is an imprecise concept and is often used as a synonym for liberalization, that is, for a lowering of entry barriers or other restrictions. More basically, it means a reduction in government-set constraints. As mentioned, deregulation can be at odds with liberalization. The entry of new competitors tends to complicate things much more than an outright monopoly and can lead to a more extensive set of rules. For example, the need to keep an interoperating system functioning requires access and interconnection rules, such as Open Network Provision in Europe and Open Network Architecture in the United States.

Typically, full deregulation is not an early option, because of the unequal power of competitors on the one hand and the politics of protecting the monopoly system on the other. Also, governments are typically unwilling to cede all control over the vital telecommunications infrastructure.

Ownership Strategies

Corporatization

Corporatization is the transformation of the PTT into a structure semi-autonomous from government, which may still be state-owned but controls its own managerial and administrative functions. The monopoly status is not touched by corporatization as such, though once the close link to the government is severed, a process is set in motion that makes further changes more likely. Sometimes the corporatized entity is described as a "private" firm, in the sense that it may be organized under private law provisions, which determines its status in, for example, contract and labor law. But that description confuses legal detail with the reality of control, which is still very much governmental. In other instances, a minority of shares may be issued to the public, though control is still retained by the state.

Corporatization may be a first step on the road to privatization. It is often sought by the PTOs themselves, who need greater managerial and budgetary autonomy to pursue long-range investment projects and the ability to raise investment capital outside of government borrowing ceilings. Corporatization may also derive from a public desire to inject new life into sleepy monopoly bureaucracies.

Because corporatization loosens direct administrative controls, it is usually accompanied by the creation or strengthening of a government regulatory mechanism. Such was the case in The Netherlands, where the Dutch PTT was split from the state control into a public corporation, with regulatory authority vested in the Ministry of Transport and Public Works. In Belgium, the RTT was renamed Belgacom and regulated by the new Belgian Institute for Telecommunications and the Ministry of Economic Affairs. After a national debate over telecommunications reform, France Télécom was corporatized in 1990. In Germany, corporatization created the Deutsche Bundespost Telekom, with its employees retaining their attractive civil service status.

Privatization

Privatization involves the government sale of shares in the PTT to private investors. However, ownership need not affect the monopoly status. In the United States, AT&T was private and a near monopoly for a very long period. In Canada, private regional monopolies exist, and long-distance competition has only recently been contemplated. Most

European privatizations are only partial. In the 1980s, the Italian government sold shares totaling 40% of the Italian monopoly local carrier SIP. It also sold 42% of SIP's parent company STET but retained overall control. In Spain, the government sold 65% of Telefónica yet still controlled the appointment of its chief executive and top management. In Denmark, the state sold 49% of the shares in the newly created TeleDenmark, but a large block was purchased by the state pension fund. Nontelecommunications concerns have often intruded into privatization decisions. Sweden put the partial privatization of Televerket on hold until the Swedish stock market recovered from a recession. In the United Kingdom, Conservatives pressed for the sale of the remaining shares of British Telecom before a general election that the Labour Party might win.

Privatization may encourage efficiencies of operation. But quality of service may fall if an unconstrained monopolist seeks cost reductions without regard to its captive customers. Privatization can also have the unintended effect of strengthening a monopoly, as shareholders become a political constituency to preserve a monopoly. Widespread shareholder involvement in the United Kingdom created a deregulatory force opposed to curbs on BT's dominance that might threaten profitability. In Spain, Telefónica is protected by the desire to assure its stock a safe status as a "widow and orphan" investment.

Ownership strategies depend on national economic development. Privatization in less developed nations derives from a need to raise capital. Indonesia, for example, offered an infrastructure role for private capital. Throughout Latin America, privatization was used as a method to reduce the heavy debt burden. In Eastern Europe, it is led by the need for foreign capital and expertise. In Malaysia, it was part of a national program to increase the ownership share by ethnic Malays in the national economy.

In contrast, in more developed nations, privatization and corporatization aim to overcome borrowing or investment restrictions on public enterprises and to provide a means to shake up bureaucratized enterprises.

International Strategies

Transnationalization

Transnationalization is a strategy of large and advanced PTOs to expand beyond national markets. As these PTOs achieved universal telephone penetration, they expanded their sights geographically. This strategy has been pursued through acquisitions, international service offerings (such as network software or management), and by establishing foreign subsidiaries. British Telecom, for example, purchased a leading U.S. value-added service provider (Tymnet) and a large stake in a major U.S. cellular carrier (McCaw) and established a firm to serve the network management needs of large multinational users (Syncordia). France Télécom acquired part of the Mexican telecommunications monopoly, TelMex, and entered the United Kingdom by providing packet-switched network service in partnership with the London Underground. Spain's Telefónica sought to leverage its linguistic affinities with Latin America through investments in the national carriers in Argentina, Venezuela, and Chile. The United Kingdom's Cable & Wireless has long been a transnational carrier, providing local service in Hong Kong and the Caribbean and international services, with the strategy of linking the world's major financial centers. It participated in fiber optic cable projects crossing the Atlantic, Pacific, and North America, and established with U.S. Sprint a global virtual private network service.

U.S. firms, specifically the Bell companies, have also sought to transnationalize their operations. Nynex provides telephone service in Gibraltar. Bell Atlantic and Ameritech acquired Telecom New Zealand. Southwestern Bell bought a stake in Mexico's TelMex. U.S. West sought to join a coalition providing trans-Siberian service. Several U.S. companies were involved in cellular services in Western and Eastern Europe and won cable television franchises in Britain.

International Alliances

International alliances offer another method for PTOs to expand their markets. Across Europe, most PTOs have entered joint ventures and service consortia. Such partnerships allow PTOs to gain some access to heavily monopolized markets where they are not allowed to compete with the local operator. Alliances also spread the risk of new service ventures across multiple participants. This has traditionally been the case with consortia such as Intelsat and Eutelsat for satellites and the transoceanic cables. The participation of multiple PTOs ensures a larger target market and customer base for new services, helps PTOs acquire expertise, and provides a defense against the entry of established foreign carriers into domestic markets. For example, competition between

France Télécom and DBP Telekom is less likely if they are engaged in multiple joint ventures and alliances.

Many advanced PTOs, for example, participate in the Infonet consortium. Infonet, whose largest shareholder is MCI, provides value-added services worldwide through 11 member PTOs that might otherwise be competitors. Other joint ventures include those between AT&T, BT, KDD, and France Télécom, and between Cable & Wireless and U.S. Sprint. Sweden's Televerket and PTT Telecom Nederland formed a joint venture, Unicom, to serve large users and for international presence. AT&T and PTT Telecom Nederland teamed up to provide long-distance service to the new Republic of Ukraine.

Harmonization

Harmonization is the coordination of telecommunications policy among countries. Harmonization may include the creation of common standards for equipment or the development of common policies for provision of service. Harmonization can be managed through regional bodies such as the European Commission and multilateral groups such as the International Telecommunications Union and its coordinating body CCITT, as well as through bilateral negotiations. It may lower barriers to entry in markets by providing a single set of regulations. But such rules may also be set in a restrictive fashion, such as a cartel-like prevention of certain forms competition to monopolies. For many years, harmonization was a code word for international restrictiveness, as exercised by PTT organizations such as CEPT and CCITT. For example, the harmonized rules of the CCITT prevented competition in telex service from indirect routing through cheap service countries. It took a challenge before the European Court of Justice to abolish this coordinated restriction. Such challenges have multiplied in recent years. Other international organizations, such as the EC, the GATT, and the OECD, have pursued harmonization on a more liberalizing basis.

Competitiveness Strategies

Industrial Policy

In almost every country, telecommunications policy is set within larger industrial development, and PTOs were given a major role in national high technology. These industrial policies tended to support the establishment of "national champion" electronics firms and implicitly assured them major shares of public procurement contracts at prices that often shared in the monopoly profits of the operator. In some cases, direct financial support for the electronics and telecommunications sectors was provided by PTTs. They also deployed and supported proprietary technologies and protocols.

France, Singapore, and South Korea have been particularly active in developing industrial policies for telecommunications. In the French government's high-technology agenda for the IT sector, the "filière electronique," France Télécom was assigned a central role. It provided a market for 45% of the French equipment industry's production and demonstrations to potential foreign buyers. The government already heavily subsidizing the nationalized electronics firms Bull and Thomson forced France Télécom to take managerial control of Bull's private data network.

In Spain, similarly, the government assigned to Telefónica a role of locomotive in high-technology development. In Singapore, the telecommunications infrastructure was funded as a platform for other high-technology industries. Even in the United Kingdom, the government spent £350 million on information technology development at the same time it espoused free markets.

Vertical Integration

In some countries, PTOs integrated vertically into the manufacturing of telecommunications equipment. In Spain, Telefónica holds a large stake in Standard Electrica, Spain's largest electronics firm, as well as several other high-tech firms. In North America, AT&T, GTE, and Bell Canada had far-reaching manufacturing operations. Eventually, the divestiture separated AT&T from the local exchange companies, GTE sold its equipment business, and Northern Telecom was partly spun off. In Italy, the network operator and largest equipment manufacturer are owned by the same partly privatized government holding company. Sweden's Televerket owns the major domestic equipment firm, Teli. Under the new wave of corporatization and privatization, other PTOs, having gained freedom, have sought to expand vertically. British Telecom bought the ailing Canadian PBX manufacturer Mitel. Equipment manufacturers also entered service markets. Alcatel, DEC, and IBM, for example, offered value-added services.

Old Wine in New Bottles?

These 11 strategies constituted the primary policy menu in the 1980s. They are often described as major steps of reform. Yet how much difference did they really make to the power of the PTOs?

In the area of market structure, liberalization had its limits. The notion of an infrastructure monopoly still has substantial political support almost everywhere. Basically, only the United States, Japan, the United Kingdom, Sweden, and New Zealand permit alternative physical non-mobile networks. Similarly, PTOs almost everywhere have also found political support for their monopoly over voice service, and its resale is rarely permitted. Brussels did not attack the PTOs' control over "basic services," which included both the provision of voice service and the physical telecommunications infrastructure. This has often changed the debate over service liberalization into nitpicking arguments over what constitutes "value added".

The actual reduction of monopoly thus tends to be exaggerated. A Danish political agreement illustrates the doublespeak: "There will be competition within all spheres of telecommunications in the next few years, apart from telex, ordinary telephony, radio-based mobile services, satellite services, the infrastructure and the use of the telecommunications network for broadcasting radio and television programmes" (Danish Ministry of Communications, 1990). In other words, "everything" is liberalized, except for the remaining 95%. Similarly, though EC laws instituted in principle the right to offer value-added services in any country, the details in many countries tended to be restrictive.

Another limit on liberalization is the pace of its actual realization. After 8 years in the U.K. market, Mercury has between 3% and 5% total market share and its core business remains serving firms in London's City as a second source for data transmission capacity and the carriage of trunk calls for businesses. Its residential service failed to gain even 1% of the market (Oftel, 1991). Where no entrenched incumbent existed, competition is better developed. For example, BT's competitor in the cellular service duopoly, Racal Vodafone, holds more than 50% of the market share. Because of the value of a headstart, the launch of second cellular carriers in competition with the national PTO was delayed in Germany, Italy, and Spain. The European Community has likewise suffered numerous delays in its efforts to implement liberalized rules for service provision. Thus, where competition with a monopoly exists, it is often a David versus Goliath contest (Kramer, 1991). In such a situation, deregulation strengthened PTOs, because operational and financial restrictions on them were lifted while competition was still embryonic.

In the equipment market, the liberalization of procurement sources actually enhanced the power of the monopoly PTOs. By opening the public procurement process to additional vendors, PTOs are in a better bargaining position to obtain favorable contract terms. They are no longer tied in to the technology developed by national champion equipment firms. Yet the larger PTOs can still dictate technical specifications to manufacturers. Only the liberalization of terminal equipment has reduced PTO powers, but such liberalization was largely an accommodation to reality. The market had already liberalized itself by numerous consumers simply, but illegally, buying cheaper and more varied equipment outside the official PTT distribution.

Similarly, devolution did not touch PTOs. Only the United States has divested its monopoly into several pieces. Similar attempts elsewhere have been resisted by PTOs. On the contrary, several countries attempted to make their carriers stronger by consolidation, such as Denmark, Italy, and Portugal.

What have been the impacts of changes in ownership and control? Here, too, reforms have increased PTO power. Corporatization substituted managerial and financial autonomy for the direct governmental operational control of PTOs and the political accountability that came with it. At the same time, the government ministries that assumed regulatory power tended to be ineffective. These ministries have only a handful of experts to confront the huge telephone organizations. In Sweden, Televerket had 42,000 employees, and the regulative ministry a telecom staff of only 6.

Similarly, privatization has strengthened PTOs. The presence of shareholders to which the PTO must answer has added new incentives for improved performance that were largely absent in the past. Privatization also curbed some market liberalization by creating a wide constituency of shareholders who oppose sweeping reforms. This used to be the case in the United States in the past and is now with Telefónica and British Telecom. Similarly, NTT's remaining shares have not been sold by the government in order not to depress the share price and hence hurt millions of investors.

The international strategies of PTOs, such as transnationalization and alliances have similarly strengthened their position. The PTOs are becoming far-flung global organizations, involved in numerous activities that cease to be transparent to governments. Competitors assert that these activities are supported by the monopoly profits from basic service. At the same time, many PTOs have also formed alliances among themselves, often as a market sharing arrangement.

Such cooperation is also manifest in policy harmonization, which also often leads to a continuation of the traditional stability. Although harmonization may eliminate restrictive national rules, it is just as likely to be used to prevent competitive behavior by establishing a policy cartel.

Virtually all countries still assign an important role in developing high technology to their telecommunications organizations. As electronics and information-intensive service industries succeed heavy industry as key determinants of national economic advancement, PTOs are an increasingly important lever to develop this sector. In some cases, regional programs, such as the EC's RACE and STAR, supplement the national efforts.

Conclusion: The End of a Golden Age?

What have these strategies and reforms meant to the traditional telecommunications organizations? As institutions, they have not been harmed, and indeed, they have benefited. PTOs enjoy a dominant position in the market. They have been energized. Their competitors are tiny, regulatory authorities are frequently ineffective, and their role is enhanced by national industrial policies. (This is not to say that some users and competitors have not also benefited. Telecommunications are a positive-sum rather than a zero-sum game.)

This suggests that reforms, instead of being instituted from the outside to curb the traditional monopolies, were rather sought by the PTOs themselves. Reforms were originally advocated from outside and at first resisted by the PTTs, which then reshaped them into accommodating forms.

Will the present PTO dominance last? Given the dynamic forces of the telecommunications market, this is unlikely. In time, PTO market share will decline as their competitors will grow in size and gain interconnection rights; eventually, unprepared regulators will become more effective; the PTO's national role in industrial development policies will be shared with other firms; and the PTO cartel collaboration will change to more head-to-head competition. New domestic entrants will seek opportunities in specialized and general markets, as will foreign entrants, some of them PTOs themselves. Liberalization at home will become critical to PTOs seeking reciprocal market access abroad. Other entrants will be specialized carriers, such as cellular companies, cable TV providers, and VAN resellers.

The notion of the single territorially defined carrier for an entire country's electronic information flows is not sustainable in the long run. The strategies followed in the 1980s and 1990s have set forces in motion that will in time assert themselves. What we are witnessing today is the golden age of PTOs, but it will not last.

References

Danish Ministry of Communications. (1990). *Political agreement on telecommunications structure*. Press release, 22 June.

Garnham, N. (1990). *Telecommunications policy in the United Kingdom*. Discussion Paper No. 1. London: Fabian Society.

Kramer, R. (1991). *A faith that divides: Competition policy in European telecommunications*. Unpublished doctoral thesis, Philadelphia, University of Pennsylvania, Annenberg School of Communication.

Noam, E. M. (1992). *Telecommunications in Europe*. New York: Oxford University Press.

Oftel. (1991). *Annual report*. London: Her Majesty's Stationery Office.

List of Abbreviations

ACTE	Approvals Committee for Terminal Equipment
AIM	Advanced Informatics in Medicine in Europe
AMRO	Amsterdam-Rotterdam Bank Group
ASCII	American Standard Code for Information Interchange
AT&T	American Telephone and Telegraph Company
ATM	Asynchronous Transfer Mode, or also Automated Teller Machine
B-ISDN	Broadband ISDN
BT	British Telecom
BTX	Bildschirmtext
CAD/CAM	Computer Aided Design/Computer Assisted Manufacturing
CADDIA	Cooperation in Automation of Data and Documentation for Imports/Exports and Agriculture
CAGR	Compound Annual Growth Rate
CAI	Common Air Interface
CAT	Customer Access Terminal
CATV	Community Antenna Television, now Cable Television
CCEET	Center for Cooperation with European Economies in Transition (OECD)
CCH	Harmonization Coordination Committee for Standardization (CEPT)
CCIF	International Telephone Consultative Committee
CCIR	International Radio Consultative Committee
CCIT	International Telegraph Consultative Committee
CCITT	International Telephone and Telegraph Consultative Committee (ITU)
CEC	Commission of the European Communities
CEN	European Committee for Standardization (Comité européen de Normalisation)
CENELEC	European Committee for Electrotechnical Standardization (Comité Européen de Normalisation Électrotechnique)

CEPT	European Conference of Postal and Telecommunications Administrations (Conférence Européenne des Administrations des Postes et des Télécommunications)
CIM	Computer Integrated Manufacturing
CNET	Centre National d'Etudes des Télécommunications
COCOM	Coordinating Committee for Multilateral Export Controls
COS	Corporation for Open Systems
COSINE	Cooperation for Open Systems Interconnection in Europe
CPE	Customer Premise Equipment
CSFR	Czech and Slovak Federal Republic
CT	Cordless Telephone
CTT	Correios e Telecommunicacoes de Portugal
DAC	Development Assistance Committee (OECD)
DBP	Deutsche Bundespost
DBS	Direct Broadcast Satellites
DEC	Digital Electronics Corporation
DECT	Digital European Cordless Telephone
DELTA	Developing European Learning through Technological Advance
DG	Directorate General (of the Commission of the European Communities)
DG I	Directorate General for External Relations
DG III	Directorate General for Internal Market and Industrial Affairs
DG IV	Directorate General for Competition
DG X	Directorate General for Information, Communication, and Culture
DG XIII	Directorate General for Telecommunications, Information Industries, and Innovation
Docdel	Document Delivery
DOD	Department of Defense
DRG	Direction de la Règlementation Générale des Postes et Télécommunications (French regulatory body for telecommunications)
DRIVE	Dedicated Road Infrastructure for Vehicle Safety
DTI	Department of Trade and Industry
DTMF	Dual Tone Multi-Frequency
E-MAC	Enhanced Multiplexed Analog Components
EBIT	European Broadband Interconnection Trial
EBRD	European Bank for Recovery and Development
EBU	European Broadcasting Union
EC	European Community
ECHO	European Community Host Organization
ECSC	European Coal and Steel Community
ECU	European Currrency Unit

EDI	Electronic Document (Data) Interchange
EDIFACT	Electronic Document Interchange Group
EDS	Electronic Data Systems Company
EEA	European Economic Area
EEC	European Economic Community
EFT	Electronic Funds Transfer
EFTA	European Free Trade Association
EFTPOS	Electronic Funds Transfer at Point of Sale
EMC	Electromagnetic Compatibility
ERMES	European Messaging System
ERO	European Radiocommunications Office
ESPRIT	European Strategic Program for Research and Development in Information Technologies
ETCO	European Telecommunications Consultancy Organization
ETS	European Telecommunications Standards
ETSI	European Telecommunications Standards Institute
EURATOM	European Atomic Energy Community
EURESCOM	European Institute for Research and Strategic Studies in Telecommunications
EUTELSAT	European Telecommunications Satellite Organization
EWOS	European Workshop for Open Systems
FCC	Federal Communications Commission
GAP	Analysis and Forecasting Group
GATT	General Agreement on Tariffs and Trade
GDP	Gross Domestic Product
GEC	General Electric Company
GEISCO	General Electric Information Services Company
GEN	General European Network
GM	General Motors
GNP	Gross National Product
GNS	Group of Negotiations on Services
GSM	Groupe Special Mobile
GTE	General Telephone Company
HDTV	High Definition Television
IBC	Integrated Broadband Communications
IBCN	Integrated Broadband Communications Networks
IBM	International Business Machines
IBN	Intelligent Broadband Network
IBS	Intelligent Broadband System
ICCP	Information, Computer, and Communications Policy Committee (OECD)
IDA	Integrated Digital Access
IDDD	International Direct Distance Dialing

IEC	International Electrotechnical Commission
IFRB	International Frequency Registration Board
IMPACT	Information Market Policy Action
INMARSAT	International Maritime Satellite Consortium
INSIS	Interinstitutional Integrated Services Information Systems
INTELSAT	International Telecommunications Satellite Organization
INTUG	International Telecommunications Users Group
IRI	Istituto Ricostruzione Industriale (Italian Industrial Reconstruction Group)
ISDN	Integrated Services Digital Network
ISO	International Standards Organization
ISR	Inter-System Roaming
IT	Information Technology
ITSC	Interregional Telecommunications Standards Conference
ITT	International Telegraph and Telephone
ITU	International Telecommunications Union
IVAN	International Value-Added Network
KDD	Kokusai Denshin Denwa
LAN	Local Area Network
MAC	Multiplexed Analog Components
MAN	Metropolitan Area Network
MCI	Microwave Communications Incorporated
MCN	Microcellular Network
MDNS	Managed Data Network Services
METRAN	Managed European Transmission Network
MFN	Most Favored Nation
MOU	Memorandum of Understanding
NEC	Nippon Electric Company
NGS	News Gathering Services
NMP	Net Material Product
NMT	Nordic Mobile Telephone
NTIA	National Telecommunications and Information Administration
NTSC	North American Television Standards Committee
NTT	Nippon Telegraph and Telephone
OECD	Organization for Economic Cooperation and Development
OEEC	Organization for European Economic Cooperation
OFTEL	Office of Telecommunications (U.K.)
ONA	Open Network Architecture
ONP	Open Network Provision
OSF	Open Software Foundation
OSI	Open Systems Interconnection
OTA	Office of Technology Assessment
PABX	Private Automatic Branch Exchange

PACE	Perspectives for Advanced Communications in Europe
PAL	Phase Alternate Line
PC	Personal Computer
PCN	Personal Communications Networks
PIT	Partners in Transition program (of the OECD)
POSI	Promoting Conference for Open Systems Interconnection
POTS	Plain Old Telephone Service
PMR	Private Mobile Radio
PRS	Premium Rate Services
PSDN	Packet-Switched Data Network
PSTN	Public-Switched Telephone Network
PTO	Public Telecommunications Operator
PTT	Post, Telegraph, and Telephone Administration
R&D	Research and Development
R&TD	Research and Technological Development
RACE	Research and Development for Advanced Communications Technologies in Europe
RARE	Réseaux Associés pour la Recherche Européene
RBOC	Regional Bell Operating Company
RSO	Regional Standards Organization
RTT	Regie des Telegraphes et Télécommunications (now Belgacom)
SDH	Synchronous Digital Hierarchy
SECAM	Sequential Couleur avec Memoire
SFR	Société Française de Radiodiffusion
SIP	Società Italiana per l'Esercizio delle Telecomunicazioni
SMDS	Switched Multimegabit Data Service
SOG-T	Senior Officials Group on Telecommunications
SOGITS	Senior Officials Group on Information Technology Standards
SONET	Synchronous Optical Network
SPAG	Standards Promotion and Application Group
SS7	Signaling System 7
STAR	Special Telecommunications Action for Regional Development
STET	Società Finanziaria Telefonica (Italy)
SWIFT	Society for Worldwide Interbank Financial Telecommunications
TCP/IP	Transmission Control Protocol/Internet Protocol
TDF	Transborder Data Flows
TEDIS	Trade Electronic Data Interchange Systems
TISP	Telecommunications and Information Services Policy Working Group (OECD)
TLP	Telefones de Lisboa e Porto
TNC	Transnational Corporation
TNS	Telecommunication Network-based Services
TPON	Telephony on a Passive Optical Network

TPSA	Telekomunikacja Polska SA
TRAC	Technical Recommendations Applications Committee
TRIP	Trade-Related Intellectual Property Rights
TRIM	Trade-Related Investment Measure
TTC	Telecommunications Technology Committee and
	Telecommunications Technology Council
UMTS	Universal Mobile Telephone System
USTR	United States Trade Representative
VAN	Value-Added Network
VANS	Value-Added Networks and Services
VAS	Value-Added Services
VSAT	Very Small Aperture Terminal
WAN	Wide Area Network
WARC	World Administrative Radio Conference
WATTC	World Administrative Telegraph and Telephone Conference

Author Index

Subject Index

About the Contributors

Jacques Arlandis is the Scientific Director of the Institut de l'Audio-visuel et des Télécommunications en Europe (IDATE) in Montpellier, France. His work studies the economics of telecommunications, perspectives of networks and services, and strategic alliances between telecommunications companies. He received a BA in sociology and a Ph.D. in Economics from the Paris business school ESCP.

Johannes M. Bauer is Assistant Professor in the Department of Telecommunication and the Director of the Institute of Public Utilities at the Eli Broad School of Management at Michigan State University. His research interests include the economics and regulation of infrastructure industries, the process of European integration, and the globalization of the telecommunications industry. He has published more than 30 journal articles and book contributions and is the coauthor of three books. He holds an MA and a Ph.D. (1989) in Economics from the Vienna University of Economics and Business Administration, Vienna, Austria.

Harry Bouwman is Lecturer at the Communication Department of the University of Amsterdam. His research interests include videotex, HDTV, interfaces, as well as the adoption and marketing of innovations. He holds degrees in Political and Communication Science from the Free University of Amsterdam and the Catholic University of Nijmegen, The Netherlands.

Laurence Caby is Associate Professor at the Institut National des Télécommunications (INT) in Evry, France, and teaches at the INT and the Sorbonne University. Her research and consulting focus on the telecommunications sector in general, with an emphasis on marketing and telecommunications. She is coeditor of a forthcoming book on technological change and the internationalization of telecommunications. She holds an MBA and a Ph.D. from the University of Paris Dauphine.

Stephen Connell is the Managing Director of IFC Research Ltd., a marketing research consultancy that serves the information and communications technology industry. He has worked on the RACE program since 1988, specializing in the analysis of applications. Prior to that he was a research fellow at the Communications Studies Group, University College London (from 1971-1974) and an international market research and forecasting manager for Rank Xerox (1974-1977). In 1977 he joined Communications Studies and Planning and CIT Research Ltd as a consultant and, in 1984, he founded IFC Research Ltd. He holds an MA in Natural Sciences from the University of Cambridge.

William J. Drake is Assistant Professor in the Department of Communications at the University of California, San Diego. He has written and consulted widely on international telecommunications and information issues, with particular emphasis on the political economy of multilateral institutions. His current projects include a book on the international telecommunications regime and an edited book on the global information economy. He holds a Ph.D. in Political Science from Columbia University.

Tim Kelly recently joined the Strategic Planning Unit in the International Telecommunications Unit (ITU). Before joining the ITU he was a Communications Policy Analyst in the OECD's Information, Computer, and Communications Policy Division. At the OECD he has worked on projects to define performance indicators for public telecommunications operators and to examine the policy implications of the convergence between telecommunications and broadcasting. He completed his Ph.D. in Geography at Cambridge University.

Richard A. Kramer is presently working for Northern Telecom in London. He received his BA from Columbia University, where he also served as Assistant Director of the Columbia Institute for Tele-Information from 1987 to 1989. He holds an MA from the Annenberg School for Communications at the University of Pennsylvania (1991), where his research concerned international telecommunications policy formation and the political economy of communications regulation.

Michael Latzer is a Researcher at the Research Unit for Socioeconomics of the Austrian Academy of Sciences in the field of technology assessment. During the past years, he conducted research on technology policy, telecommunications policy, and service development. He holds degrees in business informatics and political science from the University of Vienna, Austria.

Robin Mansell is Head of the Center for Information and Communication Technology at the Science Policy Research Unit (SPRU) at the University of Sussex, Brighton, England. She has written numerous articles on telecommunications issues and consulted frequently for the European Communities. Her present research includes the study of electronic trading networks and the process of telecommunications reform in Eastern Europe. She received a Ph.D. in Communications from the University of British Columbia, Canada.

Jürgen Müller is Head of the Division of Industrial Policy at the German Institute for Economic Research (DIW) in Berlin, where his work focuses on issues of regulation and telecommunications in particular. During the 1991-1992 academic year he was Visiting Professor at the University of Toronto, Canada. He is the author and coauthor of numerous articles and books on telecommunications policy and regulatory policy, among others the 1988 book *European Telecommunication Organizations*. He has served in numerous functions as a consultant for the German government as well as the European Communities.

Eli M. Noam is Professor of Finance and Economics at the Columbia University Graduate School of Business. He has served as Public Service Commissioner engaged in the telecommunications regulation for New York State and is Director of the Columbia Institute for Tele-Information. He has also taught at the Columbia Law School and Princeton University. His publications include over 100 articles in various legal, telecommunications, and research journals. He is the editor or coeditor of works in a variety of telecommunications topics and the recently published monographs *Telecommunications in Europe* and *Television in Europe*. He received an AB (1970 Phi Beta Kappa), a Ph.D. in Economics (1975), and a JD Law degree (1975) from Harvard University.

Pierre Sauvé is Acting Assistant Chief Negotiator for Services in the Canadian Department of External Affairs and International Trade's

Office of the North American Free Trade Negotiations. Prior to working on the NAFTA negotiations, he was an Economic Affairs Officer in the secretariat of the General Agreement on Tariffs and Trade in Geneva. He holds degrees from the University of Quebec, Montreal (BSc, Economics), Carleton University (MA, International Affairs), and Cambridge University (MPhil, Economics) and did postgraduate training at Oxford University.

Thomas Schnöring is Deputy Director and Head of the Department of Market Structure and Technology of the Research Institute for Telecommunications (Wissenschaftliches Institut für Kommunikationsdienste— WIK) in Bad Honnef, Germany. Before joining the WIK in 1983, he was a Researcher at the Institute for Regional Science at the Christian-Albrechts-University of Kiel. His research and publications center on innovation, market structure, economic development, and regional policy questions in telecommunications. He holds a Ph.D. in Economics from the University of Kiel, Germany.

Charles Steinfield is an Associate Professor of Telecommunication at Michigan State University, where he received a Teacher-Scholar award and an Ameritech Fellowship. In 1991, he received a Fulbright Research Award to study business use of videotex networks in France and was Visiting Professor at the Institut National des Télécommunications in Evry, France. In 1992-1993, he worked in Bellcore's Applied Research Laboratory, studying new approaches to business and residential information services. He has published numerous articles and book chapters as well as coediting the recent award-winning book, *Organizations and Communication Technology*. He holds a master's degree and Ph.D. from the Annenberg School for Communication at the University of Southern California.

Joseph D. Straubhaar is Associate Professor in the Department of Telecommunication at Michigan State University. He has researched and published a book and numerous articles on the comparative development of new communication technologies, including VCRs, cable, computers, and telecommunications, in several countries. He has taught for 8 years on the history and economics of U.S. electronic media and in information technologies and on comparative media and information technology systems. He holds a Ph.D. in Political Science/International Relations from the Fletcher School of Law and Diplomacy, Tufts University.

Saadet Toker has been working at the London Business School from 1986 on and is currently a Researcher at the Center for Business Strategy. She has written many articles on mobile communications in the United Kingdom and is author of *Mobile Communications in the 1990s—Opportunities and Pitfalls*. She earned her first degree in Economics in 1976 from the Middle Eastern University in Ankara, Turkey. She studied at the London School of Economics and received her MSc in Economics in 1979.

R. Brian Woodrow is Lecturer in the Department of Political Studies at the University of Guelph, Canada. He has written extensively on the political economy of international trade and the trade in services negotiations within the Uruguay Round of GATT talks.

Dimitri Ypsilanti is Head of the Telecommunications and Information Policy Section in the OECD's Information, Computer, and Communications Division (Directorate for Science, Technology, and Industry). He has specialized in telecommunications regulatory and policy analysis, including trade in telecommunication services issues and international tariffication. He studied economics in the United Kingdom and completed postgraduate studies in Canada.